The Short Oxford History of France

France in the Central Middle Ages

The Short Oxford History of France

General Editor: William Doyle

Old Regime France
  edited by William Doyle
Renaissance and Reformation France
  edited by Mack P. Holt
Revolutionary France
  edited by Malcolm Crook

IN PREPARATION, VOLUMES COVERING

France in the Later Middle Ages 1200–1500
Modern France 1880–2000

The Short Oxford History of France

General Editor: William Doyle

France in the Central Middle Ages 900–1200

Edited by Marcus Bull

OXFORD

UNIVERSITY PRESS

OXFORD

UNIVERSITY PRESS

Great Clarendon Street, Oxford OX2 6DP

Oxford University Press is a department of the University of Oxford.
It furthers the University's objective of excellence in research, scholarship,
and education by publishing worldwide in

Oxford New York

Auckland Bangkok Buenos Aires Cape Town Chennai
Dar es Salaam Delhi Hong Kong Istanbul Karachi Kolkata
Kuala Lumpur Madrid Melbourne Mexico City Mumbai Nairobi
São Paulo Shanghai Taipei Tokyo Toronto

Oxford is a trade mark of Oxford University Press
in the UK and in certain other countries

Published in the United States
by Oxford University Press Inc., New York

British Library Cataloguing in Publication Data
Data available

British Library Cataloging in Publication Data
Data available
ISBN 0–19–873185–X (pbk)
ISBN 0–19–873184–1 (hbk)

10 9 8 7 6 5 4 3 2 1

Typeset in Minion
by RefineCatch Limited, Bungay, Suffolk
Printed in Great Britain by
T.J. International Ltd., Padstow, Cornwall

General Editor's Preface

During the twentieth century, French historians revolutionized the study of history itself, opening up countless new subjects, problems, and approaches to the past. Much of this imaginative energy was focused on the history of their own country—its economy, its society, its culture, its memories. In the country's later years this exciting atmosphere inspired increasing numbers of outsiders to work on French themes, so that, more than for any other country, writing the history of France has become an international enterprise.

This series seeks to reflect these developments. Each volume is coordinated by an editor widely recognized as a historian of France. Each editor in turn has brought together a group of contributors to present particular aspects of French history, identifying the major themes and features in the light of the most recent scholarship. All the teams are international, reflecting the fact that there are now probably more university historians of France outside the country than in it. Nor is the outside world neglected in the content of each volume, where French activity abroad receives special coverage. Apart from this, however, the team responsible for each volume has chosen its own priorities, presenting what it sees as the salient characteristics of its own period. Some have chosen to offer stimulating reinterpretations of established themes; others have preferred to explore long-neglected or entirely new topics which they believe now deserve emphasis. All the volumes have an introduction and conclusion by their editor, and include an outline chronology, plentiful maps, and a succinct guide to further reading in English.

Running from Clovis to Chirac, the seven volumes in the series offer a lively, concise, and authoritative guide to the history of a country and a culture which have been central to the whole development of Europe, and often widely influential in the world beyond.

William Doyle

University of Bristol

Contents

List of Contributors

CONSTANCE B. BOUCHARD is Distinguished Professor of Medieval History at the University of Akron, Ohio. She is a specialist in the social and ecclesiastical history of France from the ninth to the twelfth century. Her books include *Sword, Miter, and Cloister: Nobility and the Church in Burgundy, 980–1198* (1987); *Holy Entrepreneurs: Cistercians, Knights, and Economic Exchange in Twelfth-Century Burgundy* (1991); '*Strong of Body, Brave and Noble': Chivalry and Society in Medieval France* (1998); '*Those of My Blood': Constructing Noble Families in Medieval Francia* (2001); and '*Every Valley Shall Be Exalted': The Discourse of Opposites in Twelfth-Century France* (2002).

MARCUS BULL is Senior Lecturer in Medieval History at the University of Bristol. His research interests include the early history of the crusade movement, aristocratic culture in central medieval France, and medieval historiography. His publications include *Knightly Piety and the Lay Response to the First Crusade: The Limousin and Gascony c.970–c.1130* (1993) and *The Miracles of Rocamadour: Analysis and Translation* (1999). His latest research project concerns the form and function of historical narratives written between *c.*1050 and *c.*1150, and he is also writing an introductory guide to the study of medieval history.

GEOFFREY KOZIOL is Associate Professor of History at the University of California, Berkeley. His primary interests are the relations between power (and powerlessness) and religion in the late Carolingian and early Capetian periods. He is the author of *Begging Pardon and Favor: Ritual and Political Order in Early Medieval France* (1992). His current research project is a revised narrative of the decline of the Carolingians after the death of Charles the Bald.

LINDA PATERSON is Professor of French Studies at the University of Warwick. She is a specialist in medieval Occitan literature and history, and is the author of *The World of the Troubadours: Medieval Occitan Society, c.1100–c.1300* (1993) and, in collaboration with S. Gaunt, R. Harvey, and J. Marshall, *Marcabru: A Critical Edition* (2000). Her latest book, written in collaboration with

C. Sweetenham, is *The Canso d'Antioca: An Epic Chronicle of the First Crusade* (2002).

JONATHAN PHILLIPS is Senior Lecturer in Medieval History at Royal Holloway, University of London. He is a specialist in the history of the crusades. He is the author of *Defenders of the Holy Land: Relations between the Latin East and the West, 1119–1187* (1996) and *The Crusades, 1095–1197* (2002). He is the editor of *The First Crusade: Origins and Impact* (1997) and *The Second Crusade: Scope and Consequences* (2001). His present research project is a monograph on the Second Crusade.

BERND SCHNEIDMÜLLER is Professor of History in the Lehrstuhl für mittelalterliche Geschichte at the University of Bamberg. A specialist in medieval French and German history, he has been a member of the organizing committees of several exhibitions on medieval subjects: on Henry the Lion in Brunswick, on Otto the Great in Magdeburg, and on Henry II in Bamberg. His books (in German) have focused on the origins of medieval France (1979, 1987) and on the self-consciousness of the Guelfs as members of the European aristocracy in the early and central Middle Ages (2000). He has edited volumes on a range of topics, including the court in the central medieval period and the dynastic history of the western empire, as well as a series of biographies of medieval French kings (1995–2001).

Introduction

Marcus Bull

This volume in the *Short Oxford History of France* series deals with some of the most important changes that took place between *c.*900 and *c.*1200 in the area that we may for convenience label 'France'. More broadly, therefore, the book addresses processes and events that are sometimes grouped together under a heading along the lines of 'The birth of France'. The problem here, of course, is that any metaphor like this runs up against the fact that there was no single moment when France came into being; what we mean by France itself is not reducible to the sort of single, coherent entity which one needs if organic analogies are to work properly. To speak of medieval France is effectively to use a piece of shorthand for a mass of concurrent ideas, myths, geographical features, historical memories, word associations, mental maps, and senses of belonging, sometimes in harmony, sometimes in conflict. To some extent France existed in the area bounded by the coastlines and land boundaries (however vague) that literally gave it shape, but it was also inside people's minds as a construct, or more accurately a host of different constructs.

Nevertheless, it is fair to say that something actually existed in 1200 which had not been there in 900, and this was recognizably the antecedent of the early modern and modern French nation. By 1200 France existed as a kingdom ruled by a newly revitalized and purposeful monarchy. Its kings were soon to make substantial additions to the areas in which their authority was effective. France had developed a political culture that had coped more flexibly and creatively than many other parts of Europe, most notably Germany, with the enormous challenges posed by movements for ecclesiastical reform and the consequent reordering of fundamental ideas about the relationship between sacred and secular authority. It was the most populous part of Europe. Culturally and intellectually it was enjoying unparallelled prestige. A vocabulary to describe and extol Frenchness and the associations growing around it was developing. And the king's greatest rival, Richard the Lionheart, king of England and lord of a vast swathe of western France from the Pyrenees to the Channel, had just died in a freak accident of war. God, it seemed, was on France's side.

This book, then, is about a process of formation. Its aim is to help readers to develop an understanding of the profound changes that took place in the three centuries covered by the volume. It also attempts to avoid the impression that there is a dominant thread in medieval French history which must be followed—what more critical-theory-minded scholars would label a 'metanarrative' about the rise of France. Even in more modest terms, this book does not aim to examine the central medieval period in order to set up what comes next—the world of St Louis, the Black Death, and the Hundred Years War. The intention is to identify and explain more or less coherent patterns of change within their own terms of reference, and without turning them into scenes in a grand 'emplotment', a story whose beginning and middle serve the interests of explaining the end.

This is an obvious point to make. But it is noticeable how tenaciously an attachment to a narrative of gestation, birth, and growth persists to give direction, and by extension meaning, to the story of France. In large part this boils down to the inertia of popular understandings of the past, which are far more resistant to scholarly fashion than professional historians like to believe. It is worth bearing in mind that France is a country which takes the teaching of *its* history in its schools very seriously. And like all Western societies, France draws its identity from images and ideas associated with the Middle Ages to a greater extent than most people, not least many historians who work on later periods of history, consciously realize. In part, too, the whiff of teleology, with all its associations with old-fashioned history-writing, still hangs around central medieval France as a curious result of the trendiness of French historiography since the second quarter of the twentieth century. French scholars have been pioneers of many exciting and salutary reorientations of what medieval history ought to be about. New perspectives associated with scholars such as Marc Bloch, Georges Duby, Jacques Le Goff, and Jean-Claude Schmitt have focused attention on social and economic issues and on cultural history—the domains of *imaginaire* and *mentalité* (both terms, significantly, whose meanings are imperfectly captured by their closest equivalents in English). For many years political history was frozen out, or at least pushed to the margins. In addition, scholarly attention was focused on localities and regions: units such as kingdoms were seen as unwieldy objects of study and, worse, as entities compromised by their prominent place in old-fashioned, nation-centred historiography. But the results proved paradoxical. When interest in the kingdom as a unit and in politics at the national level began to resurface in the late 1980s and 1990s—Le Goff's publication of a book on the reign of St Louis (1226–70) in 1996 was treated as quite a landmark event—it became clear that the political history which was thawing out of its *annaliste* ice age was a well-preserved relic of an older, simpler time. In particular, a narrative thread of clear development and progress, the sort of plot which historians of medieval England have long since written out of their national story, had not quite gone away. As some of the steam runs out of scholarly focus on the French regions as opposed to the national level, and as the once disparaged *histoire événementielle* (history as a series of events) catches up with modern historiographical approaches, it will be interesting to see where the study of medieval France goes. The contributions to this volume seek to distil and explain some of the main issues and debates that have interested historians in recent decades, while also communicating the open-endedness of a subject that will doubtless shift many times in the future.

The history of France was traditionally the staple of school and university courses that dealt with medieval Europe beyond the British Isles. So much so, in fact, that many of the accepted truisms about medieval civilization as a whole turn out on closer inspection to be extrapolations of predominantly French (and more typically northern French) conditions. Since the 1980s a reaction has set in to make other places better served by English-language textbooks and monographs: Spain, Germany, and Byzantium have been notable beneficiaries of a process which has also extended to most parts of the Christian world. A consequence has been that France has risked becoming downplayed; the perfectly valid revision of historians' priorities can sometimes create its own new distortions. Fortunately, a counter-reaction has been signalled by the publication of new editions of two of the three books which between them have provided the fullest introduction to France in the period covered by this volume. Elizabeth Hallam's *Capetian France 987–1328*, first published in 1980 and revised, with the collaboration of Judith Everard, in 2001, is particularly valuable for its consistent focus on the French kings and their many interactions with other powerful individuals and groupings in their kingdom. While stronger on the period after 1200, in that the accounts of the reigns of St Louis and Philip the Fair (1285–1314) amount to the climaxes of what goes before, this is a clear and reliable starting point for further study. Jean Dunbabin's *France in the Making 843–1180*, republished in a second edition in 2000, is very strong on France as a composite of its constituent parts. It is the best book-length synthesis in English of the work that historians have done on the French regions. And it strikes an intelligent balance between doing justice to the sheer variety of the political, social, economic, and cultural experience within the regions and arguing that French medieval history does not simply dissolve into a riot of idiosyncrasies and centrifugal tendencies. The third book is Georges Duby's *France in the Middle Ages 987–1480*, a 1991 translation by Juliet Vale of a French original that appeared in 1987. As one would expect in light of the author's interests, the book is particularly useful in its treatment of social and economic conditions and of the grass-roots experiences of the 'silent majority'. Its treatment of politics and the Church is, equally expectedly, a mixture of stimulating insights into issues such as perception and ritual alongside some less effective narrative.

The aim of the present volume is to complement the coverage built up by these and other works. This is done by re-emphasizing the importance of certain events and processes, downplaying some issues that have perhaps enjoyed too much scholarly attention, and filling some gaps. Three aspects of the coverage offered by the book deserve particular explanation. First, it has been a deliberate editorial decision not to include a discrete chapter dedicated to the history (or rather, histories) of French women in this period. This was a difficult decision because there can be no doubt that the study of women's history has been one of the most dynamic features of medieval historiography in recent decades. But in a sense the success of this endeavour, which has resulted in the publication of many accessible and varied treatments of the subject, is what decided against the inclusion of a chapter here. It seemed doubtful whether a piece on women could go much beyond some of the generalizations—many of them applicable to conditions in western Europe generally, not just in France—which can be found in the numerous textbooks on medieval women. More importantly, it was felt that it would misrepresent the progress made by the study of medieval women and its offshoot concept 'gender' if the subject were corralled into a separate chapter. Rather, the brief to which contributors have worked has been to integrate the discussion of women within the particular parameters of each subject area, as appropriate. This inclusive approach, it is hoped, better conveys the complexity and diversity of women's experiences in this period.

Second, there is a deliberately undogmatic approach to what does or does not constitute France or qualifies as French. This is for the very simple reason that these concepts were themselves forming in our period, meaning that any prescriptive definitions would prejudge the very issues that need to be considered. In practical terms, what this means is that the contributions in this volume focus on, and draw most of their material and examples from, those areas that were within the space variously describable as 'western Francia' or 'the kingdom of France'. Most of modern-day France (about two-thirds of the surface area) overlaps with this circumscription, and the two entities are in many respects in direct line of descent. So the kingdom of France has first claim on the title of the progenitor of modern France. But it is important not to push this too far. For one thing, the kingdom of our period extended beyond the modern-day borders, northwards into Flanders and southwards over the eastern Pyrenees into Catalonia. Catalonia was a somewhat 'semi-detached' part of the French polity after the late tenth century, when its appeals for help against its Muslim neighbours went unanswered in the north. But it was formally within the kingdom until the thirteenth century, and before then its destinies had been intricately bound up with the affairs of the French Midi. Flanders and neighbouring areas now in Belgium were important parts of the medieval French political and economic landscape. To exclude them from a discussion of medieval conditions on the basis that their 'Frenchness' has now receded would be perverse. More delicate is the question of what to do with the large north–south corridor in what is now eastern France, extending from Alsace and Lorraine down through eastern Burgundy, the Jura, Savoy, the French Alps, and Provence. (And one should not overlook the French-speaking part of Switzerland, nor those areas of modern-day francophone Belgium which were never within the medieval kingdom of France.) The regions making up this eastern corridor were not part of the French kingdom in our period, nor were they to be incorporated within France for many more years. Much of Provence came to the French crown in the fifteenth century, for example, and it is always salutary to remember that somewhere that seems as quintessentially French as Nice only became French soil for good in the 1860s. In addition, anyone familiar with nineteenth- and twentieth-century European history knows very well how the national identity of Alsace and Lorraine has been a highly charged issue in modern times. The process of transition from the central medieval to the modern boundaries of France was, moreover, piecemeal and intermittent, which means that the whole eastern zone cannot even be treated for the sake of convenience as a single entity defined by its being in some sense 'France in waiting'. The approach of this volume, therefore, has been to focus on the kingdom without erecting unreal barriers between it and the areas to the east, which were, after all, populated by people who spoke Occitan, Franco-Provençal, or northern French dialects and had numerous cultural, economic, dynastic, religious, and political ties with the kingdom. Thus, to analyse the Midi, for example, as Linda Paterson's chapter reveals, is to enter a zone in which the political border between French Languedoc and imperial Provence was only one among numerous boundaries, physical and cultural, that facilitated contact and identification as much as they served to separate groups of people.

Third, the constraints of space have made it impossible to devote specific chapters to a number of deserving topics. The main absentee is perhaps the history of French towns in this period. Urban history has been one of the most popular areas of medieval studies in recent decades. But in the absence of a chapter devoted to towns, it seemed useful to integrate them as appropriate within the subject areas covered. Thus towns feature here in various guises: for example, as among the arenas in which political culture was played out; as prizes and resources in political competition; as cultural and intellectual centres; as bishops' sees; and as markets for the products of the rural economy. This, it is hoped, does justice to their varied roles. On the other hand, it is important to bear in mind that urbanization affected different parts of France to very different degrees, and that even after migration to towns accelerated in the later eleventh and twelfth centuries, the overwhelming majority of the population remained based in the countryside and locked into the agrarian economy. Constance Bouchard's chapter on the rural economy and society, therefore, takes us to the essential building-blocks of France in this period.

Another regrettable absentee is a separate treatment of 'minorities'. If one downplays their significance, it is easy to create a picture of medieval society that looks more homogeneous and unified than was actually the case. One group that deserves particular attention is heretics; and they are considered in their appropriate place, in Linda Paterson's chapter on the south, because it was in twelfth-century Occitania that the effects of heresy were most keenly felt within the space and period covered by this book. In an ideal world, a chapter on Jews would have been welcome, for they have an interest which transcends the fact that they were a small part of the population and were not evenly spread across France. In very schematic terms, the history of French Jewry over our period is a story of increasing marginalization and insecurity, a consequence of various wider developments such as shifts in attitudes to 'otherness' within the majority society, changes in religious sensibilities, new tensions created by the growth of a money economy, and changes in how political leaders exploited the resources of those over whom they ruled. Early in our period, Jews were relatively widely integrated within many social and economic functions. By the end, their status and image had mutated into the forms that would feed the stereotyping and persecution that are familiar from the later Middle Ages and beyond. An important watershed was reached during the preaching of the First Crusade in 1095–6, when French Jewish communities, for example that in Rouen, were among those victimized by would-be crusaders who had been encouraged to express feelings of vengeance against the enemies of the faith but failed to differentiate between the intended targets, the Muslims of the Middle East, and the non-Christians on their own doorstep. By the later part of the twelfth century, one finds early indications of the sort of scare stories of ritual murder and desecration that would inflame Christian attitudes to the Jews in later centuries, and of the systematic manipulation of Jews by kings.

Given the fact that it is impossible to cover everything, the subject areas tackled by this volume are intended to strike a good balance between depth and breadth, and to introduce readers to some new perspectives as well as tackling more obvious topics such as the Church. Bernd Schneidmüller's chapter on the emergence of ideas about France and Frenchness is a valuable summary of questions and issues that have attracted the attention of French and German scholars (mindful, no doubt, of how the complex intertwining of French and German history continues to resonate in the modern European experience) but have seldom filtered through into English-language introductory treatments. Geoffrey Koziol digs beneath the narrative of political events to consider some of the fundamental issues beyond the surface story—how the people with power viewed themselves and others, how they expressed their ideas through ritual, in short how politics was a matter of cultural attitudes and behaviours. A book of this length cannot do full justice to the results of all the work done on the regions in recent decades, but Constance Bouchard's chapter effectively synthesizes the principal lessons that have been learned, and draws attention to the similarities that connected the multiplicity of places that made up medieval France. One 'super-region' worthy of separate treatment is the south, which has sometimes not received the attention it deserves in discussions of France as a whole. Linda Paterson's chapter introduces us to a political and cultural world in which its link to the rest of France and its sense of distinctiveness were held in a dynamic tension until just after the end of our period, when the Albigensian Crusade and the re-entry of royal power effected a complete transformation in southerners' perceptions.

Jonathan Phillips's chapter addresses an important aspect of the medieval French experience which is often overlooked in inward-looking treatments of France itself: that is, the remarkable diaspora of French-speakers in the latter part of our period into the British Isles, Spain, southern Italy and Sicily, and Syria and Palestine. These people took their languages and their social conventions to the places that they conquered or settled. They effectively represent an enormous expansion of 'France' understood, not in territorial or political terms, but as the leitmotif for a wide range of cultural, artistic, literary, social, and linguistic trends. In the first half of the twentieth century, French scholars were drawn to the apparent similarities between, on the one hand, the experience of medieval French crusaders and settlers in the Levant and, on the other, the French colonial presence in the Middle East and North Africa of their own day. The eleventh and twelfth centuries became, in their eyes, the first phase of France's special relationship with the Arab world. Postcolonial attitudes now make this sort of perspective look very outmoded, of course. But it remains important to keep an eye on France 'beyond itself', for the experience of French warriors, ecclesiastics, merchants and settlers in other countries was much less marginal to the history of France overall than is sometimes supposed.

The remainder of this Introduction offers a brief political narrative viewed from the royal 'centre'.[1] This is intended simply to serve as a chronological framework for the following chapters. It is hoped that it does not fall into the teleological trap that was mentioned earlier: what follows, it must be emphasized, is one possible framework among many others. But given the role that the kings play in much of what this book addresses, and the convenience factor of using reigns as chronological 'punctuation' to break up what was in reality a continuum, this narrative helps to preface the discussions in the following chapters.

A good place to start is the volume's time-span. The terminal dates, 900 and 1200, should not be taken as hard and fast, nor should any particular significance be attached to these years as opposed to others immediately before and after them. The year 1200 bisects an important reign, that of Philip Augustus (1180–1223), and falls just before momentous shifts in the scope and range of royal power which were rooted in long-term factors, of course, but also owed much to unforeseeable short-term circumstances. The year 900 is even more imprecise as a chronological marker. As Bernd Schneidmüller's chapter argues, we need to look back into the ninth century in order to understand the origins of the entity we call France in the slow and haphazard fragmentation of the Carolingian empire. If there is one key date close to 900 that can be singled out, it is 898, the year in which King Odo died. Ten years earlier, the elites of the western portion of the former empire had broken with tradition and elected a non-Carolingian, Odo, to be their king. There was a Carolingian claimant, but he was a small boy, and what was needed more than anything was strong and effective leadership in the face of Viking incursions. For all Odo's strenuous efforts to have his authority

---

[1] My warmest thanks to Geoffrey Koziol, who generously wrote an outline political narrative on which I have drawn for what follows.

recognized and respected, however, the existence of a potential Carolingian rival compromised his achievements; indeed, that rival, Charles, was himself anointed king in 893 in defiance of Odo's status, and he was to succeed to the throne on Odo's death.

Charles, burdened by the uninspiring tag 'the Simple', which actually refers to an uncomplicated, naïve nature rather than mental deficiency, is one of those kings who suffered from a bad press in old-fashioned historiography. The fact that he was deposed in 922, and eventually died a prisoner of Herbert II of Vermandois after a six-year captivity, suggests that his reign had been, to say the least, problematic. But he had made serious attempts to bolster royal power. For example, he came to terms with one of the principal Viking warbands in order to regularize their presence within parts of the area that would in due course mutate into Normandy. He also had ambitions to extend his power eastwards into Lotharingia, the resonant homeland of the Franks and the location of Charlemagne's old capital and tomb. In this Charles overreached himself, his favouritism towards Lotharingians incurring the magnate opposition that was to be his downfall. But at least monarchical power had been sustained to the point where effective kingship remained something worth fighting for.

The seventy years after Charles's deposition appear, with the benefit of hindsight, like a liminal phase between two periods of dynastic continuity, though of course this is not a perspective that those at the time could have shared or even imagined. Charles was succeeded by Odo's brother, Robert of Neustria (922–3) and then by Robert's son-in-law Raoul, duke of Burgundy (923–36). After Raoul's death, the Carolingians staged what on the face of it looks like a comeback in the persons of Louis IV d'Outremer (936–54) (he is so called because he had spent his childhood exiled 'overseas' in the care of his mother's family, the kings of Wessex), his son Lothar (954–86), and Lothar's son Louis V (986–7). But the family of Kings Odo and Robert remained an important factor in political affairs, especially thanks to Robert of Neustria's son Hugh the Great (d. 956), whose power and status were entrenched by Louis d'Outremer in return for the support that he gave the new king. Hugh was granted the *ducatus Francorum*, not a duchy in a strictly territorial sense but a form of viceregal authority over the whole kingdom. Though Hugh himself never got beyond nursing ambitions to become king, the pre-eminence that he achieved would be the foundation for his son Hugh Capet's rise to the throne a generation later.

The west Frankish kingdom was not an entity developing in isolation. On the contrary, its history was intricately bound up with that of its eastern neighbour, Germany, which was itself heir to part of the former Carolingian empire. The German connection assumed particular importance in the generation after the deaths of Louis IV and Hugh the Great in the 950s. The eastern Frankish king Otto I (936–73) was the brother-in-law of both men. Yet, for all the superiority displayed by Otto I and Otto II (973–83), the essential fact remained that the west Frankish kings were Carolingian and they were not. (The reign of the last Carolingian to be king of Germany had ended as far back as 911.) The obvious proving-ground for the relative strength of the western and eastern Frankish monarchies—the place where a self-respecting Carolingian simply had to reassert himself in relation to his Ottonian neighbours—was Lotharingia. When Otto II died leaving an infant heir, the opportunity seemed to present itself to revive Charles the Simple's interest in that area. But this was in fact to prove the Carolingians' undoing, for it threatened the interests of two groups which, in combination, were to prove too powerful: the magnates of northern Gaul, in particular Hugh Capet, and the influential, pro-Ottonian bishops of prestigious and strategically vital sees in the north-east of the kingdom with close ties to Lotharingia. The central figure proved to be Archbishop Adalbero of Reims, who responded to a charge of treason against himself by taking the offensive against Lothar and, after the king's accidental death, his successor, Louis V. When Louis himself died in 987, Adalbero orchestrated the manoeuvrings which excluded Louis's uncle Charles from the succession and secured the election of Hugh Capet.

With the benefit of hindsight, we now know that this event marked the beginnings of a royal dynasty, the Capetians, that was to rule uninterrupted until 1328 and in a cadet line was to retain the French throne until the sixteenth century. This long-term success would not have been apparent at the time, of course, and the possibility of a Carolingian *revanche* hung over the early Capetian kings. More than this, the period covered by the reigns of the first four Capetians, Hugh Capet (987–96), Robert the Pious (996–1031), Henry I (1031–60), and Philip I (1060–1108), has traditionally been treated as the nadir of the French monarchy. This, it used to be accepted, was the time when an institution already weakened by its late Carolingian incumbents went into yet steeper decline. The typical caricature of Robert, for instance, was that he was weak and easily dominated by his wives and by the monks he favoured; Philip, with a little more secure warrant in the evidence, has been castigated as an inert figure who allowed marital escapades—he abducted the count of Anjou's wife, earning himself an excommunication—to interfere with effective rulership. Worse still for historians of an older, nationalist stripe, these were the kings who allowed the power of the dukes of Normandy to expand to the point that they could destabilize the delicate equilibrium that existed among the principalities of northern France by becoming rulers of the rich, well-governed, and all-too-close kingdom of England.

Revisionist historiography has generally been better disposed to the first four Capetians. The fact, for example, that Robert the Pious fought successfully to secure the duchy of Burgundy for his brother is seen as an indication of strategic thinking and a willingness to make the most of opportunities as they presented themselves. Similarly, Henry I, whose reign was long considered to be the absolute low point of Capetian power, is now understood to have pursued intelligent policies in trying to balance the different princely interests that pressed on the royal domain—the spheres of influence of the dukes of Normandy and the counts of Flanders, Blois, Champagne, and Anjou. Henry acted in ways which suggest that, even if he sometimes backed the wrong horse and lacked the resources to make the decisive difference in regional contests, he had a developed appreciation of how politics worked and how royal status was in theory unique, and should be seen to be so, even if its practical impact remained limited.

Despite the rehabilitation of the early Capetians, the traditional view still persists that sees the reign of Louis VI (1108–37) as finally reversing the slide in royal power. Much of this reputation rests on the fact that Louis is the subject of the first full 'biography' of a Capetian king (written by Abbot Suger of Saint-Denis) to engage meaningfully with the issues of political power and military might. (The earlier account of Robert the Pious by Helgaud of Fleury is much more in the mould of a saint's Life.) So, to some extent, shifts in the nature and depth of the available source material may be creating an appearance of change that masks underlying continuities. But that said, there can be little doubt that Louis brought new vigour to the prosecution of kingship, building on strategies that he had developed before his father's death to make himself undisputed master of his own 'back yard', the area from north of Paris down to the Orléannais which historians now refer to as the royal principality. This was the zone in which the kings had most of their own family resources, and more broadly it was where they could expect to exercise authority, not just *qua* kings as such, but also along the same lines as a duke of Normandy or a count of Champagne might wield power in his own respective territory. The key problem that Louis tackled, and substantially resolved, was the subjection of the minor counts and castellans of this area, the Île-de-France. Indeed, by the latter part of his reign it had become more realistic to intervene beyond the zone of immediate Capetian influence in areas which had been little touched by royal power for many years, sometimes centuries. Louis helped the bishops of Clermont, for example, in their disputes with the counts of Auvergne. And when the count of Flanders was struck down by assassins in 1127, leaving no obvious successor, the king tried to exploit the ensuing power vacuum to insert his own candidate into the county. This endeavour met with only short-term success, but the fact that royal intervention was attempted is perhaps more significant than its actual outcome.

The appearance of an outward-looking monarchy keen to project itself further afield was sustained in the early years of Louis's son Louis VII (1137–1180), thanks in large part to his marriage to Eleanor, the heiress to the vast duchy of Aquitaine/Gascony in south-western France. But having started out as part of the solution, Eleanor ended up part of the problem. Marital difficulties surfaced, though it is very hard to penetrate beyond the chroniclers' salacious rumours to find out what was really going on. Soon there was a full-blown crisis. Divorced by Louis, in part because she had failed to produce sons, in 1152 Eleanor married Henry Plantagenet, soon to add the title of king of England to the string of titles and honours that he held in France: duke of Normandy, count of Anjou, and now, of course, by right of his wife, duke of Aquitaine. Henry was Louis VII's nemesis but also, paradoxically, a beneficial presence in that, in learning how to survive against a much more powerful, over-mighty vassal, the Capetians accentuated the uniqueness of their status and prestige. They also received a schooling in how to play for much bigger stakes than they had ever done before. This lesson was learned to the extent that the eventual defeat of Henry's 'empire', and the conquest or annexation of much of it in the first decades of the thirteenth century, actually represented the biggest single step taken by the medieval French monarchy in becoming the dominant political force within its own kingdom.

This is why the king who effected this transformation, Philip Augustus, is traditionally accorded pride of place in the story of the Capetians before they get to their shining star, St Louis. Having earned the unofficial title *Augustus* (with its echoes of imperial might) for increasing (the Latin verb is *augere*) the royal domain in the north-eastern part of the kingdom in the 1180s, it was Philip who dealt the decisive blow against Henry Plantagenet's son, King John, by taking the side of one of John's Aquitanian vassals in a dispute against his lord. This allowed Philip to declare John's French lands forfeit once the English king, as everyone expected, had failed to obey a summons to the French royal court. By 1204, two years after the initial sentence against him, John had lost Normandy and most of the rest of his father's northern French inheritance; most of Poitou was to be lost later, leaving a rump in a shrunken Aquitaine/Gascony which scholars of the next two centuries differentiate from its predecessor with the name 'Guyenne'. In 1214 Philip won a shattering victory over a larger army which was led by the German emperor Otto IV and included rebellious north-eastern barons such as the count of Flanders, as well as forces supplied by King John (who was not present himself). This victory, at Bouvines, is a landmark event in the French historical consciousness in the same sort of way that people in England have heard about Hastings and 1066 even if they profess no other knowledge of the Middle Ages. Like all such supposed landmarks, the significance of a day's fighting one Sunday in late July 1214 can be exaggerated, but Bouvines is a useful point at which to bring the political narrative of this period to a close. Its symbolic meaning was appreciated at the time as much as its geopolitical consequences, and when it is taken together with the Capetian penetration of the deep south which was soon to get under way as the kings filled the power vacuum left there by the Albigensian Crusade, it is clear that the first decades of the thirteenth century reconfigured the political scene in France to a degree unmatched since the ninth century. As the era between periods of particularly rapid and convulsive change, therefore, the centuries between 900 and 1200 form a useful unity as an object of analysis.

1

Constructing identities of medieval France

Bernd Schneidmüller[1]

Constructing a medieval nation

France is a creation of its medieval history. Its emergence between the ninth and twelfth centuries was not a direct result of linguistic, ethnic, cultural, or religious identities. Nor did it originate within a homogeneous geographical space. In the central Middle Ages, the idea was forged, with the benefit of hindsight, of an ancient, continuous, and distinguished history that belonged to the French. The aim of this chapter is to analyse this process by investigating the disjunctions between medieval constructions and modern perspectives while also examining how France came into being in practice.

Identities do not remain constant over the course of centuries. They constantly develop new forms which are often historically grounded but always, more importantly, represent responses to the challenges of the present. Political structures and conditions, shaped by the limits of possible action, brought about a transformation which changed the kingdom of the Franks into the kingdom of the French. In the process, identities were forged out of diverse elements. The forms and functions of these identities are not to be understood as operating solely in the realm of ideas, but rather as the

[1] Translated by Marcus Bull.

combined result of political change and of how it was perceived and interpreted.

The political community of the Middle Ages was not represented by all the inhabitants of a given kingdom. On the contrary, it only consisted of the monarchy, the nobility, and the ecclesiastical elite. The Latin sources called this the *regnum* (kingdom). In the case of the greater *regnum* of the Franks—and then the French—this was made up of many other *regna*. It was a combination of heterogeneous regions with traditions which can be traced back to the early Middle Ages (*Francia, Neustria, Burgundia, Aquitania, Britannia* (Brittany), *Gothia, Wasconia* (Gascony)) and newly created political units (*Normannia, Flandria*). It was within this space that the French people, a nation forged in the central medieval period, came into being, integrating within itself the older peoples of the Franks, Burgundians, Aquitanians, Goths, and Gascons.

The French nation as it emerged in the Middle Ages was certainly not identical to its modern-day counterpart, a concept that first assumed significance at the time of the French Revolution. Important distinctions are evident, the function of differences in the social diffusion of a sense of national belonging. Whereas the modern nation requires this sort of awareness from everyone, its equivalent in medieval and early modern France was limited to the political elites in particular—the monarchy, nobility, and Church, which were later joined by urban elites. The stages by which the medieval French identity was constructed constitute part of a long series of ethnic formations. This development is evident in both French and European history more generally from the fifth to the twenty-first century. In terms of how the development of French consciousness emerged, the creation of the nation in medieval France was shaped by political and social configurations alike, with the result that it has an interesting bearing on the study of the history of political consciousness in the Western tradition.

France is frequently held up as a durable model for the process of national formation in Europe. Here, so the argument goes, the kingdom (*regnum Francorum*) gave birth to the nation in a deliberate act that involved building on various ethnic, regional, cultural, and linguistic foundations. These variegated historical roots can still be seen today influencing the French national consciousness. It is not something based on uniformity of descent, language, or religion. Rather, the sense of belonging can be conceived as a permanent act of volition on the part of each individual, which is what Ernest Renan was referring to in the nineteenth century when he addressed the issue of the nation as a 'daily referendum' (*un plébiscite de tous les jours*).

Viewed from a Europe-wide perspective, the emergence of the French nation in the Middle Ages in fact appears more like an exception than the norm. Concepts and ideas only give the appearance of having remained constant over the course of centuries, whereas the reality is that they were invested with different meanings at different times. The single most dominant people, the *Franci* (the Franks, the French), gave their name to the kingdom, and gradually this term became superimposed over the ethnic diversity. The theoretical authority of the kings, the *reges Francorum*, was recognized throughout the kingdom, which functioned as a 'zone of acknowledgement', whereas their actual power remained effectively limited to one part of northern France—the 'sanction zone'. It was only in the twelfth century that the monarchy succeeded in consolidating the royal domain, and only in the thirteenth, when its power had extended to the whole kingdom, that the crown could assume the role of the institutional representation of realm and nation.

Before that point was reached, the geographical continuity of the king's rule in the Île-de-France had already served to encourage an emphasis upon the long-term historical connectedness of the Franks and the French. These historical traditions were cultivated and developed in spiritual centres such as Saint-Denis, Saint-Rémi, Reims, and Saint-Martin, Tours. It was here, in milieux close to the Carolingian and Capetian kings, that there emerged an awareness of the particular worth of the Franks/French within both secular and sacred history. A 'royal religion' assigned to the kings a pre-eminence over all the other monarchs of Europe and stimulated the notion of the French as a people favoured by God. In terms of its consistency, this identity remained unique in European history, growing out of various roots and embracing different elements in an extended and far from uniform process that stretched between the ninth and early thirteenth centuries. This chapter will now discuss the most important stages of this development.

The formation and development of the Carolingian kingdoms

The first area to consider is how the Carolingian family created its kingdoms. The divisions of the Frankish empire between the sons of Emperor Louis the Pious (814–40) marked critical turning points in the history of medieval Europe. For centuries before then, the Merovingian and Carolingian kings had divided the Frankish realm among all their legitimate sons: each received a portion of *Francia*, the heartland located between the Rhine and the Loire, and a part of those lands south of the Loire which the Franks had gained by conquest. The unity of the Frankish dominions was guaranteed by the unity displayed by the royal family. And it was only the accidents of dynastic succession, as well as murders and premature deaths within the Merovingian and Carolingian families, that repeatedly served to unify the Frankish polity.

In 800 Charlemagne received the imperial crown in Rome. In the process he acquired a status that transcended the limits of the Frankish realm. The new fusion of Roman *imperium* and Frankish kingdom demanded new approaches to the issue of succession, for the imperial title was indivisible. As a consequence, tensions arose between the traditional claims to the Frankish polity of all the ruler's legitimate sons and the notion of an individual succession by a single emperor. Charlemagne and Louis the Pious attempted different resolutions of this problem in 806 and 817 respectively, but neither produced a clear solution. From 829 Louis found himself engaged in a struggle with his sons over the Frankish empire. Louis's original intention had been to leave the core of the Frankish dominions, along with the imperial title, to his eldest son, Lothar: the younger brothers were to be junior to him and provided with subordinate kingdoms in Aquitaine and Bavaria. The brothers, however, successfully contested this arrangement. In the Treaty of Verdun in 843, Emperor Lothar, King Louis ('the German'), and King Charles ('the Bald'), together with the leading nobility, worked out a division of the Frankish empire which was to change the face of medieval Europe.

The division of 843 was rooted in the principle that each brother should receive a politically and economically equal portion of the

Frankish empire. In the process no consideration was given to the presence of existing economic, ecclesiastical, linguistic, cultural, or ethnic boundaries. Each brother was, as a matter of course, to rule over a part of the most important people within the empire, namely the Franks. A consequence was that the imperial title lost its force for cohesion. Lothar retained the imperial office and a long, narrow kingdom in the middle of the former empire that extended from Frisia in the north, down the Rhône valley, and as far south as central Italy. Emperor Lothar and his son King Lothar II gave their name to this 'middle kingdom' north of the Alps: the *regnum Lotharii*, Lotharingia. Louis II (his usual designation as 'the German' is anachronistic) received a kingdom east of the Rhine and north of the Alps. Charles II, the Bald, ruled the western part of the old empire, from the Channel down to northern Spain. His kingdom's eastern border roughly comprised the Meuse, Scheldt, and Rhône. When Emperor Lothar's three sons died without heirs, new divisions were negotiated in 870 and again in 880. The Treaty of Ribemont in the latter year provisionally set the seal on the creation of the kingdoms in the area once occupied by the Frankish empire: Lothar's entire realm, comprising Lotharingia, Provence, and Italy, fell to the eastern kingdom.

The kingdom that came to Charles the Bald, like those of his brothers, did not become a unified entity in the ninth century. It had acquired its shape simply as a result of decisions driven by dynastic concerns, a fact which manifested itself in the uncertain and inconsistent ways in which its space was given conceptual expression. The fact was that Frankish kingdoms had emerged out of the Frankish empire, and each preserved the traditions of the Frankish past and present. To begin with, the western kingdom took its name from its ruler: *regnum Karoli*, Charles's kingdom. Historians nowadays, when writing about the ninth and early tenth centuries, often use the designation 'west Francia' in order to register the fact that people long continued to regard it as part of the larger Frankish realm. There was an awareness of the many divisions and reunifications that punctuated Frankish history, and as a consequence contemporaries did not set much store by the durability of the particular arrangements made at Verdun or Ribemont. It was only the unfolding of events over the following decades, and indeed centuries, that endowed these contingent arrangements with the appearance of permanence.

How did the situation stabilize itself? How could a new identity emerge in a kingdom that was so heterogeneous? And how durable would the divisions actually prove? Sufficiently long to permit the development of strong political structures? In the beginning the prospects for Charles the Bald's kingdom looked bleak. He was forced to fight long and hard before he was able to make his position generally recognized within his kingdom. Regular invasions by the Vikings in the north and west, the Magyars in the east, and the Saracens in the south proved a long-term disruption to the political order. The king failed to fulfil his most important responsibility, which was to ensure the protection of his subjects. To compound matters further, the leading nobles had interests that were not confined within the kingdom's borders. After 843 the kings naturally demanded that their nobility should give them exclusive loyalty; but the nobles for their part repeatedly stressed their right to participate in political decision-making and to share power. Leading noble families regularly withdrew their allegiance from the west Frankish kings, in 854 and 858/9 going so far as to invite the east Frankish king to become their ruler in the west.

The belief in the unity of the empire remained strong for a considerable period. When in 884/5 there were no suitable candidates to be found among the surviving members of the western Frankish branch of the Carolingian family, the nobles called on Charles III ('the Fat'), the ruler of the east Frankish and Italian kingdoms, to come west. For three years Charles united the old Carolingian polity once more. But his period of rule also demonstrated that the parts of the former empire had gradually been developing separate identities over the preceding forty years. Charles's regime foundered and he was deposed; the old Frankish political order now broke up definitively. Five kings succeeded to Charles III's inheritance. The west Frankish kingdom was one product of this disintegration, surviving a change of ruling family in 888 when no suitable Carolingian was available. Instead the nobility elected as king Odo (888–98), the count of Paris and margrave of Neustria, who belonged to the Robertian family (the forerunners of the Capetians) and who had successfully led the struggle against the Vikings. The old lustre enjoyed by the Carolingian line was dimmed by its kings' many failures, and now it was a non-Carolingian who offered the best prospects for protection and peace.

So what held the west Frankish kingdom together in 887/8? Why did it not fragment, as the old empire had done, into several pieces— into, say, *Francia* (the area between the Loire and the Meuse), Burgundy, and Aquitaine? Clearly this period of forty or so years had sufficed to allow a feeling of solidarity to develop within the west Frankish nobility. The leading men of the kingdom resolved in favour of the unity of this new kingdom that Charles the Bald had brought into being. What, then, had brought about this rapid integration despite all the dangers that were faced? What had prompted this first step towards a west Frankish identity?

The operation of political contingency was far too significant to permit a straightforward answer to this question. Nonetheless, attention can be drawn to certain individual elements of west Frankish self-awareness, especially in light of the fact that the France that becomes recognizable later in the Middle Ages emerged as a result of foundations initially laid in the ninth century. Later historians, writing in the twelfth century, saw in Charles the Bald the founding figure of the kingdom: from his reign onwards, the notion of the empire (*imperium*) became detached from that of the kingdom (*regnum*). On the other hand, people back in the ninth and tenth centuries were not in a position to share this historical perspective. The process of integration, rather, emanated from the kings' entourage: from the chancery, which produced their documents and increasingly preserved the memory of the acts and privileges granted by the Frankish kings of old; and more especially from bishops, abbots, clerics, and monks, who propagated and extended the idea of a self-evident continuity running through a unitary Frankish-French pattern of history.

The identities so formed did not remain constant. On the contrary, their efficacy was dependent on the ability to make flexible adaptations when confronted with new political challenges. Geographically and politically the political elites remained closely linked to the monarchy. Their collective consciousness was preserved in the old Frankish royal monasteries and in the northern French bishoprics where royal influence was strong: centres such as Laon, Soissons, Reims, Sens, Orléans, and Tours were crucial. It crystallized around powerful and enduring beliefs about the venerable nature of Frankish history with its origins in antiquity, about the particular quality of the Frankish people, and about its superiority over other peoples.

Origins in both continuities and crises

The greatest achievement of Charles the Bald and his entourage was perhaps the affirmation of these traditions and their gradual absorption within the notion of the west Frankish kingdom. In practical terms, it was here that most of the pre-eminent sites of Frankish history were located: centres of the old Merovingian and Carolingian kings such as Reims, Sens, Paris, Orléans, Soissons, Tours, and Saint-Denis. These places functioned as the core of the old *Francia*, focal points of Frankish settlement since the fifth century and also the cult centres of the great saints who were closely linked to royal power such as Martin at Tours, Remigius at Reims, and Dionysius at Saint-Denis. Pippin and Charlemagne had, of course, enormously extended the Frankish realm by conquest in the eighth century; and they had shifted the centres of gravity of royal power eastwards to places such as Aachen, Prüm, Paderborn, and Frankfurt-am-Main as well as south to Pavia and Rome. After the ninth-century partitions the west Frankish kings no longer had access to these more recent centres of Carolingian imperial rule, so they resumed an emphasis on the old focal points of memory that were situated in their own *regnum Francorum*. It was these continuities in terms of places, names, and ideas that were to set their seal on subsequent west Frankish/French history.

The intensive nurturing of tradition evident under Charles the Bald was a result of his political weakness. As the youngest son of Louis the Pious he had been forced to fight hard to assert his position in relation to his brothers. It took a strenuous effort, for example, to secure Aquitaine by conquest. In 859 he was abandoned by the west Frankish nobles, who invited his brother Louis II, king of the east Frankish realm, to take his place. At this critical moment Charles was only saved by the west Frankish bishops, who asserted the idea that no layman could depose an anointed king. The close alliance that the monarchy forged with the Church, exemplified in the theological underpinning of rulership developed by Archbishop Hincmar of Reims, helped it to ride out periods of political weakness. When the throne was beset by conflict, it was often the sense of Carolingian tradition and the confidence-boosting belief in God's favour that remained the only supports that ensured the survival of the weak kings. From the beginning, then, the monarchy's self-confidence was born of crises.

Over the course of the ninth and tenth centuries the western kingdom laid claim more and more insistently to the idea that it alone embodied the continuation of Frankish history and of the line of Frankish kings. Charles the Bald projected himself as the successor to his grandfather Charlemagne, thereby drawing attention to the great status that attached to his authority. The royal court was the setting for the greatest achievements in Carolingian art and for the culmination of the cultural reform that Charlemagne had instigated and Louis the Pious had carried further. Images of rulership and Latin poetry created by artists and writers assembled in the court portrayed Charles as the ideal Christian king (*rex christianus*). The royal culture of representation celebrated the notion of Carolingian continuity; for example, the chancery deliberately adopted the signifiers of royal power used by Charles's predecessors, in particular Charlemagne's monogram, which was skilfully imitated. From 848 onwards Charles saw to it that his consort and children were anointed by archbishops from his kingdom. The notion of the king as the 'Lord's anointed' (*christus Domini*) was based on Old Testament and early Frankish models (Saul and David, Pippin and Charlemagne); on being anointed, the ruler assumed a sacral status and became a mediator between God and his people. Charles's repeated staging of this act cemented the biblical and Carolingian tradition of anointing in the west Frankish kingdom. In contrast, the first Saxon king of the east Franks, Henry I (919–36), refused to be anointed. It was only his successors, starting with Otto I (936–73), who treated the act of anointing as a rite of passage, as the Anglo-Saxon kings were already doing. Yet this was a practice that King Pippin had introduced for the Frankish rulers as far back as 751, and one that Charles the Bald from 848 onwards had consolidated for his successors on the west Frankish throne.

In perfect keeping with the traditions of the Carolingian family, Charles the Bald made a bid for the imperial title when a favourable opportunity presented itself. He was crowned emperor by Pope John VIII in Rome on Christmas Day 875—exactly seventy-five years after Charlemagne's imperial coronation. However, the attempt to gain Italy for the west Frankish realm, and thereby to secure for the west Frankish Carolingians an imperial political orientation, proved abortive. After Charles died in 877, no other ruler of the west Franks/ French would attain the imperial throne until Napoleon I. With the imperial coronation of Otto I in 962, the destiny of the empire came to be linked—for more than 800 years, in the event—to the eastern Frankish/German kingdom.

In the west Frankish kingdom, on the other hand, the successors of Charles the Bald were conscious of the Frankish imprimatur of their royal office and of their great predecessors such as Clovis I, Dagobert I, Pippin, and Charlemagne. Charlemagne was remembered above all as a king of the Franks; in the French tradition, the newly established western imperial office was of secondary importance. The lustre of their Carolingian origins helped to keep even weak kings on the throne up to the 880s. When Odo was elected as the first non-Carolingian king of the Franks in 888, he too had recourse to the same concept of the royal office and the same means of rulership that his predecessors had applied. For a century (888–987) two royal dynasties fought for the west Frankish throne, until in 987 Hugh Capet, a member of the Robertian family, finally prevailed, in the process founding a dynasty which took his name as the 'Capetians'. All these rulers exploited the traditions of their office and reaffirmed in their documents the desire to reign like their predecessors. In this way the notion of the Frankish monarchy was sustained, even as it gradually became detached from the Carolingian family itself. Indeed, the monarchy's institutional aspects—transcending the fluctuations of political affairs and changes of personnel—became the basis of political stability.

Transformations of names: *Franci* and *Francia*

This consideration brings us to the issue of nomenclature, for the durability of the names applied to people and kingdom is a significant factor. In the early ninth century *Francia* still denoted the broad area of early medieval Frankish settlement, extending from the Loire to the lower Rhine and the upper Main. After the various partitions of the empire one can observe important processes of conceptual contraction centred on the two parts of east and west. From the tenth century, in the usage found in the west Frankish kingdom, *Francia* only referred to the area situated between the Meuse, the Loire, and the Oise—in other words, a portion of northern France with the later Île-de-France at its centre. This zone was distinguished from Aquitaine and Burgundy to the south and Flanders and Normandy to the north and north-west. And this was the stage on which was played out the high politics of kingly and noble interaction. The rulers' field of operation was now constrained within narrow limits, and they no longer travelled to the other parts of their kingdom. Thus outside *Francia*, especially in southern France, the kings lived on only as a memory. People living beyond *Francia* were certainly aware that they belonged to the French kingdom, the *regnum Francorum*, but it would be hundreds of years before they ever saw their king again. It was only in the twelfth century that the kings began to be a presence once more south of the Loire. In the east Frankish kingdom a similar contraction occurred: the label *Francia* at first became focused on the region centred around the middle Rhine and the Main, subsequently narrowing to the area around Würzburg and Bamberg. When the name *Francia* became established as the designation for France in the eleventh and twelfth centuries, the terminology underwent a further process of precision in the east: this area now became referred to as *Franconia* and its inhabitants as *Francones*.

The conceptual continuities evident in the west and the need for neologisms in the east were a consequence of the definitive disintegration of the Frankish polity and of various processes of identity formation. In the east Frankish realm Frankish traditions became less significant from the tenth century onwards, thereby facilitating the exclusive appropriation of the Frankish name by 'France'. In the eastern kingdom the centres of gravity of royal power shifted, in the first instance towards Saxony. Moreover, with the imperial coronation of Otto I in 962, Roman traditions came to supervene, leading to the application of Roman-based terminology to the empire (*imperium Romanum*) and subsequently to the emperor/king (*imperator Romanorum, rex Romanorum*).

By way of contrast, the terminology of Frankishness survived with marked tenacity in the west Frankish kingdom: the correspondences in the vocabulary enabled a celebrated people's historical and political traditions and its pre-eminence to be transferred to its successor.

To begin with there was the belief that the Franks were especially loved by God, a notion expressed in the prologue to the early medieval Frankish law code, the *Lex Salica*. To this was added the idea that the Frankish race had a venerable ancestry—from the seventh century a descent was traced back, like that of the Romans, to Troy. These sorts of descent myths were active in France from the tenth century onwards (and indeed into the modern era). Each new king became part of a tradition connected with his office that traced its origins back to the Trojan monarch Priam. In addition, much was made of the particular freedom that the Frankish people enjoyed, their name being understood as a synonym for 'the free' (*Franci* = *ingenui, liberi,* free and noble men). People were proud of the Franks' great political successes: they had defeated Rome in the fifth century, and from their original starting point in Gaul had expanded to create a powerful empire that, by the time of Charlemagne, subsumed almost all of western Christendom with the exception of the British Isles. Finally, a particular adornment was the belief in the Franks' orthodoxy and piety. At Clovis's baptism they had become the first Germanic people to adopt Catholicism, thereafter never tolerating heresy and keeping unbroken faith with the Roman Church.

The key elements of this Frankish self-consciousness had already emerged in the Merovingian and Carolingian eras. They were then transmitted to the France of the central medieval period, where from the tenth century onwards they were further developed. It became a given that Frankish history was being seamlessly continued. The reduction of the greater *Francia* of the Carolingian period to the *Francia* situated between the Meuse and the Loire was a slow process that excited little comment; but it was a thoroughgoing change. The terminological shrinkage involved can be clearly seen in a comparison of the Carolingian annals of the ninth century with the tenth-century historical writing of two authors linked to Reims: the canon Flodoard, who died in 966, and the monk Richer, who wrote towards the end of the century. Over the course of this period one finds that the older *Francia* situated between the Loire and the Main had given rise to a newer version of itself in the west. From the old *Franci* (Franks) had emerged the new *Franci* (French). The names stayed the same but their meanings changed.

The strength of Carolingian tradition, the unity of the realm, and the relations between empire and kingdom

The rivalry over the Frankish name and Frankish history was mostly generated by the western kingdom. Charles III ('the Simple', 893/898–922, d. 929), the posthumous son of the Carolingian king Louis II ('the Stammerer') from a marriage that had been canonically controversial, initially faced severe opposition because of the doubts surrounding his legitimacy. He was twice passed over for the succession to the throne and then had to fight the Robertian king Odo for five years to secure the crown. The problems surrounding his accession help to account for his persistent attention to the ideas associated with the royal office. His consistent use of Carolingian traditions was a response to the constraints placed on the monarchy by its restricted power. In this merging of practical weakness and elevated claims, Charles placed a distinctive stamp upon the self-conception of the later French monarchy. Thus, his supporters were exploiting the memory of a great past when they elected the young man king on 28 January 893—the anniversary of Charlemagne's death—in opposition to King Odo.

From 898 Charles III's royal chancery had recourse to charters dating from the eighth century, enabling it to imitate the formulas applied in the documents issued by Pippin and Charlemagne. This too situated the current Frankish monarchy in the context of a great past. Increasingly, tradition became a force for legitimacy. In competition with the other kingdoms that had emerged after the splintering of the empire in 888, Charles projected himself as the sole continuator of Frankish history. When the last Carolingian king in the eastern kingdom, Louis IV ('the Child'), died in 911, the nobility in Lotharingia refused to accept his successor, Conrad I, and attached themselves instead to the Carolingian in the west. As a result Charles extended his rule over prestigious sites associated with the former Frankish realm—Aachen, Prüm, Metz, and Verdun—and thus over the area around the Meuse and the Moselle which constituted the old homeland of the Carolingian dynasty. He understood this enormous expansion of his kingdom as the entering into rightful possession of his 'greater inheritance'. Thenceforth Charles styled himself 'king of the Franks' (*rex Francorum*) in his documents, in contrast to his predecessors who had been referred to simply as 'king'. From 911 onwards the west Frankish/French royal chancery propagated the notion of an exclusive claim to rulership over all the Franks.

Charles III's ambitions to rule once more over the whole Frankish polity came to nothing, for the process of fracture between the west and east Frankish kingdoms could no longer be reversed. As early as 925 the east Frankish king, Henry I, reconquered Lotharingia; thereafter it was to be an integral part of the empire for the rest of the Middle Ages. In reality Charles's claims to exercise his kingship over all the Franks were limited to west of the Meuse and Rhône. Here the names of the kingdom (*regnum Francorum*) and of its king took root. The product of a fortuitous combination of circumstances, the royal title developed into a clear sign of right and continuity. For many centuries to come the French kings would use the title *rex Francorum* in their seals and diplomas. When documents also came to be written in French in the thirteenth century, the formula *rex Francorum* was replaced by 'king of France' (*roi/roys de France*). Thus, the conscious appeal to the tradition of the Frankish kings and the exclusive preservation of the Frankish royal title proved the wellspring of the formulations of French identity that one encounters in the Middle Ages. The kings gradually freed themselves from their older and geographically more extensive antecedents, even though, as we have seen, the mutation is difficult to chart with chronological precision since names and concepts remained outwardly the same while their inner meanings changed.

The traditions surrounding the royal office that Charles III had secured were available for exploitation by all his successors, including those who did not belong to the Carolingian family. Charles's rival for the throne, King Raoul (923–36), similarly styled himself *rex Francorum*, as did the rulers belonging to the Robertian/Capetian line. In this way, the title of king became detached from the person of a single ruler and from association with the Carolingian dynasty. In fact, the Carolingians ruled between 936 and 987 in an unbroken sequence comprising the son, grandson, and great-grandson of Charles III; and this helped to cement the connection between royal line (*stirps regia*) and kingdom. But the kingdom was no longer the exclusive property of this one dynasty. Moreover, the position of the monarchy came to depend on the act of election by the nobility whenever the son succeeded his father. In a development similar to what also happened in the Burgundian and east Frankish kingdoms in 912 and 936 respectively, the royal succession was no longer divided among all the king's legitimate sons. Thus, the unity of the kingdom triumphed over the old principle that there should be partition among all the sons, an important precondition for the ability of loyalties to endure in the long term and to be readily transferable from one individual to the next. When King Louis IV died in 954, the kingdom fell to just his eldest son, Lothar (954–86), and the claims of Lothar's younger brother Charles were passed over. Lothar secured the succession during his own lifetime by having his son Louis V (986–7) made co-king and using his authority to steer the nobility's choice. The securing of the succession within the royal family and the principle of the indivisibility of the royal dignity, then, represented decisive stages in the development of the unity of the kingdom.

Thus were the foundations laid for the Capetians' succession to the throne. When Hugh Capet was elected king by the nobles in 987, he entered into the full traditions of his Carolingian predecessors, and immediately secured the succession within his own family by making his son Robert II co-king. The French monarchs were to use this technique to bolster their dynastic position up to the twelfth century. Philip II (1180–1223) was the first to abandon the practice of engineering the election of one's son by the nobility. By the thirteenth century it had become self-evident that only a Capetian prince could become king. Louis VIII succeeded his father in 1223 without any formal process of noble election. Thus, between the tenth and thirteenth centuries the unity of the kingdom and the succession within the Carolingian and Capetian royal lines had become central pillars of French history.

The challenges posed by the Ottonians were a further factor in the formation of France. As it evolved as a discrete entity, France nonetheless continued to be long bound up in its connections with east Francia, Burgundy, and Italy. Competition with the Ottonian and Salian rulers of the east Frankish kingdom had a significant impact on France in its formative phase. Up to the mid-eleventh century the west Frankish Carolingians and Capetians remained interested in the idea of conquering Lotharingia, the old core of the Frankish realm which they conceived as the 'land of their fathers' and consequently their rightful inheritance. In the event, their attempts at expansion came to nothing, a demonstration of the power of the east Frankish realm. From the eleventh century, therefore, the French kings accepted east Frankish/German rule over Lotharingia. Indeed, it was not until the seventeenth and eighteenth centuries that the ancient claims were revived by King Louis XIV in his policy of recuperating the area between the Meuse and Rhine. Moreover, it was not until after the French Revolution that the notion of the Rhine as a national frontier was to resurface.

Defeats in the struggles for the whole Frankish polity forced a concentration over the course of the tenth century upon the northern part of France, the *Francia* between the Loire and Meuse. Here the kings' royal domain confronted areas controlled by noble and ecclesiastical lords. At some points the late Carolingians possessed scarcely anything more than the episcopal city of Laon; and for their part the early Capetians did not have the power to exercise any measure of consistent control over *Francia*. The identity of the French monarchy developed, then, at a time of *de facto* weakness, for these adverse circumstances led, thanks to rivalry with the nobility, to a progressively more consistent accentuation of the unique status enjoyed by the kings.

The discrepancy between real power and what was claimed becomes particularly apparent in the period 940–87, during which time the Carolingians survived in their many struggles against noble opposition only thanks to the massive support given them by the Ottonian kings. Otto the Great's two sisters were married to the Carolingian Louis IV and the Robertian Duke Hugh the Great. For a generation, high politics amounted to a 'family business'. The theatre of operations created by the old Frankish realm continued to influence the scope of cross-border activity on the part of kings and noble kindreds. Otto I celebrated this dynastic cohesiveness in 965 at a solemn court at Cologne, where his brother Bruno was the archbishop. The emperor had recently returned north after an extended stay in Italy, where he had received the imperial crown in 962. Now the re-establishment of the *imperium* was to be celebrated at Cologne with the whole family, from east and west Francia alike. Among the guests were the widowed west Frankish queen Gerberga and her son King Lothar, Otto's nephew. During the celebrations at Cologne, the young king was betrothed to a daughter of the new empress, Adelheid, by her first marriage. In this way, it was hoped, the ties of relationship would ensure the unity of the incipient Frankish kingdoms into the next generation.

But the differences in status between Otto I and King Lothar, between an Ottonian dynasty newly risen from its Saxon homeland and the old, enfeebled Carolingian line from *Francia*, furthered Lothar's ambitions for independence. Not long afterwards he made a bid to be regarded as an equal, at first by imitating Otto I's new imperial seal. Then in 978 decades of cooperation came to an end when Lothar launched a sudden attack against his cousin Otto II and attempted to take Aachen, the site pre-eminently bound up with the memory of Charlemagne. Lothar's campaign in Lotharingia ended in failure, as did Otto's retaliatory strike that took him up to the gates of Paris. Clearly, the conflict over Lotharingia and the rivalry between the two rulers could not be resolved by military means. Nonetheless, one minor and rather insignificant victory of Lothar's in a clash near the River Aisne was able to evoke quite new emotions: the king, it was said, had put the emperor to flight! The emphasis upon the proper dignity of the king assumed even greater significance: the impression that the kings were subordinated to the emperors was not to be encouraged either in the symbolic representations of royal power or in meetings between the two rulers. The system of routine contacts between the two courts, regular marriage links, and frequent meetings between rulers increasingly broke down from the late tenth century onwards. The accession of the first Capetian, Hugh Capet, did not mark the rupture: this had already begun during the reigns of Lothar and of his son Louis V. By the eleventh century the intimate connections between emperors and kings had been completely broken. After 1056 it would be nearly a century before the French and German rulers again met face to face. This separation was to have considerable implications for political perceptions and for the fashioning of new, discrete destinies.

In letters, histories, and the canonistic literature emanating from Reims and Fleury, the king was presented as standing on an equal footing with the emperor. The titles 'emperor' (*imperator*) and 'king' (*rex*) were treated as simply those that attached to the east and west Frankish rulers respectively, denoting no difference in status. The Ottonian emperor was now regarded in France as a foreign ruler.

Consciousness of belonging to a separate kingdom with its own dignity informed political behaviour and discourse. France and Germany—successors of the old extended Frankish polity and long conjoined in a shared history—were now striving to become discrete entities. The border between empire and kingdom became a clear dividing line.

One possible root cause of this shift was the imperial coronation of Otto the Great in 962 and the greater status conveyed by association with the Roman emperors. When the Ottonians extended their rule into Italy in 951 and revived the *imperium* eleven years later, they effectively exploded the system of kings distributed around the Frankish kingdoms and possessed of equal powers. In France this led to the perception that the kingdom had its own distinctive status, encouraging the formation of identities corresponding to this perspective. In their emphasis upon their own kingdom, the kings sought their own distinctive path beyond the world of communal activity associated with the old Frankish realm. Henceforth we should talk in terms of 'France', not 'west Francia'. Of course, this distinction is necessarily a construct: the official titles of 'kingdom' and 'king' did not change, and the shifts in identity took place imperceptibly, which means that we cannot fix on a specific date for the 'birth' of France. Awareness of possessing a particular individuality, of having one's own place in history, and of the independent dignity of the kingdom emerged as part of an extended process. For many decades a sense of shared Frankish history remained important, running in parallel with the gradual development of a French identity up to the second half of the tenth century. Within this extended process it is only possible to identify certain critical moments: the foundation of the west Frankish kingdom from 843; the election of the first non-Carolingian king in 888; the harking back to the specifically Frankish quality of one's own monarchy from 911. Forces for integration and separation mixed together over a protracted period until, in the final decades of the tenth century, the fact of partition became more clearly fixed in people's minds.

The French kings now consciously differentiated themselves from the emperors and focused their political attention upon their own core element of the former Frankish realm, not on its totality. This readjustment was reflected in political thought and in historiography. The years either side of 1000 became a period of intellectual and conceptual experimentation. Thus, the chancery of Hugh Capet (987–96) and Robert II (996–1031) looked for new ways to express notions of rulership, kingdom, and legitimacy. The greatest experiment in the context of the writing of history was undertaken by the historian Richer in the monastery of Saint-Rémi, Reims, in the final decade of the tenth century. Richer wrote a chronicle specifically focused on the Gauls rather than the Franks. To do this, he drew on the ancient formulation popularized by Caesar, according to which the Rhine divided Gaul from Germania. In taking this approach, however, Richer did not simply intend to show off his learning. More importantly, he was using borrowed Latin terminology to link his notion of a kingdom of Gauls under a Gallic king with the new realities of the late tenth century. There is some debate as to whether this chronicle (which only survives in his autograph copy) is informed by the perspective of an outsider. We can be sure that it was written in Reims, one of the most important centres in the kingdom; and it was dedicated to Richer's teacher, Gerbert of Aurillac, who was the greatest scholar of his age, the counsellor of kings, archbishop of Reims and Ravenna, and finally, as Silvester II, pope. In other words, the issue of the Gallic identity of the kingdom was not an issue being discussed on the political periphery. Significantly, Richer began his history with the year 888 and the kings Odo and Charles III. Moreover, Frankish history was limited to Gallic soil, thereby corresponding to the geographical range of Capetian rulership.

Richer's chronicle made no attempt to portray the Carolingian expansion into the regions east of the Rhine. Gallo-Frankish history and the Frankish/French present appeared identical, concentrated on *loci* of memory such as Reims, Tours, and Saint-Denis. The other key cities and regional centres of early Carolingian rulership (for example Pavia, Rome, Aachen, Frankfurt-am-Main, Saxony, Bavaria, and north Italy) dropped out of this Gaul-centred frame of reference. This helps to explain Richer's many 'mistakes', which were a corollary of the aims behind his writing of history: he was crafting his chronicle not as an expression of Frankish togetherness, but from the perspective of projecting his new French present back into a Gallic past. On the basis of Caesar's geographical classifications, Richer conceived of Gaul as the space which was his home and to which he belonged, and of Germania as the foreign neighbour beyond the Rhine. The geographical concepts were still fluid, however, and

Richer's notion of 'Gaul' as the suitable name for the kingdom did not gain general acceptance. But the historiography's concentration on a new France centred on Laon, Soissons, Reims, Orléans, and Paris did correspond to political realities. In imparting an exclusively western quality to the history that led up to his own day, Richer was pointing, perhaps unwittingly, to an important stage in the process of forgetting the Frankish past and of forging new identities.

Dynastic unity and royal sanctity

Richer's chronicle did not remain unique in its approach. Histories written in the monastery of Fleury and the archbishopric of Sens in the early part of the eleventh century also linked actuality to a past that was geographically compressed within west Francia. These histories did not draw on the concept of a Gallic space; rather, they exploited popular perspectives connected to notions of Frankish-French identity. For example, Aimo of Fleury construed the French nation (*natio Francorum*) from its distinguished Trojan descent. His Franks/French were conspicuous thanks to their great virtue (*virtus*), their love of liberty, and their talent for dominating other peoples (*domina multarum nationum*). The *Historia Francorum Senonensis*, an anonymous chronicle written in Sens, arranged the history of the Franks and the French according to the succession of three families, the Merovingians, the Carolingians, and the Capetians. This first attempt at a dynastic interpretation of history took root in France and continued to be developed, since this model of the three royal families was easy to grasp and generated a sense of complete historical unity connecting the Franks and the French. Already in our period historians and even the royal chancery were beginning to harmonize the dynastically discontinuous history of the ninth and tenth centuries. The Robertian kings between 888 and 923, despite being the forebears of the reigning Capetian line, were excised from the sequence of legitimate rulers because they interrupted the pattern of Carolingian continuity between 751 and 987. In this way the great crises that had beset the monarchy in the mid-eighth century and at the end of the tenth were elegantly 'finessed'. Consequently, neither the early Capetian kings nor their contemporaries perceived the transition from the last Carolingian to Hugh Capet and his successors as an effective break. It was only in later centuries, once the principle of dynastic succession to the throne had become firmly established, that commentators came to express shock at Hugh's 'usurpation'. Indeed, in the fourteenth century his name was even deleted from the line of direct royal succession, and no future French king was to bear the name of the founder of the dynasty.

Nevertheless, at the close of the tenth century it was the continuities that were predominant. Hugh Capet maintained the traditions of the royal office that his Carolingian predecessors had bequeathed to him. His son Robert ('the Pious') cemented the new monarchy, not only thanks to a long reign but also because of a reputation for great religiosity which contemporaries extolled. In his biography of the king, the monk Helgaud of Fleury went as far as to attribute to Robert the personal ability to heal the sick. This particular favour appeared initially to be confined to Robert. Moreover, theologians remained uncertain about the notion of a layman possessing thaumaturgical powers. A hundred years later Guibert of Nogent reported that the king of his own day, Louis VI (1108–37), was able to cure scrofula (a form of tuberculosis of the skin); in addition, Guibert claimed, Louis's father, Philip I (1060–1108), had at times possessed this ability, only to keep losing it. Historians nowadays reject the idea that these statements represent the survival of ancient beliefs about fertility magic or the wonder-working powers of kings. On the contrary, this is an instance of myth and legend becoming caught up in the process of monarchical institutionalization. In fact, in the twelfth century the ability to cure scrofula (the 'royal touch') was also accredited to the kings of England. The French monarchs first adopted the legend officially in the thirteenth century, whereupon the Capetian court was able to combine numerous and diverse traditions that had come to it from different sources in order to construct a coherent theoretical basis for the claim. Once the Hohenstaufen imperial dynasty came to an end (1254), the kings of France could, thanks to their 'royal religion', lay claim to be the highest-status monarchs in Europe.

This long process of development originated, as we have seen, with the healing gift ascribed individually to Robert II. This is one demonstration of the larger fact that the numerous elements that contributed to the transformation from Frankish history to French actuality were to be found in the circles within which the monarchs moved, above all in the writings of ecclesiastics working in the large bishoprics and monasteries within the royal domain. In this way, an awareness of the connecting thread in Frankish-French history remained limited to restricted elites. It was here, rather than in the numerous parts of the kingdom that were remote from the king, that the historically grounded identities were forged. However, it is also worth noting that memories and loyalties were genuinely preserved in those other places as well. In the Pyrenean region, for example, the memory of Charlemagne was cultivated by the locals as a validation of their own freedom and Christian identity, which were threatened by the Spanish Moors; as a result, people recognized the distant authority of the French king, at least on a theoretical level. On the other hand, it would take many centuries for the sort of political consciousness that was present in and around the royal court to penetrate all parts of the kingdom; when France was still in its formative phase, political identity remained essentially confined to a small group of political leaders in the north.

The chosen people, the sweet land, the Most Christian Kings, and the rediscovery of Carolingian roots

It is not just the monarchy that facilitated the process of identity formation that we have been examining. The people and the kingdom also served as points of connection. This became clear in the histories of crusades and the vernacular poetry that were written in the twelfth century. The key event was the success of the First Crusade (1095–9), in which French knighthood played a central role. In the Holy Land the crusaders were referred to by the Byzantines as well as by the Arabs as 'Franks' (*Franci*), and they too used this collective term to identify themselves. On the other hand, back in Europe the notion of the 'Frank' had long been limited to the inhabitants of northern France. The double meaning was exploited by crusade historians from that region such as Guibert of Nogent and Robert the Monk, as well as by the authors of numerous crusade songs, to praise their own people: God had chosen the crusaders (*Franci*) to be the instruments of his will on earth in the liberation of the Holy Places. And because the French (the *gens Francorum*) were particularly dependable fighters in defence of the Christian faith, they were glorified, in the formulations of French historians writing in the twelfth century, as a people with a special mandate within God's plan for mankind. As God's representatives, the popes looked to France for consistently loyal support. This had begun at the time when the papacy was threatened by its Lombard opponents back in the eighth century, and it extended up to the preaching of the crusade by the first northern French pope, Urban II, in 1095. In Old French epic poetry France was portrayed as the best and most ideal country in the world, the home of noble knights and great Christian heroes. Poets and troubadours made 'sweet France' (*dulce France*) the focus of positive emotions. In the *Song of Roland*, Roland dies fighting the Moors for his homeland and for Christendom. And from this France the ideal monarch, Charlemagne, holds sway over his empire and subjugates the pagan Saxons east of the Rhine.

These potential forces for identification were also used in the twelfth century by the French kings and their ecclesiastical circle. Although individual kings such as Philip I repeatedly incurred the wrath of the popes, the monarchy as an institution did not become the focus of controversy. Much as they had protected the popes in the Carolingian period, the kings continually proved themselves trustworthy supporters of the papacy in its conflicts with the Salian and Hohenstaufen emperors. In their own estimation as well as in papal rhetoric the French monarchs became the 'most Christian kings' (*reges christianissimi*).

Thus, when Pope Paschal II found himself under pressure from King Henry V in 1107, what he did was to travel to France. There he met King Philip I and his heir, Louis (the future Louis VI), at the abbey of Saint-Denis, pope and king renewing the old alliance against the oppressors and enemies of the Christian Church which Pope Stephen II and the Frankish king Pippin had forged 350 years earlier. In his account of the life of Louis VI, Abbot Suger of Saint-Denis propagated the idea of a French self-assurance which resulted from that event and which flowed from the convergence of many older notions: for Suger, France would be the culmination of Carolingian traditions. Frankish royal right would also require that Germany and

England should be subjected to the French. In this way France would reign supreme as 'mistress of the lands' (*domina terrarum*).

Working with Abbot Suger, King Louis VI skilfully used these sorts of sentiments when the emperor, Henry V—the 'German tyrant' (*Teutonicus tyrannus*) according to Suger—planned an invasion of France in 1124. In the face of this danger, the relics of the saints venerated at Saint-Denis—SS Dionysius, Rusticus, and Eleuterius— were solemnly raised up, and the king ritually placed himself under St Dionysius' lordship. He then symbolically received a church banner from the altar of the monastery church, thereby turning himself into the standard bearer of St Dionysius, who now functioned as the patron saint of the whole kingdom. In this way the king united 'the whole of France' (*tota Francia*) against its German opponents, who duly decided against pressing their attack any further.[2] Over the course of the twelfth century the flag became identified with the *oriflamme*, the 'golden flaming' banner held by Charlemagne and taken into battle against the heathen by Roland. Right up to the fifteenth century the French kings were to take the *oriflamme* with them on their military campaigns as a symbol of victory.

In 1124 the immediate interests of the monastery (claims to lordship in the Vexin, the area north of Paris, which the banner symbolized) and those of the monarchy (to project St Dionysius as the protector of France) momentarily coincided. The French kings also exploited cults and their related traditions from other places in order to enhance themselves. For example, as far back as the ninth century the church of Reims had claimed possession of a holy chrism which, it was believed, a dove had brought down from heaven in an ampoule for the anointing of King Clovis (481–511) by Bishop Remigius of Reims. From the ninth century onwards, the archbishops of Reims propagated belief in this chrism in order to establish an exclusive right to consecrate the French kings, a claim that was contested by the archbishops of Sens. This dispute meant that the kings came only hesitantly to adopt the claim made by Reims, even though it was clear that the heavenly chrism would lend the person being anointed a special status. The kings' reservations stemmed from a concern not to make the monarchy too dependent on a single prelate for the

---

[2] Suger, *Vie de Louis VI le Gros*, ed. H. Waquet (Les classiques de l'histoire de France au moyen âge 11; Paris, 1929), 220.

performance of their coronations. Indeed, up to the twelfth century the kings had themselves anointed by the archbishops of Reims *and* Sens. In this way, neither archbishop was able to exploit the early crisis years of the Capetian dynasty to achieve a dominant position. Only in the twelfth century did the monarchy become sufficiently secure institutionally to allow itself to be reliant on a single prelate conducting the crowning ritual. Accordingly, the thirteenth-century kings took hold of the Reims story of the heavenly ampoule and incorporated it within their coronation *ordo*. Until well into the modern period, the anointing of monarchs at their coronations lent them a particular lustre and a particular status as mediator between God and the people.

So, the 'royal religion' that emerged from the fusion of different elements served to raise the king above his subjects and to give the French people a means of identification that was rich in potential. The status of the monarchy was still further enhanced through the recourse made to Charlemagne as the ideal Christian king of medieval Europe. The trauma of the Capetians' violent usurpation of authority from the Carolingians gradually eased with the passage of time. Nonetheless, the victors of 987 continued to be burdened by the negative implications of a prophecy attributed to St Valerius, to the effect that Hugh Capet and his successors would only occupy the throne for seven generations. Once the passage of more than a hundred years had granted it some sense of distance, the new dynasty gradually began to forge connections with its Carolingian predecessors. King Philip I was the first to revive the name Louis for his son— a name that had long been associated with Merovingian and Carolingian royal naming practices. From the time of Louis VI onwards, this name, which evoked memories of Clovis, of Louis the Pious, and of the last Carolingian Louis V, became very popular within the Capetian line. A further hundred years later, the name Charles also re-entered use, in the first instance being applied to an illegitimate son of Philip II, and then as a second name given to one of Louis VIII's sons, the Charles of Anjou who would later bring about the destruction of the Hohenstaufen dynasty in southern Italy.

From the twelfth century onwards, increasing use was made of dynastic arguments; and the court thereby came to adopt a structural vision that had developed elsewhere. Thus Andrew of Marchiennes organized his history of the French kings, a work completed in 1196, around the schema of three dynasties, the Merovingians, the Carolingians, and the Capetians. This historian attached particular importance to the marriage of Philip II Augustus to Elizabeth of Hainaut, for she was a member of the Flemish comital house which traced its descent from Charlemagne: in their son, Louis VIII (1223–6), the blood of the Carolingians and the Capetians was duly merged. After seven generations, Louis VIII represented the Carolingian line's return to the throne, a process known as the *reditus regni Francorum ad stirpem Karoli Magni* (the reversion of the kingdom of the French to the bloodline of Charlemagne). Thirteenth-century historiography written within the circle of the French kings picked up and developed this Flemish connection. The cult of Charlemagne already had a long history thanks to twelfth-century vernacular poetry. Now it became a central feature of royal representation, propagated in the official historiography of the kingdom. Starting in the late twelfth century, monks from the royal abbey of Saint-Denis collected historical works and spliced them together to fashion a single chronicle account of the kingdom, the people, and the monarchy. With the support of the royal court, this Latin compilation was translated into French in the second half of the thirteenth century. The *Grandes Chroniques de France*, copies of which were numerous, successfully spread their version of national history and in the process cemented a binding historical consciousness.

According to the vision expressed in these works, the particular worth of the people was a corollary of the kings' political successes. From 1204 onwards Philip Augustus and his successors expanded their authority beyond the narrow royal domain between the Loire and the Meuse into the whole kingdom. In 1214 Philip won a great victory at Bouvines over the emperor, Otto IV. Philip and his son Louis also overcame King John of England. The king and his historians exploited these triumphs in order to parade their superiority. As Philip's biographer William the Breton observed, Philip had defeated the Saxons just as Charlemagne had done. Accordingly, he merited the honorific title of *augustus*, the augmenter of the kingdom. Similarly, Gerald of Wales argued that Philip bore comparison with Charlemagne: for would he not restore the former Frankish empire to its full extent? Philip had Giles of Paris compose a mirror of princes for his son Louis to aid him in his education as a ruler. The book bore the title *Carolinus* and portrayed Charlemagne as the ideal model for all subsequent kings. Once again, then, the venerable history of the Franks served the present-day interests of the central medieval French. In the thirteenth century King Louis IX (1226–70) definitively rearranged the tombs of the kings and queens at Saint-Denis. Now the rulers buried there formed two rows close to one another, with the Merovingians and Carolingians on one side and the Robertians/Capetians on the other. Between the two rows stood the tombs of Philip Augustus and his son Louis VIII like connecting limbs. In them the blood of the three lines had come together again to create the unified dynasty of the *reges Francorum*, the kings of the Franks and of the French.

Conclusion: constructing identities of medieval France

Medieval France was not shaped by a single identity. The growth of an awareness of the significance of place in the unfolding of history, and of the particular qualities of one's own people, was a slow and not always unitary process. It involved the fusion of diverse elements rooted in both continuity and renewal. Changes in ideas reflected political needs and contingencies. Periods of weakness generated intensive historiographical reflections on the question of self-evaluation, which people in times of strength were able to pick up and exploit to redevelop their own identities. This is why this chapter has combined a consideration of the development of political frameworks with a description of the various elements that contributed to the emergence of French self-awareness in the central medieval period. The ecclesiastical circles in and around the royal court were instrumental in shaping this process, setting the monarchy on the course that it would follow over the medieval period, first of all in asserting itself in relation to the Empire to the east, then in its struggles against the aristocratic forces within its own kingdom, and finally in competition against the Anglo-Norman kings. In the thirteenth century the diverse developmental strands were pulled together to create a theory of monarchy based on the concept of the royal nation. This did not mean, however, that the development of political thinking in France came to an abrupt end. The great status enjoyed by the

French kings in Europe corresponded neatly with the self-assurance that was given direction by the 'royal religion': the long history of the Trojans, Franks, and French, the special mission which the people had in the world, the monarchy's importance in the scheme of salvation, distinguished symbols such as the Oriflamme, and widely recognized rituals such as the unction with holy oil or the royal touch—all these pointed the way ahead for the nation.

In comparison with other kingdoms, the French experience reveals an unusual degree of consistency. Its success resulted from its capacity to react to challenges in flexible ways, and to retain a core of values and concepts bearing on its sense of worth. Equally significant was its ability to adopt new elements of tradition derived from diverse sources, and then to develop them still further in the context of a greater whole. Viewed in terms of its impact, the creation of French identity in the Middle Ages proved unique in European history.

2

Political culture

Geoffrey Koziol

In 754, three years after Pippin the Short had deposed the last Merovingian to become king of the Franks, Pope Stephen II levelled a curse good to the end of time against any who would ever choose a king from outside Pippin's line. Some 130 years later, in the face of a pressing Viking threat and mindful that the four previous Carolingians had proven themselves arrogant, incompetent, or simply fatally unlucky, the northern magnates of the west Frankish kingdom did just that, overriding the claims of the three-year-old Charles, great-great-great-grandson of Pippin, and electing as king Odo, count of Paris and margrave of Neustria. Judging by the next 300 years of west Frankish history, God must have taken Stephen's curse seriously, for Odo's reign (888–98) begins a sorry story. Civil wars and treacheries followed in an endless succession that numbed even contemporaries. Alliances, truces, and treaties were repudiated at first advantage. Kings were imprisoned or deposed, counts, bishops, and court favourites assassinated, and conspiracies and intrigues abounded. The wonder of it is that the Franks kept doing it, over and over, for three centuries, swearing oaths they knew would be broken, anointing kings they would conspire against, accepting safe conducts they knew could be violated.

In considering these 300 years of failings, affronts, and defeats, the still greater wonder is that the kingdom remained a kingdom at all. If one looks at the tenth and eleventh centuries, every predictor indicates that 'France' should have become nothing more than a small, rump kingdom comprising territories between the Loire and the Aisne, a vestige of Carolingian greatness. Surrounding it would be the entirely separate kingdoms of Aquitaine, Normandy, and Flanders. Even as late as the middle of the twelfth century, one can easily imagine something like a grand-palatinate duchy of Champagne developing in the east, while the south became an Italian-style jumble of atomized lordships and city-states. And in the west, north-west, and south-west, the joining of England, Normandy, Aquitaine, and Anjou under the rule of Henry II Plantagenet in 1154 could have created a lasting empire that either dwarfed France, absorbed it, or annexed it outright.

So close was 'France' to developing along these lines that in the late tenth and eleventh centuries, chroniclers did, in fact, speak of Aquitaine, Flanders, and Normandy as kingdoms, while the counts and dukes who ruled those 'kingdoms' appropriated a host of attributes, privileges, and rituals taken directly from royal models that made them appear extremely kingly. Yet they never became kings. Though Flanders could be referred to as a monarchy, its ruler was always a count, at best a marquis, but never a king; and the same was true for every other principality. Even the dukes of Normandy, after 1066 often kings of England, ruled in Normandy only as dukes and did some sort of homage to the kings of France for their duchy. The single surest sign that no matter how much power devolved to the great territorial princes their principalities would not become kingdoms is the fact that, though these rulers were often fêted in ways that were reminiscent of royal honours, not a single one was ever anointed, or even tried to be. The kings did not enforce this rule; they did not have the power to. The magnates had the power to repudiate the rule; they did not. Somehow, the magnates themselves recognized a line between being a count or duke exercising regalian rights and privileges over a county or duchy, and being the anointed king of the Franks, and no one tried to erase it or cross it. There was a kingdom of the Franks, it could have only one king, and everyone knew it.

In trying to understand what it was that kept the idea of a French kingdom or French kingship intact, as Bernd Schneidmüller's chapter reveals, historians have emphasized the idea of the sanctity of the royal office, the belief that the royal office was instituted by God, that by virtue of an anointing modelled on the Old Testament anointings of the kings of Israel and ritually similar to the anointing of a bishop, kings took on something of the grace of God. A king became literally God's *christus*—his 'anointed one'. In token of this 'christomimesis', every solemn entry of a king into a city of his dominions was choreographed as a formal religious procession imitative of Christ's entry into Jerusalem before the Passion. And on great feast days a king would enter a church, perhaps cloaked in a purple mantle studded with stars and emblems of the Apocalypse, and kneel to deposit his crown on the high altar over which hung a crown, in recognition that the king held his crown from God, the King of kings.

Though true to a significant extent, any explanation for the durability of west Frankish kingship based on the religious aspects of the office cannot be the whole story. It does not explain why such beliefs retained currency when so much reality went against them. It assumes that the Latin prayers offered at a king's anointing by the literate clergy of Reims were believed by lay counts as ruthless as Arnulf I of Flanders (d. 965), Fulk Nerra of Anjou (d. 1040), and William II of Normandy (d. 1087). In fact, it is hard to find any great respect for the Lord's anointed in the magnates' treatment of Charles the Simple (898–922) and Louis d'Outremer (936–54) during the tenth-century civil wars, while explicit articulations of disrespect to kings were fairly commonplace. This is particularly true of the Capetians, and particularly jarring, since the Capetians worked so hard to develop a religion of monarchy. Unusually solicitous of their reputations as defenders of the Church and the reformed papacy, the twelfth-century Capetians especially took strong stands against the antipopes sponsored by the German emperors, and welcomed popes fleeing Italy for extended stays in the royal domain. Louis VI (1108–37) milked this papal alliance for all it was worth, appearing with the pope or his legates in ecclesiastical councils as Rome's devoted servant, gaining ecclesiastical sanction for his military campaigns, and even having his son anointed in a plenary council by Innocent II himself. Louis VII (1137–80), the son Innocent anointed, used Henry II's quarrel with Thomas Becket to represent himself as more loyal to the cause of ecclesiastical reform than the pope himself by adopting an even harder line towards Henry than the pope wanted. Nor was the piety of these kings a mere pose. Louis's crusade in 1147–9 was probably associated with his belief, or the belief of those around him, that he was the Last Emperor, who would lay down his crown in Jerusalem in anticipation of the return of Christ the King. And Robert the Pious (996–1031) and Louis VII both made care for the sick and the poor central to the public rituals of their reigns.

Yet against such high-minded sentiments, we have to place the jokes and taunts that circulated about the Capetians. 'Who made you count?' Hugh Capet and his son are said to have asked Aldebert of La Marche. 'Who made you kings?' was Aldebert's sly retort.[1] The monks of Fleury celebrated Robert the Pious as something close to a saint, but the bishop of Cambrai referred to his *imbecillitas*, a word that connoted both feminine incapacity and monkish prudery.[2] Almost no one had anything good to say about Philip I (1060–1108), French, Norman, and Burgundian chroniclers alike depicting him as wallowing in lust and gluttony and utterly useless to the kingdom. The reputation of Philip's son Louis VI has always benefited from his having a sympathetic biographer in Suger, abbot of Saint-Denis; but though Suger liked Louis immensely and respected his devotion to the Church, he knew his weaknesses, and if he veiled them he did not omit them. Louis was reckless, lacked foresight, and was too in love with the romantic ideal of a swashbuckling knight to be a great king; besides, by the end of his life he had become as fat as his father. As for Louis VII, his first wife, Eleanor of Aquitaine, complained that he was more a monk than a man, and for all his high ideals, his leadership during the Second Crusade was such a disaster that his brother returned from the Holy Land and mounted a campaign to depose him based on his demonstrated incompetence. However, what is perhaps most surprising is that the kings made fun of themselves, as when Louis VII spoke jokingly of Henry II of England, who had everything a king could want—warriors, horses, gold, silk, jewels, fruit, game—'while we in France have nothing but bread and wine and gaiety'.[3]

Clearly we are missing something. It cannot simply be (as more than one historian has claimed) that the kings were such nonentities that no one bothered to depose them. Nor can it simply be (as Odo II of Blois actually said of Robert the Pious, in yet another joke at a king's expense) that the magnates thought it less profitable to be king than the king's master. After all, Odo's political career ended with repeated disappointment and defeat, while Robert annexed half of Burgundy and had a life written of him that portrays him as a just

---

[1] Adhemar of Chabannes, *Chronique*, ed. J. Chavanon (Collection de textes pour servir à l'étude et à l'enseignement de l'histoire, 20; Paris, 1897), 205.

[2] 'Gesta episcoporum Cameracensium', *Monumenta Germaniae Historica Scriptores*, ed. G. H. Pertz et al. (Hanover etc., 1826–), vii.474.

[3] Walter Map, *De Nugis Curialium*, ed. and trans. M. R. James, rev. C. N. L. Brooke and R. A. B. Mynors (Oxford, 1983), 450.

and holy king who could heal lepers simply by making the sign of the cross over them. Raw power cannot have been the only measure of successful kingship in this society, nor can a common language, a common law, and common institutions have been the only sources for a sense of belonging to a community. The durability of France and French kingship lies elsewhere: not in power or institutions, but in a shared political culture of which kingship was an expression.

Fundamental assumptions

By the Treaty of Verdun, Charles the Bald (840–77), youngest son of Louis the Pious, received his brothers' recognition as king over the western regions of the Carolingian empire. But all the treaty did was give Charles a claim. Making good that claim entailed a different set of tasks, and it was not a foregone conclusion that Charles would succeed at them. In November 843, for example, three months after Verdun, Charles faced continued resistance in Aquitaine from his nephew Pippin II, a growing feud among the Neustrian aristocracy, defection by the Bretons, and renewed invasions by Vikings. Sensing Charles's weakness and their strength, a group of magnates met and agreed on a platform among themselves, less a list of demands than a set of expectations and principles they wanted Charles to accept before they would support him. Young, proud, and indignant that he should have to kowtow to anyone, Charles wanted to reject such pressure tactics, but that would have been political suicide. So with the smoothness he habitually displayed, the twenty-year-old king went to Coulaines, on the Neustrian–Breton frontier, and accepted the demands while representing them as his own decision in a royal administrative decree (a capitulary). Changing the form, however, could not change the fact. The magnates had banded together as a group, established an agreement among themselves (a *convenientia*), and the king had had to accept it. The final article of the text states this fact clearly: though issued in the name of the king, the capitulary actually recorded a treaty (*foedus concordiae*) between the king and the magnates, to which the king himself subscribed as a party. According to the terms of this treaty, the magnates agreed to reverence Charles's authority, give him aid and counsel, and avoid factionalism. In turn, Charles agreed to protect the Church, its properties, and the privileges of the clergy. He agreed to maintain the law of every individual of any administrative grade, to deprive no one of his honour save through just judgement, and to deal fairly with everyone. And should he stray from these ideals, he agreed that he would listen to the warnings and remedies of his magnates. Whatever his rhetorical spin, at Coulaines Charles made promises. He continued to make the same promises at every critical juncture of his reign, and his magnates reciprocated with their own.

The idea that magnates could bind themselves by negotiated agreements (*convenientiae, pactiones, concordiae, foedera*), the idea that the same sorts of agreements could bind kings and magnates to specific obligations towards each other, the idea that a king's rule could even be made contingent on such consensual agreements—these became some of the most distinctive elements of west Frankish politics, enshrined in the oaths of good governance that, beginning with the contested accession of Charles's son Louis II, 'the Stammerer' (877–9), kings were required to swear aloud, subscribe to in writing, and deposit on the altar before being anointed. These were the first principles of what might be considered the 'unwritten constitution' of the west Frankish kingdom as it developed in the second half of the ninth century.

Another fundamental principle also came out of ninth-century developments. Odo's election as king in 888 was a recognition that the dynastic right of the Carolingians was not the only consideration in making a king: bravery, skill, and military leadership were also important, and in emergencies could be determining criteria. Odo more than satisfied these other criteria, for, like his father, he had been the count responsible for defending the march that fronted the Vikings. But this meant that Odo thought like a marcher lord rather than like a king, so that even as king he assumed that counts had rights and privileges, and that those rights and privileges were necessary for effective defence. Rather than seeing strong counts as a weakness, Odo saw them both as a necessity and as a good in itself. Far from obstructing the accumulation of power by regional princes as a Carolingian might have done, Odo therefore furthered it. In effect, he gave the counts of Auvergne and Autun unusual leeway, and unusual perquisites. He allowed them to control the appointment of bishops within Aquitaine and Burgundy, to add to the numbers of counties they directly controlled in these territories, and to bring secondary counts and nobles into their clientage through homage, dependent marriages, and appointment to honours such as viscounties and prelacies.

Odo also gave each control of an important monastery: Saint-Julien at Brioude for William the Pious, count of Auvergne (d. 918); Saint-Germain in Auxerre for Richard the Justiciar, count of Autun (d. 921). The importance of these monasteries for defining the authority of the two territorial princes cannot be overstated. Though a layman, the count who controlled the monastery became its abbot. As abbot, he gained the right to administer its extensive temporalities as he saw fit and to use those temporalities to reward himself and his supporters. Even more important, by virtue of their lay abbacies, William and Richard became something more than ordinary counts—no longer just viceregal figures in terms of their military and judicial power, but viceregal figures in terms of their relationship to the Church. Though not kings, Richard and William became, like kings, responsible for protecting the Church, the clergy, and the poor. They acquired a king's responsibility for ensuring the proper obser-vance of the cult activities that propitiated the saints who gave vic-tory, fertility of crops, and security from disease within territories traditionally recognized as sub-kingdoms. They also acquired, like kings, something of a sacred aura. They presided over liturgical cere-monies in the abbey, used the abbey's relics and emblems for their battles, sat in the abbot's seat to give properties to vassals or hear complaints and grievances of the oppressed. And they began to issue charters, modelled on royal diplomas, that awarded them honorific titles and epithets, titles invented to make them less than kings but more than counts, epithets that had normally been the prerogative of kings. They were 'princes', 'dukes', 'margraves', 'rulers' (*principes, duces, marchiones, rectores*), 'most glorious', 'most serene', 'most illus-trious', 'excellent beyond compare'. They claimed to rule 'by the grace of God', as did kings, bishops, and abbots; and ruling by the grace of God, their faithful approached them in prayer, as they would God or these rulers: prostrate or kneeling, hands outstretched, beg-ging for an act of grace, entreating for mercy, clamouring for justice against oppressors. And these prerogatives must also have stemmed from Odo's sense not just of what was necessary but of what was right, for even before his elevation to the throne, as lay abbot of

Saint-Martin of Tours, he had issued charters with exactly the same language.

These are the two foundational principles of west Frankish political culture: the right of magnates to be honoured by a king as they would honour him; and the right of magnates to rule territories with viceregal authority, with privileges and prerogatives that imitated royal privileges and prerogatives, yet were founded not just on a royal grant but on a divinely ordained order that sanctioned the power of kings and magnates alike.

Agreements like Coulaines, coronation oaths like Louis the Stammerer's, and the formation of the first territorial principalities under Odo: it was once thought that these were the first steps on the road to the collapse of royal power in west Francia—a fragmentation of power and authority to the benefit of magnates that hamstrung both kingship and French unity for centuries, and required the tough-minded aggressiveness of Philip Augustus to set right. Certainly one cannot deny that kings did lose power, insofar as power is manifested by a monarch's unquestioned right to intervene everywhere in his kingdom. It is equally certain that the result of these developments was to place an unusually complete array of powers in the hands of magnates, beginning the dissolution of the kingdom into an assortment of territorial principalities that functioned with such autonomy that France became essentially a 'mosaic kingdom'. However, the important point in understanding French political culture is that this devolution of authority was not thought wrong. Magnates did not want strong kingship. They wanted just kingship. And just kingship was defined as both embodying and protecting an order in which magnates ruled their territories in imitation of kings and by the grace of God.

How this worked in practice was shown in 924, in the aftermath of Charles the Simple's deposition, when William II (d. 926), duke of Aquitaine and successor to William the Pious, refused to recognize Raoul's anointing. Raoul finally gained his adhesion not by conquering William but by treating with him. Going to the Loire, the king waited with his retinue on his side of the river, while William and his retinue waited on theirs, each side sending negotiators back and forth for an entire day until they reached an agreement: William crossed the river, rode into Raoul's camp, dismounted, and approached the king, who was still mounted on his horse. Then, after receiving

Raoul's kiss, William returned across the Loire. After a week of further negotiations, William did finally do homage to Raoul; yet Raoul never did cross the Loire into Aquitaine, and by respecting that boundary implicitly recognized William's control over the region. It was not (or not simply) a matter of William's power and Raoul's lack of it; it was a matter of a just and well-ordered system of governance. How could it have been otherwise, when Charles had been deposed by a coalition of magnates led by Robert of Neustria, Odo's brother, and Raoul himself, Richard the Justiciar's son?

Once introduced into political discourse, these principles became overdetermined, meaning that the principles shaped political geography, while that geography, now become a fact of life, embedded the principles more deeply within west Frankish political culture. In the late tenth century, when a pro-Capetian apologist like Abbo of Fleury stated his expectations for the new dynasty, his fundamental presupposition was recognizably an outgrowth of Coulaines: the magnates will reverence their kings, because kings will reverence their magnates. Looking back with the benefit of hindsight on the failure of the Carolingians, early Capetian writers saw the downfall of the dynasty as its kings' failure to respect the principle of consensus and the right of magnates to rule. Dudo of Saint-Quentin therefore explained Louis IV's humiliating captivity in 945–6 as the result of the king's failure to respect the honour of Hugh the Great and the young Richard I, respectively duke of the Franks and duke of the Normans. Richer of Reims identified the trigger for Charles the Simple's deposition as the king's attempt to oust Robert of Neustria and other west Frankish magnates from his counsels, to rule not only against their advice but without their advice. As for Hugh Capet, he is shown by Richer in the years immediately before and after his anointing as deserving to be king precisely because he made no decision without seeking the advice of his own followers. To contemporaries, then, Hugh was neither a weak king nor a vacillating leader. He was, like his great-uncle Odo, at heart a territorial magnate, and shared the territorial magnates' fundamental assumptions: a just and good king recognized that kings and princes each had their proper spheres, and the proper sphere of a king was to protect and respect the rights and privileges of dukes and counts.

The mimetic power of kingship

Charles the Simple and Louis d'Outremer had to deal with a handful of territorial princes: the dukes, margraves, and counts of Aquitaine, Burgundy, Flanders, Vermandois, Gothia—and of course the duke of the Franks. By the second half of the tenth century, these principalities were themselves in a state of decomposition. The dukes of Burgundy and Aquitaine and the margraves of Gothia had lost effective control over the counties of their territories, leaving local power in the hands of counts, viscounts, bishops, chapters, and monasteries, often a single city being torn between rival lords. Inheritance and marriages by the sons and grandsons of Herbert II of Vermandois (d. 943) had fragmented and recombined his vast dominions into a grouping of only loosely affiliated counties at Troyes, Saint-Quentin, and Blois. Even the dukes of the Franks were subject to the trend, as their viscounts at Angers and Tours established strong counties in Anjou and Blois and acted quite independently of, and often antagonistically towards, their nominal lords. During the late tenth and early eleventh centuries the fragmentation proceeded further still, beneath the level of county and viscounty to the castellany.

Many historians have seen the process by which castellans established *de facto* autonomy from counts as one of complete anarchy. Revisionists have recently criticized this assessment as excessive; but even they recognize that at some point in the eleventh century, almost every region in the kingdom suffered some critical period in which castellans and local counts acted as if they were entirely free of any superior control, using their castles, revenues, and control of manpower to create new jurisdictions, no longer delimited by the boundaries of the old Carolingian *pagus* but by the area that could be dominated by a single family from its castle. Still, the revisionists are right to point out the speed with which moments of anarchy were righted and a new equilibrium established. Though the locus of power was no longer the county or *pagus* but the castellany, the majority of castellanies were controlled by descendants of the same families that had been prominent in the retinues of tenth- or even ninth-century counts and viscounts. More important, by the early twelfth century, a handful of great princely families had once again come to dominate political life. If the first fact speaks of the surprising resilience of the oldest aristocratic families and the care with which they husbanded their vast economic resources, the second speaks of the resilience of the fundamental principles of west Frankish political culture inherited from the Carolingians and reinterpreted for an age of castles.

In effect, when kings, dukes, and great counts were confronted with the proliferation of castles, they responded by re-emphasizing the ideological principle that had been the original foundation of their authority. The presupposition was that whether a castellan's power derived from delegation, agreement, or simple brute force, it remained mere power. In contrast, the rule of the great princes represented legitimate and legitimating authority, established by God and modelled on God's qualities of rulership. The princes therefore fulfilled a divine ministry, with all the responsibilities attendant on those who ruled by the grace of God: to govern justly; to maintain the peace; to protect the defenceless. The programme was enunciated in great public trials, often staged in a church, everything calculated to highlight the immutability of public authority, as monks and clergy came before the ruler and fell to their knees, making a tearful clamour against the castellans and knights who did violence to them. Receiving the complaints mercifully, the ruler gave them to a select group of his greatest barons, the judgement a foregone conclusion; or the prince heard the complaints in the company of bishops, who collectively excommunicated the malefactor. In either case, the result was a public triumph of the old alliance of prince, prelates, and monasteries.

Even more famous as a vehicle for this programme of political renewal was the movement known as the Peace of God. It had begun developing in the last decade of the tenth century (exactly contemporaneously with the first great proliferation of independent castles) at the instigation of bishops and abbots, as a way to limit the depredations of castellans and their knights. The idea was simply to force these warriors to swear oaths that they would leave certain classes of people out of their conflicts—again principally the defenceless: clergy, monks, pilgrims, women and children, unarmed peasants, and merchants. In the second decade of the eleventh century, one finds the great rulers taking over the initiative, or at least jointly presiding with bishops over the assemblies where the oaths were sworn. The dukes of Aquitaine and Normandy, the count of Flanders, the king himself, all sponsored Peace councils, open-air assemblies outside the towns of their dominions at which princes and bishops surrounded themselves with relics of saints brought from monasteries, all gathered together in another public triumph of God's order of earthly governance.

This is why Aquitaine, Flanders, and Normandy came to be called 'kingdoms' (*monarchiae, regna*). The usage did not mean that these principalities were free of the kingdom of the west Franks. It meant that the governance of these territories was *imitative* of the kingdom's. Thus, the rites and prerogatives developed by eleventh-century princes to exalt their authority were not aimed at diminishing the authority of the king; they were intended to use the idea of royal authority to legitimate the princes' own authority over their own subjects. So just like kings, the dukes of Normandy and the counts of Flanders were fêted with chants known as *laudes* ('praises'). Just as in a royal *adventus*, the entry of a count into one of his cities was celebrated with a liturgical procession of monks and clerics chanting hymns. And though the great territorial magnates were never anointed as kings, they were still installed with formal liturgical rites that echoed the investitures of new kings.

Quite apart from the reactive reassertion of princely authority, there was a second brake on the 'anarchy' associated with the rise of castellans. True anarchy being inherently unstable, rogue lordships being difficult to sustain over a long period of time, eventually the castellans themselves became legitimate powers in the political landscape. At that point (roughly, after the First Crusade) one finds castellans acting like little counts. Just as a royal or ducal palace of the tenth century was distinguished by the conjoined presence within a single large enclosure of assembly hall, fortification, and church, so every castle enclosed tower, eating hall, and church of secular canons. Just as every princely family had one or more churches closely tied to its dynastic memory that acted as necropoles, so members of the castellan dynasties were buried in the churches of their castles, their funerals accompanied by a cortège of knights, clergy, and townspeople, a microcosm of the three social orders over which the castellan ruled, as a king ruled over the three orders of the kingdom. And within this microcosmic political order, there was again an expectation of consensus, as the knights of a castle gathered around their lord to give him counsel in matters of justice, warfare, and diplomacy.

The political culture of France was therefore fundamentally and thoroughly mimetic. Understanding this, we can begin to answer the question posed by west Frankish political history: why did kings and kingdom remain intact when kings were weak and the kingdom disunited? The most elemental reason is that a duke or margrave could not repudiate the legitimacy of a king's office, a count repudiate a duke's, a castellan a count's, without repudiating the very basis of his own authority over his own subalterns. And a society without any foundation for any authority—that was an anarchy dreaded by all, for it could have no winners.

The balance of power

Emphasizing not what kings lacked with respect to their territorial magnates but what they shared suggests other reasons for the durability of kings and kingdom. Reading of the rebellions against Robert the Pious and Henry I (1031–60) or of the trouble Philip I and Louis VI had controlling their own castellans and counts (let alone the dukes of Normandy and counts of Champagne), one is led to focus on how weak the kings were and wonder how they remained kings. But this misses an obvious point: at one time or another, every territorial prince had exactly the same trouble with his counts and castellans that the kings had with theirs. The trouble was not constant, to be sure, but that was true of the kings, too. Where historians have tended to narrate Capetian history as a story of the kings' endless difficulties with a restive local nobility, in fact, rebellions, insurrections, and simple troublemaking usually occurred only at transitions of reigns—exactly what was true in every single county and castellany in the kingdom. Everywhere, a minority, the extinction of a line, or even a simple succession led to the testing of limits and, quite often, open civil war. This was true even in the strongest of principalities: in Normandy during the minority of William the Conqueror (1035–47) and after the deaths of William Rufus (d. 1100) and Henry I (d. 1135); in Anjou, when Fulk le Réchin expelled his brother from the county (1068); in Flanders after the death of Baldwin VI, when Robert the Frisian usurped the county from an under-age nephew (1071), and again after the murder of Charles the Good left the county without any clear successor by patrilineal right (1127).

When we read Suger's history of the wars fought by Louis VI to impose his authority over the counts and castellans of the Île-de-France, we are amazed at how many different contending powers Louis had to master: the counts of Beaumont, the counts of Rochefort, the lords of Crécy, Corbeil, La Roche-Guyon, Le Puiset, Montmorency, Mouchy, and Montlhéry—all within an area no more than fifty kilometres from Paris. If the kings could not control their own domains, how could they control the kingdom? Again, however, the trouble Louis VI had with these lords came almost entirely towards the end of his father's reign and at the beginning of his own, when he was trying to escape the network of alliances that had supported his father and build up his own network that would allow him to be his own king. Equally important, the thick undergrowth of minor counties and castellanies that characterized the royal domain also characterized most other principalities. The duke of Aquitaine, for instance, had to contend with the lords of Mauléon, Lusignan, Thouars, Châtellerault, and Talmont, each with multiple castles to buttress his power—and this just within his core county of Poitou.

The fact is that, apart from Normandy and Flanders, no lord's dominion formed a coherent territorial jurisdiction akin to a modern governmental circumscription, within which administration and justice are uniform within defined and consistent limits. Within the territories we speak of as the royal 'domain', the kings possessed this village but not the neighbouring one; had in a village all rights of justice or only rights of justice over major crimes; exercised a monopoly over fishing rights above a town but not below it; held this castle but not the next one; held minting rights in this city but shared them with the bishop in the next. Nor was the distribution of the kings' rights isomorphic throughout their domain. They had very dense personal possessions north-east of Orléans, but many fewer north and north-west of it; a large number of estates along the Seine between the Burgundian and Norman frontiers, but many fewer as soon as one moved away from the river. The royal domain was like Swiss cheese, substantial but perforated with great holes. Within those holes, local counts, castellans, knights, bishops, chapters, and abbeys all had their domains, as varied and fragmentary as the domain of the kings: villages or portions of villages; tolls or fractions of tolls; forests or only the right to graze herds in the forest. And once again, the same was true for every other ruler in the kingdom. The domains of the counts of Anjou, Blois, Troyes, Mâcon, Poitiers, and Angoulême, for example, were all as fragmentary and piecemeal within their principalities as was the royal domain, and as were the domains of their own castellans and knights.

The king was therefore not in as bad shape as one might think. He had his strengths and weaknesses, which changed over the course of a single reign almost like a life cycle: hard times in the early years, stability in the middle years, restive jockeying for position before an impending death at the end. But the same was true of every other ruler, even the strongest. This simple fact was of immense importance for the conduct of politics: it meant that politics became the art of maintaining a balance of power between one's allies and one's enemies, and knowing how and when to shift allies and enemies according to changes in their power and one's own. What everyone could be sure of is that over the medium term, the equilibrium would remain no matter how much alliances changed in the short term. The best example is perhaps Henry I, simply because he is often taken as the weakest of all Capetians, his possessions hemmed in to east and west by the domains of Odo II of Blois (d. 1037), the very magnate who said openly (of Henry's father) that he wanted to be the king's master, who formally rebelled at the beginning of Henry's reign in an insurrection so serious that the new king was forced to flee to Robert of Normandy for refuge. However, the fact remains that, in alliance with Robert, Henry mastered Odo's rebellion, as Henry's father had isolated Odo with the support of Fulk Nerra of Anjou, and as after Odo's death Henry mastered a rebellion of the counts of the Île-de-France with the support of Fulk Nerra's son, Geoffrey Martel. Of course, these alliances were not free; Henry had to give Robert of Normandy the county of Dreux, Geoffrey Martel permission to conquer Tours. But allowing Geoffrey to conquer Tours meant that Henry had shifted the balance of power in Geoffrey's favour; so Henry restored the balance by distancing himself from Geoffrey and supporting Robert of Normandy's young heir, William II, during the troubles of his minority. When William, secure in power thanks to Henry's help, began to manoeuvre against Henry by allying with the count of Flanders, Henry moved back to Geoffrey, while at the same time fomenting rebellions among William's barons, just to keep William off balance.

Nor were the magnates any different. They made and broke pacts as cavalierly as did the king, used the king just as the king used them. Our perception of royal weakness is again falsified by focusing on the king rather than on the political culture of which kingship was a part. Restricting our frame of analysis to Henry's domains, we cannot help but see the fragility of his position with respect to Odo II of Blois. Widen the frame and we see that from Odo's perspective, it was *his* position that was fragile, since his core dominions around Blois, Chartres, and Châteaudun were themselves hemmed in by the royal domains on his east, Norman domains to his north, and Angevin domains to his west. What protected Odo was what protected the king: an ability to make the enemies of his enemies his friends. And Odo could maintain that balance because the dukes of Normandy and the counts of Anjou were themselves rivals for control over Maine, the buffer county between their territories. In other words, to Blois, Anjou was a greater enemy than the king, as Normandy was a greater enemy to Anjou. For all three, Henry I was more useful as an ally than an enemy. Indeed, most of Odo's insurrections and intrigues were intended not to crush the king, nor even weaken him, but simply to detach him from his Angevin alliance.

The material foundations of power

Over the course of the 200 years between Hugh Capet's election (987) and the great conquests of Philip Augustus (1203–6), alliances changed in the short term within a balance of power that was fairly stable in the medium term. Over the long term, however, the entire structure of power shifted noticeably towards the greatest princes, ultimately favouring the king above all, and thereby making Philip's conquests possible in the first place. One can see the shift clearly in the changes undergone by so-called 'feudal' relations: the commendation of man to lord known as homage, which made a man the vassal of a lord; the oath of loyalty by vassal to lord known as fidelity; and the grant of a fief by lord to man. In the late tenth and early eleventh centuries, such feudal ties were an agent in the disintegration of political loyalties, as knights and castellans did homage to and received fiefs from a multiplicity of greater lords, allowing them to play off their lords against each other. In the early twelfth century, however, feudal relations became an agent in the consolidation of political order around kings and princes, as priority homages and a hierarchy of fiefs came to be recognized, and the lesser nobility came to be more vulnerable to the confiscation of a fief by a single lord. What made these different outcomes possible were changes in the material conditions of power within which feudal ties operated.

To put it simply, the transformative story of the eleventh and twelfth centuries was the economic and governmental colonization of formerly underdeveloped and undergoverned internal spaces. In counties, castellanies, and fiefs of all sorts, the number of towns, villages, and parishes increased, forests were cleared, new fields planted, and markets founded. The economy grew richer and more intensively exploited. Lordship grew richer and more exploitative. The effects on power were dramatic. In the late tenth century, when armies were small and domains inefficiently exploited, it took little for a wildcat lord to build a castle of the 'motte and bailey' type: a tower (the 'keep'), occasionally of stone but more often of wood, surrounded by a few wooden outbuildings in a yard (the 'bailey') enclosed by a wooden palisade, all atop an artificial mound of packed earth no more than ten metres high (the 'motte'). A fortification so simple would never suffice against a large army, but it was never intended to. It was meant only to make a ruler think twice before attacking and, more than that, to serve as a base from which to harass the local peasantry and attack and defend during feuds and military rivalries with neighbouring lords, all of them doing exactly the same thing. Beginning in the second half of the eleventh century, and absolutely by the first half of the twelfth century, the motte-and-bailey castle became outmoded. It could not hold against the stone keeps (*donjons*) that were becoming the military norm. By the second third of the twelfth century, and even more by the last third, stone keeps themselves could not hold against the great castles being built on the model of fortifications in the Latin East—castles like Richard the Lionheart's Château-Gaillard, built in 1197–8 to defend his Norman border from French attack at a cost of £21,203—roughly the entire annual ducal income from Normandy. Who but the greatest princes could afford such castles—remembering especially that a castle was built not in isolation but as part of a tactical network comprising multiple fortifications of different functional types? Who else could afford the manpower to garrison the castles, the supplies to provision them, the labour to maintain the road system that connected them? Who else could afford the mercenaries that fought in advance of them? Who else could afford the diplomacy that laid the groundwork for wars—like the £1,000 a year paid by Henry I of England to Robert of Flanders as a money-fief to neutralize Robert's support of Louis VI?

The rising cost of the technologies of power—military and administrative alike—worked to concentrate power in the hands of the king and the very greatest magnates, making it impossible for any castellan, however legitimate his power, to maintain his autonomy, making it difficult enough for a small-time count to maintain his. The greatest lords simply had more lands, villages, and towns, in more profitable locations, and more ways of exploiting them; and when resources failed, they had access to more and wealthier creditors (and more irresistible means of putting political pressure on them to advance loans). Castellans and small counts could not compete. Inevitably they began to fall into the orbits of the great princes. Their sons entered the princes' households and administrative service, becoming their seneschals, bailiffs, judges, and counsellors. They surrendered to the great lords their patrimonial lands and castles and received them back as fiefs, placed themselves on stipend to the lords by receiving annuities from them as fiefs, and fought for them as mercenaries. To gain more lands they might do homage to several lords, but they had to agree that their greatest lord would be their 'liege', that service to him would have priority before service to any other, and that any default of service would be sanctioned by loss of the primary fief.

Despite the magnitude of these changes, the degree of continuity is equally impressive. Not only did France remain a mosaic kingdom comprising territorial principalities, but the principalities actually gained cohesiveness and identity. Whether 'feudal' relations were structured to the advantage of vassals or lords, they were always enunciated in negotiated agreements, called (just like the capitulary of Coulaines) *convenientiae*, that defined the reciprocal obligations of each party to the other. From the courts of kings to those of castellans, decisions were made by public consensus. Such continuity is another indication that from the ninth century until the twelfth, there was a distinctive west Frankish political culture within which change was articulated. It is not so much that this culture spread throughout the aristocracy and the kingdom as that acting according to its assumptions defined both aristocracy and kingdom. It is what eventually made the west Franks French.

Queens and countesses

Women in the ruling elite may also have found it more difficult to compete in this newly avaricious politics. Unfortunately, sources that reveal something of the roles, powers, and positions of public women are subject to so many contradictions, inconsistencies, and qualifications that this or any other generalization is false or misleading. What one can say is that tenth-century sources reveal several women of high public profiles, especially but not exclusively queens. Emma, Raoul's queen, was so sure of herself that when her husband ordered her to hand over the city of Laon to her former enemies, she refused and continued to garrison it herself. Adelaide, daughter of Fulk the Good of Anjou, was undeniably instrumental in the expansion of Angevin power in the later tenth century and a central figure in the politics of the kingdom throughout her long life. Above all there was Gerberga, sister of Otto I and queen of Louis d'Outremer, who single-handedly mobilized the alliances that kept her husband from being deposed during his captivity, and who was clearly one of the three major political players in the kingdom during the first years of her son's rule.

And yet, there are countervailing indications. Emma was the daughter of Robert of Neustria; her father married her to Raoul to seal their alliance against Charles the Simple. Adelaide had four successive marriages, each one advantageous to her brother, Geoffrey Greymantle. As for Gerberga, Louis married her in order to offset Hugh the Great's alliance with Otto I, an alliance sealed by Hugh's earlier marriage to Gerberga's sister. And though Gerberga did protect her husband, her most powerful weapons in doing so were her brothers Otto and Bruno, the latter archbishop of Cologne, duke of

Lotharingia, and the agent of Otto's hegemony in west Francia. In other words, the apparent power of Emma, Adelaide, and Gerberga cannot be separated from their political usefulness to the men who headed their families. And politically useful is what many marriages in the tenth century and after seem to have been. From this perspective, women seem to have been nothing but counters in a game of alliances played by men.

And yet, there are countervailing intuitions to these countervailing indications. To begin with, though we might regard even the most powerful women as being constrained by their social roles, it is not clear that most men were any less constrained—not when the name a son was given at birth destined him to a particular office, not when he could be required to change that name if his destined office changed. Modern assumptions about the integrity and autonomy of the individual simply do not fit the Middle Ages, either for men or for women. For both, the individual served the needs of the family. Given that fact, we cannot be certain that sisters and daughters did not participate in the game of alliances as partners of their brothers and fathers, rather than as their tools. Judging by contemporary Ottonian and later French and English experience, west Frankish aristocratic women might also have believed they had a crucial role to play as wives in political marriages: maintaining communication between their natal and their marital families, passing information back and forth between the two, shaping policies and patronage to suit the needs of the alliance, and often making very delicate decisions if the alliance began to fail. If Gerberga needed her brothers' power, her brothers needed her influence. Moreover, political roles were strongly gendered, with women's roles generally being not in law courts and on campaigns but within the household and palace. The fact remains that household and palace were public institutions, of great symbolic and practical importance. Queens interceded with their royal husbands for mercy, cared for the sick, distributed alms to the poor, and wove the ceremonial mantles worn by kings and the altar cloths given to royal churches. None of these were 'private' activities. All were part of the representation of kingship as merciful, beneficent, and pious. Kingship without queenship was not only literally sterile; it was not complete.

In any case, women do seem to have exercised real and considerable influence over political affairs. Of course, influence is not the same as power. Our sources implicitly distinguish and gender the two, showing a queen's or countess's influence being manifested subtly and privately—through her privileged access to her husband's private thoughts and her ability to shape those thoughts through her own skilful use of language (language often being represented as a feminized/clerical power distinct from the masculinized/lay power of arms). As described by men, a queen's or countess's powers of persuasion could be beneficial to the community by leading her husband to acts of mercy and piety. On the other hand, they could also be a vice. In an openly competitive, militarily combative society in which consensus and rivalry between men were played out in public forums and public rituals, men feared women because they could use language to manipulate rivalries in secret. Women were therefore always imagined by men as being at the centre of intrigues, and their weapons were imagined as unmanly weapons, wielded in secrecy, that took the virtuous attributes of women and turned them vicious: instead of the medicinal herbs women used to give life, poison that took it; instead of the faithful sexuality that continued legitimate dynastic lines, the faithless adultery that corrupted them. Of course, since nearly all of our sources were written by men of the clergy, we cannot really know whether wives and stepmothers did resort to poison and adultery; they were, however, often at the centre of court intrigues. Fulk Nerra of Anjou had Robert the Pious's palace count assassinated because he was a favourite of Robert's second wife Bertha, widow of Fulk's mortal enemy the count of Blois. Robert's third wife, Constance, was central to almost every major uprising against her husband and their son Henry. Suger, abbot of Saint-Denis, hated Philip I's paramour Bertrade not just because her relationship with Philip was sinful but also because she was opposed to Saint-Denis's influence over the king, and Philip's love for her made her antagonism policy.

Such examples suggest a final consideration in evaluating the role of women of the ruling class: they *were* women of the ruling class, at least in the tenth and early eleventh centuries. Simply because political power was shaped by marriage alliances among kings and the greatest magnates, queens and countesses were usually the equals, near-equals, and sometimes superiors of their husbands. They carried themselves with the confidence of those who had powerful kin groups standing behind them: to offend Emma or Gerberga was to offend Hugh the Great and Otto I. They also carried themselves with the sense of entitlement of those born to power. An eleventh-century bishop of Chartres renowned for his intelligence and political skills was terrified of going to court, for fear of the queen's anger at him. No wonder: upon discovering that her chaplain was a heretic, the same queen struck him with her staff, killing him on the spot. Adela, countess of Blois, made it clear to her husband that she, daughter of William the Conqueror, would not be married to a coward who had fled the siege of Antioch in 1098; she sent him back to the Holy Land, where he died.

Although we continue to find politically active and independently powerful women in the twelfth century, the same long-term trends that disadvantaged castellans and knights also disadvantaged women, and here too a material substratum shaped the trends. It is likely that the high profile of tenth-century queens and countesses was supported by real material power, if we can assume that many of the patterns of the eighth and ninth centuries continued into the tenth. In that case, tenth-century queens and countesses would have received substantial estates as dowries from their fathers or dowers from their husbands, and administered those estates in their own right, for their own purposes, with their own agents. They would have used this wealth to build up their own clienteles of supporters. And they would have played an important role in administering the agricultural domains of their husbands, at least to the extent of making sure that provisions from the domains reached the court and that palaces were provisioned as they should be. All this changed over the course of the eleventh and early twelfth centuries. As the great noble families realized that their territorial possessions were not infinite, they began to develop techniques to preserve a set of core patrimonial lands intact, usually by assigning them to the eldest son. In order to create larger and more compact domains, lords increasingly married into the families of their own regional vassals. And the same growing emphasis on the protection of patrimonial estates led to an increasing definition of the aristocratic family as a lineal dynasty that descended through males and males only. Finally, as political, economic, and military administration became more complex and systematically exploitative, it became increasingly professionalized and specialized—meaning masculinized.

All these trends worked against the direct exercise of power by women of the ruling class. The more rigorous protection of patrimonies meant that husbands and fathers were no longer willing to give wives and daughters the large dowers and dowries that had once materially supported a wife's clientele, nor would they allow them independent control over what they did receive. Less commonly of equal status to their husbands, wives could no longer bank on the support of a powerful kin group to shore up their power within their husbands' households. Most important of all, whereas in the tenth century the fact that women came from outside the husband's family had been essential to a political system construed as a network of alliances between powerful families, now the lineage was seen as an integral, autonomous, enduring whole, defined entirely by the lineal descent of sons from fathers and grandfathers. Wives became problematic outsiders, necessary to the perpetuation of the lineage, but foreign to it. In the context of all these changes, the power of women to circumvent a male administration and to undermine the public decisions of men at court became more and more feared, and the fear focused as never before on what women allegedly did in secret, in bedrooms: whispering, seducing, poisoning. And as the purity of a male lineage of kings, counts, and castellans came to be more and more the defining characteristic of a dynasty, the possibility that a wife's secret sexual liaisons could introduce tainted blood into the male line came to terrify the nobility.

It would be a mistake, however, to think that men therefore relegated women to private rooms under constant supervision. Women still exercised influence. They still intrigued at court over the positions of heirs and favourites. They still acted as regents during the minorities of sons. They might still rule a county in the absence of a direct male heir, and as lady receive and perform homages. One can make no generalization about the role, power, and position of public women in the twelfth century that is not false or misleading, except to say that for men, women were charged: loved and feared, respected and marginalized, admired for their virtues, despised for their vices. As to what women themselves thought, we do not really know.

Political values

When medieval historians think of the values that underwrote political authority, they tend to think in terms of the religious values that underwrote sacred kingship, values espoused in a king's anointing, for example: the king was the protector of the Church, the defender of the poor and weak, and a partaker in the ministry of bishops. All this is true—or at least, all this was taught to be true by ecclesiastical ceremonial. But there were other values, no less important for political activity, that almost never appear in a religious context; indeed, some appear to have been almost self-consciously articulated in opposition to clerical teachings—this being especially true of the rites and values of chivalry as they developed in the early twelfth century. At almost every turn they seem to stand clerical and monastic virtues on their heads: pride rather than humility; largesse rather than poverty; long flowing hair and brightly coloured clothes rather than clerical tonsure and drab dress; a purportedly oral literature in the vernacular rather than a literature written in Latin; brotherhood rather than hierarchy; youth rather than age; a bath rather than baptism; a slap by the lord for the new entrant into knighthood instead of a bishop's solemn laying on of hands for the new entrant into priesthood. The possibility of such a self-conscious anti-ethos is important to keep in mind, since it demonstrates the extent to which the laity could be motivated by values that were fundamental to determining political actions and yet, being consciously opposed to the Church's teaching, are nearly invisible in our sources because of the Church's near-monopoly of writing.

There were, therefore, other values; and though these values can be found in other kingdoms, they seem to have been particularly pronounced among the Franks. As outsiders more easily see the obvious to which insiders are oblivious, so it is Muslim writers who quickly noted the traits that distinguished the Franks from other European peoples: great warriors, the Franks were imbued with a deep sense of honour they would fight to the death to avenge, though in avenging it they were prone to a certain reckless foolishness. To these perceptions we might add one other. Convinced of the special virtues of those whose blood imbued them with honour and prowess, the nobility had an occasionally sadistic puritanical streak, simply because they saw the body as the repository of honour and shame. They therefore punished affronts to honour with humiliating desecrations of the body, reserving the worst for traitors and adulterers, perpetrators of the worst dishonours imaginable.

Although the nobility's language of honour and vengeance came from feuds, after the tenth century military activities did not really have a strong feuding component, in the sense of conflicts transmitted from generation to generation. Nor were there the finely detailed rules of early medieval law codes that once supposedly governed compensations in feuds by balancing every possible insult and injury to body and body part. But the attraction of the schema remained, as is clear from epics like *Raoul de Cambrai*, a late twelfth-century song about the ruin that ensues when fathers and nephews avenge sons and uncles beyond measure. More to the point, chroniclers and contemporary historians consistently described military conflict and posturing in terms of a language of feuds. Suger, for example, was well aware of the geopolitical stakes of Louis VI's wars. Yet when he describes their motivations, it is consistently in terms of affront and revenge, honour and dishonour. And though among ecclesiastical chroniclers Suger was unusually taken with the language of vernacular epic, such language was second nature to many. The *Deeds of the Bishops of Cambrai* explains the plundering expeditions of two brothers, sons of a former count, as a war 'to avenge the injury' they had suffered in being denied their father's lands.[4] According to William of Poitiers, the count of Ponthieu fought against the Normans at Mortemer in 1054 because he wanted 'to avenge his brother', killed by the Normans in battle the year before.[5]

While it is possible to see such language as no more than an acceptable rhetoric covering considerations of *Realpolitik*, that is an unlikely explanation, because the pursuit of honour and vengeance was also described as motivating the most ordinary legal and political activities. Killings naturally gave rise to killings by avenging brothers, sons, lords, or vassals, all slayers claiming to be moved by anger (*ira*) and hatred (*odium*), where 'hatred' was something like a state of

---

[4] 'Gesta episcoporum Cameracensium', 440.
[5] William of Poitiers, *Gesta Guillelmi*, ed. and trans. R. H. C. Davis and M. Chibnall (Oxford, 1998), 48.

ritually declared public hostility. Yet it was not just blood crimes that gave rise to expectations of vengeance. The discourse of feud was the discourse of legitimate legal procedure at all levels of the aristocracy, in all regions of the kingdom, as plaintiffs enforced their perceived rights with armed seizures of the property claimed or forcible exercise of the rights alleged. More often than not, such conflicts were settled, again like feuds, with acts of peace (*concordiae, pactiones*) imagined as establishing 'friendship' and 'brotherhood' between the parties (*amicitia, fraternitas*). But before the friendship came the violence, too bloody to be dismissed as mere posturing. Peasants were expelled from lands, their cattle and personal belongings seized, their crops burned. In such cases, a plaintiff was essentially waging a feud (*inimicitias exercuit,* one charter calls it),[6] and though acts of violence would harden antagonisms, not acting violently would convey lack of conviction in one's claims and moral weakness in acquiescing in insult and injury to the honour of oneself and one's family.

This was not simply a violent society; the men of the ruling elite loved violence, and defined their reason for being in terms of war, honour, revenge, plunder, and booty. It is hard to get at these motivations, because almost the entire corpus of our texts was written by churchmen, in Latin, many removes from what kings, counts, castellans, and knights talked of in their vernaculars while drinking, hunting—and fighting. But in those rare sources in which the lay aristocracy speaks with its own voice, in its own language, this is how they speak, what they sing of, what they love hearing sung. This is how the troubadour Bertran de Born expressed it:

> I tell you there is not so much savour
> in eating or drinking or sleeping,
> as when I hear them cry out,
> 'There they are!' on both sides,
> and I hear riderless horses
> neighing in the shadows,
> and I hear cries for 'Help! Help!'
> and I see them fall among ditches,
> little men and great men on the grass,
> and I see fixed in the flanks of the corpses
> stumps of lances with silken streamers.

[6] *Cartulaire de l'abbaye cardinale de la Trinité de Vendôme*, ed. C. Métais (5 vols., Paris, 1893–1904), i.337–8.

Barons, pawn your castles,
and your villages, and your cities,
before you stop making war on one another.[7]

Odo and the territorial magnates who rose to power with him believed that God stood behind their success, and to show it they cloaked themselves in mantles of religious liturgy and moral obligation. But what had legitimated their success in the first place were their military victories, for the first principalities had nearly all coalesced around the leaders of the west Frankish defence against the Vikings. Astonishingly, the same relationship between military victory, legitimacy, and religion held true two and three centuries later. An unimpeachable source is the short history written or dictated shortly before the First Crusade by Fulk le Réchin, count of Anjou, in which he recalls his ancestors' origins and rise to power. Religion is hardly absent from Fulk's history. In particular, one can sense the apocalyptic worry that may have motivated Fulk to dictate his history in his list of 'signs and prodigies' that had suddenly appeared over the course of the preceding year: disease, death, and bad weather, all following the portent of stars falling from the sky, this only a few years before the turn of the year 1100 and the crusade in which the Franks, as the new Chosen People, would return in victory to Jerusalem. For the rest, the piety is the conventional sort one would expect from a French magnate, as in Fulk's recollection that his grandfather Fulk Nerra had twice gone on pilgrimage to Jerusalem, or that before dying, his uncle Geoffrey Martel had become a monk in the monastery of Saint-Nicolas built by his father and endowed by him. One also finds the unmistakable pride of the territorial prince harnessed (as usual) to religious pomp, in Fulk's account of Urban II's visit to his capital at Angers, when the pope dedicated the church of Saint-Nicolas and oversaw the 'translation' of his uncle's body into the church—'translated' as one would the body of a saint. Nor can one mistake Fulk's obvious pleasure in the gold coin Urban gave him, with the injunction that the counts of Anjou always keep the coin with them. Yet the pilgrimages, monastic foundations, and papal visit—these are like award ceremonies that prove the success achieved by Fulk and his dynasty. In Fulk's received memory, what actually

---

[7] *Lyrics of the Troubadours and Trouvères*, trans. F. Goldin (Garden City, NY, 1973), 244–7.

achieved the success were his ancestors' military victories, and God is directly and personally important in Fulk's history primarily because these victories show how much He favoured the Angevin counts. The dynasty itself began with the military victories of the earliest counts—Ingelgerius, Fulk the Red, and Fulk the Good—who created a county by 'wresting Anjou from the pagans and defending it from Christian counts'.[8] The military glory continued with the victories of Fulk's great-grandfather, Geoffrey Greymantle, over the dukes of Aquitaine and Brittany. Then came Fulk Nerra, who defeated Odo II of Blois and Herbert Wakedog of Maine and slaughtered 1,000 Bretons, including their count Conan. But greatest of all was Geoffrey Martel, victor over the counts of Poitou, Maine, Blois, and Normandy, and called 'Martel' because he smashed his enemies like a hammer. Finally, there was the single moment of Fulk's greatest pride, the day his uncle, this same Geoffrey Martel, girded young Fulk as a knight, the only day besides Urban II's visit that Fulk remembers right down to the day, year, and place: Angers, on the feast of Pentecost, in 1066, when Fulk was seventeen years old.

Violence was inherent in the aristocracy's code of feud, in the ordeals and trials by battle of its ordinary judicial procedures, in the looting and arson that were its normal tactics of warfare. Violence was inherent in the forcible seizures with which good and honourable men were required to stake their legitimate legal claims, not despite being good and honourable men but to show that they were. And violence, physical cruelty, and outright assassination were instruments of power—extreme instruments, to be sure, but predictable ones nonetheless. When Theobald of Blois refused to give up Tours to Geoffrey Martel of Anjou, Geoffrey imprisoned him under conditions so harsh that Theobald gave in after only three days and surrendered the city. Geoffrey's father, Fulk Nerra, had the king's palace count assassinated because he led the court faction opposed to him. Fulk Nerra's grandfather, Fulk the Good, gained control of Brittany by assassinating its young count, even though he was the boy's stepfather and guardian.

Of course, the Angevins were a notoriously ruthless dynasty. On the other hand, so were the dukes of Normandy and the counts of

---

[8] 'Fragmentum Historiae Andegavensis', ed. P. Marchegay and A. Salmon, *Chroniques d'Anjou* (Paris, 1856), 376.

Flanders. Most princes were ruthless when it suited their interests. And many churchmen accepted this, both because they believed that only violence could tame violence, and because they felt that violence in a just cause was not a vice but a virtue. In a famous deathbed speech, William the Conqueror apologized for the harshness of his reign by arguing that the Normans needed disciplined rule, for with it they fought resolutely, but without it, 'they tear each other to pieces and destroy themselves'.[9] Though the speech was fictitious, the conviction was real enough. What Suger, like many others, respected in Henry I, as both duke of Normandy and king of England, was that powerful men feared him: 'To those who plundered he promised nothing but the ripping out of their eyes and the swing of the gibbet.'[10] Though the Capetians were careful to cultivate a reputation for piety, fairness, and consensus, they were no different when necessary. Faced with the assassination of a castellan on the Norman frontier, Louis VI's garrison had the assassin's supporters mutilated, disembowelled, and thrown from the window of the tower where they had taken refuge, while the assassin himself had his heart ripped from his body and impaled on a stake—then all of their bodies were tied onto jetsam and cast into the Seine to float downstream into Normandy, so that Henry I's border castellans could see what the French did to traitors. Nor, in a culture of royal mimesis, were lesser rulers different from greater. After capturing a town that harboured his enemies, Vulgrin II of Angoulême had the ringleaders beheaded and everything in the town burned but the church. The nobles of Flanders thought their young count, Baldwin VII, would be unable to enforce the peace because no one was afraid of him; so Baldwin summarily executed a knight in a cauldron of boiling water for taking two cows from a poor woman. Now men were afraid of him, and he was seen as a great count.

If there is something larger than life in such stories, there was meant to be, and not just because people believed that terror needed to be public to be an effective deterrent. Rulers were supposed to be larger than life, for another salient characteristic of west Frankish and

---

[9] Orderic Vitalis, *The Ecclesiastical History*, ed. and trans. M. Chibnall (6 vols., Oxford, 1969–80), iv.82.

[10] Suger, *Vie de Louis VI le Gros*, ed. and trans. H. Waquet (Les classiques de l'histoire de France au moyen âge, 11; Paris, 1929), 100; Eng. trans. R. C. Cusimano and J. Moorhead, *The Deeds of Louis the Fat* (Washington, DC, 1992), 70.

French political culture is the aristocracy's susceptibility to the pull of legend, romance, and epic. Again, the power of the heroic ideal operated at all levels of society and in all venues. For example, one of the most common ploys in an ordinary trial was for a knightly defendant to challenge his opponent to trial by battle, only to withdraw at the last possible moment when mediators sued for peace. In a precisely analogous fashion, it sometimes seems as if no French siege would be complete without a lord or knight stepping up to the walls and daring some brave soul within to settle the war by single combat. As a young man, Louis VI himself did it repeatedly. Of course the challenge would be refused; the point is, the challenge had to be made for the besiegers to act out an ideal narrative of heroic behaviour, for the besieged to be represented as cowards. French nobles acted as if the legends of their past heroes were true, and a true model for their own comportment.

We should not underestimate the ideological appeal of such ideals, beginning with their capacity to smooth over the growing strains within the lay aristocracy. At a time when the relative power and wealth of princes were growing and those of castellans and knights declining, the fervent belief that loyalty, largesse, and prowess were the characteristic virtues of those born to power made it possible to ignore the new reality: that men fought for pay and did homage to acquire property, and that wars were financed by increasingly grasping administrations run by men who knew how to read, write, and do accounts, even if their ancestors had been serfs. The very idea that a prince like William IX of Aquitaine could sing bawdy songs with the best of his 'boys', could promise in those songs to let them in on his secret seductions, hid the enormity of the real distance between them. The idea that, if a younger son is truly loyal and fights really well and is just handsome and smart enough, he will gain the hand of the beautiful daughter of a powerful lord—that is a fiction worth believing if one is merely one teenager in a crowd of bachelor knights dubbed in a great collective ceremony and then cast out, each to find his own fortune. It may well have been a fiction the lords themselves wanted to believe.

The remarkable thing about early twelfth-century France is the way in which the Church bought into this 'chivalourization' of political culture. To be sure, here too there were strains and cleavages. It was hard for monks and clerics to shift gears and give knights and castellans a legitimate place in the political order when they had spent so much of the eleventh century castigating them as godless tyrants. In the early twelfth century, they continued to criticize the culture of young knights, with their long hair, curl-tipped shoes, and promiscuous sexualities. Even so, a remarkable number of overlaps appeared, not least in the literature of love developed among monastic reformers, most notably the Cistercians, many of whose earliest recruits were taken from exactly the class of young knights longing for an *aventure* that promised happiness, brotherhood, and the protection of a Lord that would last beyond the next campaign or tournament. We also know that monks of more ordinary aspirations than the Cistercians, cloistered though they were, still dreamed nostalgically of the world they had left. As for secular canons, being uncloistered, they still saw a good deal of the world in the courts of the lords whom they served as notaries and administrators. And as ecclesiastical reformers constantly remind us, secular canons were sometimes hard to distinguish from knights. They liked the same colourful clothes. They liked riding and hawking. They liked power.

Quite apart from these points of overlap between chivalry and religion, monks and clerics had always been the ones who moulded God and the saints in the image of power. They did so again in the twelfth century. A knight going on pilgrimage to Saint James of Compostela could stop in Gellone and see the relics of William of Orange, hero of the epic cycle and one of Charlemagne's legendary twelve peers. In monasteries outside Bordeaux he could visit the tombs of the heroes of the *Chanson de Roland*: Archbishop Turpin's at Saint-Jean, Sorde; Oliver's at Belin; Roland's at Saint-Romain, Blaye. In northern France, writers at Waulsort and Ribemont made sure that their churches' histories were the backdrop for the great feuds of *Raoul de Cambrai*. Indeed, *Raoul* itself is a kind of a pilgrim's guide to the epic history of northern France, so conscientiously does the song find a place for every significant local church in the history of the great feud between the Vermandois and Cambrésiens. Even battle cries were nothing but appeals to the local saints—for the warriors of the Vermandois, for example, 'Saint Quentin!'

Monasteries had been the authors of the liturgification of princely authority in the regalian image of the King of kings. Now they were the authors of a mythology of power that was all the more desirable at a time of social fission in that it fused epic, romance, and religion into a single grand expression. Thus, the earliest extant prayers for the dubbing of knights come from the churches of Reims and Cambrai, which created them for *their* knights. Monks and clerics in the dynastic churches of counts also re-imagined the histories of princely dynasties to take account of popular romance tropes. The monks of Marmoutier, for example, wrote histories of the counts of Anjou that turn the first counts into virtual knights errant, seeking adventure and finding romance and fortune. And when counts made solemn entries into their cities, though they were still greeted by clerics bearing candles and singing lauds, now the clergy was preceded by young knights playing war games on horseback.

Since political culture in France was founded on the mimetic capacity of kingship, royal monasteries naturally developed a similar mythology for kings, and nowhere with greater impact than at Saint-Denis under Suger. Abbot of one of the most prestigious abbeys in all Frankish history (to him, of course, the most prestigious), builder of a Gothic church more splendid for its time than most cathedrals, counsellor of two kings, twice regent, Suger was also the biographer of two kings; and in his life of Louis VI and in the diplomas he wrote (and some probably forged) he was also the great architect of French political ideology. At the core of this ideology was St Dionysius and his monastery, the saint the special protector of the French king and the French people, his monastery the hallowed burial place of the royal dynasties of France. The monastery also became the special repository of the regalia used in coronations—under Suger the royal crown; after him the sceptres, sword, and mantles. Of course, all this fell well within the precedents of the traditional west Frankish alliance between monasteries and princely authority. The innovation of Suger and Saint-Denis was to infuse sacred kingship with romance and epic. Perhaps already in Suger's time, but certainly soon after, the *vexillum* of Saint-Denis was believed to be the *oriflamme* of the *Chanson de Roland*—the very standard under which Charlemagne was supposed to have fought his battles against infidels. By the time of Philip II, Saint-Denis had not only Charlemagne's *oriflamme* but also his crown and his sword *Joyeuse*. The name of the sword was again taken from *Roland,* as was the battle cry of the royal army—'Montjoie et Saint Denis!' Finally, to validate and sacralize all these relics of a profane oral literature, the monastery produced a chronicle of

Charlemagne's crusade-like victories in Spain (the *Pseudo-Turpin*), probably written at the beginning of Suger's abbacy in the name of the very archbishop of Reims who, in the *Chanson de Roland*, fought alongside Roland.

The power of this synthesis is shown in Suger's account of one of the most famous events in medieval French history. In 1124, Louis VI assembled the greater number of French magnates to defend the kingdom from a threatened invasion by Emperor Henry V. True, the invasion never materialized, so neither did the campaign. Still, the army did mobilize at Reims. That alone has long been judged important, simply because it shows that the territorial magnates could set aside their differences and unite under their king against a perceived common danger from a foreign enemy. Beyond this, the event as related by Suger reveals how different components 300 years in the making had come together to make a distinctive French political culture. So in 1124, the individual integrity of the kingdom's territorial principalities was of course respected, as the army mobilized by duchy and county. The search for consensus was fundamental, as the leading magnates forged a unified strategy through public discussion of conflicting battle plans. The sacred was harnessed to the martial, as throughout the campaign the relics of Saint-Denis lay on the high altar while the monks performed continuous rites of entreaty on behalf of the army. And the nobility adopted the martial postures of their epic heroes: anger at an enemy's insult; eagerness to avenge that insult; and proud vauntings of violence and reckless courage as the knights goaded themselves with the prospect of filling the field of battle with the dead bodies of their enemies. Suger's account reveals less an ideology than a mythology whose attractive power came from the fusion of the epic, the sacred, and the romantic into a flexible, all-encompassing whole in which the epic became sacred and romantic tropes governed political displays and decisions, rather in the ways that the crusades (largely French themselves) blended epic, romance, and religion. It is therefore only too fitting that while their myth held these French to be heirs of Charlemagne, in 1124 the kingdom's real west Frankish founder, though unmentioned, was very much present; for when Louis took the *vexillum* from the high altar of Saint-Denis, behind him rose the great red marble tomb of Charles the Bald.

This was the political culture of France, a fragmented country governed by a fractious aristocracy united not by laws, language, or institutions, but only by its shared mythology and common values born of three centuries' experience making war and peace with each other.

3

Rural economy and society

Constance B. Bouchard

An appreciation of the French rural society of this period requires a discussion of both aristocrats and peasants, both of whom underwent major transformations in position and status during the eleventh and twelfth centuries—changes that were linked. In addition, monasteries were very much part of the society and economy of the countryside at the time, serving as landlords and, especially in the case of houses of Cistercian monks, as innovators in the economic sphere. The current scholarly understanding of these topics has been developed in a series of regional monographs over the last generation or two. Curiously, most of these monographs concluded that their particular region was somehow 'different' from the rest of France. In fact, the various regions (at least those north of the Mediterranean—and even the Mediterranean basin is now understood to be less different than once thought) have all turned out to be remarkably similar. Older paradigms and timetables have had to be modified, but the consensus now emerging is of a highly dynamic period of economic growth and social opportunity.

The aristocracy

French rural society between the tenth and twelfth centuries was dominated by the aristocracy, by knights and nobles. Although the epics and romances enjoyed by these aristocrats portrayed them at war, at the hunt, or engaged in courtly dallying, their most important social and economic function was as landlords. Sometimes in opposition to the peasantry, sometimes in partnership, they played a crucial role in the rapid agricultural expansion that marked the central Middle Ages and made the period's cultural and urban growth possible.

Even without the fictitious 'terrors of the year 1000', it is clear that at the end of the tenth century and beginning of the eleventh French social structures underwent rapid changes. Both castles and knights first appear in the documents in the 980s, as does the Peace of God, the movement, originally run by the bishops, which sought to restrict the increasing violence of armed men. The long-standing relationship of loyalty and clientage between the most powerful and those who attended them took on a new complexion in the 1020s with the first appearance of fief-holding. The changes that ensued both among the aristocracy and among the peasantry have led some scholars to term the decades on either side of the year 1000 as a time of 'feudal revolution'. Such terminology is certainly overblown, yet there can be no doubt that society underwent profound change at this time.

One of the most fundamental changes was the first appearance of knights and castles, which emerged together at the end of the tenth century. Although in the popular imagination knights and castles may seem characteristic of the entire Middle Ages, in fact they were new developments then, unlike any that had preceded them in France. Both were fundamentally military phenomena and represent a growing militarization of the aristocracy. Nobles had always had the power to command, but under Carolingian rule armies had been, at least theoretically, composed of all freemen, most of whom fought on foot. With castles and knights, military strongholds became the preferred residence of the wealthy and powerful, and fighting was increasingly done by men on horseback. Not surprisingly, the initial result was the increased power of the lords of castles over the surrounding countryside.

The term *castrum* had been in use for centuries to refer to a fortification of any kind, but in the 980s it began to be used in a much more specific sense, for what would now be called a castle in English: something that combined an elegant house for a lord with a defensible structure. (The 'elegance' of course was relative; by later standards eleventh-century castles would have seemed dark and cramped.)

Earlier lords had ruled from palaces, and fortifications had been used only in times of war, but these two functions were combined in the first castles. A number of early castles were of the 'motte and bailey' variety encircled by a wooden palisade. Quickly, however, lords began building entirely in stone.

The first castles were built by counts. Indeed, Fulk Nerra, count of Anjou (987–1040), built many of the first and most formidable castles in his territory of the lower Loire valley. In Anjou, therefore, castles were used to strengthen comital power, but in other areas the rapid spread of castles was an indication of the weakening of that power. In most of France, the *malus*, the public Carolingian court over which the counts had usually presided, disappeared at the end of the tenth century. With weaker oversight from the counts, other theoretically lesser but powerful lords of a region might exercise their own power by building castles, or might appropriate ones put into their hands. The difficulty with such admirably defensible structures was that they could be held against the man who had built them in the first place. Count Fulk was fairly successful in retaining the loyalty of the castellans to whom he gave the command of his castles, but in other cases counts returned after several years to discover that these lords had found temptation too strong and had made the castles their own.

It should be noted that castles were not built during the more violent period of the ninth and tenth centuries, for the excellent reason that one cannot construct a castle in the middle of an invasion or a war. Although castles certainly became centres of violence, from which knights could ride forth to terrorize and to which they would then return with impunity, they also, perhaps ironically, became a stabilizing force. Because for several centuries defensive technology developed faster than did offensive technology, it was often not even worth attacking a castle. Symbols of militarism and bloodshed, their grim presence often served to deflect outbreaks of fighting.

Such castles needed warriors to staff them, and, also beginning in the 980s, knights began to appear in the records, men called *milites* in Latin, or sometimes *caballarii*. It is significant that neither castles nor knights were found in Britain before the Norman Conquest, but that the French conquerors quickly introduced both together. The word *miles* itself, simply meaning soldier, went back to the Roman empire, but it had fallen out of use until it was revived in the final decades of the tenth century with a new meaning: a fighter on horseback. *Caballarius*, meaning someone on horseback, was even more specific.

Although scholars once assumed that knights and nobles were always identical, more recent scholarship has made clear that these were in origin very different groups. The French nobility of the central Middle Ages had roots in the late Roman empire. Although of course the families that considered themselves noble had undergone major changes by our period, those characteristics thought most typical of nobles scarcely changed at all: they were considered to be the wealthy and powerful who were born with noble blood. There was, one may note, no necessary militaristic element in this self-definition.

The knights, in contrast, who first appear in the documents half a millennium later than medieval nobles, were always defined by their military function. They served the nobles, especially by fighting on horseback, but they were not in the eleventh century nobles themselves. Instead, they seem to have been of rather unexalted background, brought into the castles and issued weapons in order to assist the castellans in exercising authority over the countryside. Because their weapons and horses were given to them by their lords, these cannot be taken as indicative of the knights' own wealth. Almost exactly contemporaneous with the first appearance of the knights in France was the rise of the Peace of God movement, intended specifically to combat knightly violence. Incidentally, the proliferation of swords, armour, and horseshoes, all of which knights required, was accompanied by a greater amount of ironworking at the end of the tenth century compared to earlier centuries.

Both the dangerous possibility that a castellan might turn against the count who had given him his castle and the concern that these castellans felt in keeping control over rambunctious knights led to a rethinking and reworking of the oaths of loyalty that went back centuries. For the first time, fiefs appeared in the documents, grants of property or rights made in return for promises of perpetual fidelity. The Carolingian kings had delegated counties to their counts on what was termed a precarial basis, temporary grants of rule made to their most powerful clients, but these had always been short-term arrangements. Fiefs, in contrast, were granted for a lifetime. The earliest description of a fief and of the oaths offered in return for it, and one which attests to how novel and fluid the institution was in the early eleventh century, is found in a letter of Fulbert of Chartres.

According to this letter, dating from the early 1020s, Fulbert had researched, on behalf of the duke of Aquitaine, classical precedents in the practice of Roman clientage in an attempt to establish exactly what the duke might expect from a vassal to whom he had granted a fief. His need to research the topic indicates how unusual fiefs were in the 1020s, even though his search for classical antecedents—as eleventh- and twelfth-century thinkers sought classical precedents for much of what they saw around them—has often confused modern scholars into thinking fief-holding was substantially older than it in fact was.

Fief-holding developed fairly rapidly in the eleventh century, so that by late in the century many nobles were vassals, that is, they held at least some of their property in fief. However, fief-holding remained rather ad hoc and never became an orderly 'pyramid' of the type too frequently encountered in non-scholarly surveys. An exchange of fiefs and oaths of homage was often used to cement a peace between two men of comparable status—who might, in fact, also be reversed in the roles of lord and vassal for a different piece of property. Indeed, the kings of France, who one would have expected to be at the top of such a pyramid had it existed, did not try to attempt to persuade the great French dukes and counts that they were royal vassals until well into the twelfth century. In England, in contrast, King William the Conqueror (1066–87) ordered all the great lords—including the bishops—to do homage to him for their lands, but even there any sense of tidiness broke down once one passed beyond the upper levels of society. Moreover, William's descendants, who continued to be dukes of Normandy as well as kings of England until the thirteenth century, were vassals to the French crown for Normandy once the vassalage of French dukes became expected.

Fiefs, it should be noted, were both granted and held by nobles and knights exclusively, not by most of the population. The system of fief-holding was once called 'feudalism', a term which has recently been abandoned by medievalists, at least in the English-speaking world. It is worth some space to explain why this term has lost all utility. Although it might at first glance seem perfectly valid, as it comes from the Latin *feudum*, meaning 'fief', it is in fact not a medieval word, having been coined only in the seventeenth century. Part of the difficulty with its use is that its '-ism' ending suggests something orderly and universal, whereas in fact fief-holding, as already indicated, was rather ad hoc and far from orderly. It was also far from universal; even men who held much of their land as fiefs normally owned other land outright, *in allodium* as it was put in Latin at the time, and some great lords were entirely allodists or, as they said, held their land only from God. In addition, fiefs were part of medieval society for a relatively short period, not being found before the eleventh century and losing all significance by the fourteenth.

Even more seriously, the term 'feudalism' has, since the seventeenth century, taken on a plethora of other meanings that have nothing to do with fiefs, thus making it very difficult to use without having to explain which of the various contradictory meanings one has in mind. During the French Revolution, 'feudalism' was given the meaning of hereditary legal privileges, precisely at the moment when these privileges were being abolished; they had moreover all been established originally in the seventeenth and eighteenth centuries, long after the period of fief-holding. For example, the *fleurs-de-lys* and seventeenth-century coats of arms which were struck from public buildings in the first years of the Revolution had been condemned as 'signs of feudalism'. In contrast, in nineteenth-century Marxist thought the term 'feudalism' was applied to a form of economic exploitation of peasants, of a sort that had begun in the sixth century—a good half-millennium before the first appearance of fiefs. In the twentieth century, 'feudalism' was generally used, when describing medieval France, as a synonym for anarchy and a weak central government, even though, at exactly the same time, 'feudalism' was seen as an organizing and centralizing force in English politics. More weakly but even more pervasively, 'feudal' has been used as a synonym for 'noble' or even for 'medieval', so that every castle becomes a feudal castle, the crusades an exercise in feudal warfare, and the entire Middle Ages an 'Age of Feudalism'. Such imprecision, of course, obscures rather than elucidates, which is why it has seemed easiest to modern medievalists to discuss fiefs without resorting to use of the word 'feudalism'. (Modern French has two words where English has only one, *féodalité* to mean fief-holding and *féodalisme* for everything else, but even the 'everything else' can become remarkably imprecise.)

The proliferation of knights and castles in early eleventh-century France, accompanied by the initial spread of fief-holding, used to lead historians, as already suggested, to characterize the period as one of 'feudal anarchy', when all power was local and the early Capetian kings were virtually helpless to direct events in their kingdom. More recent scholarship has disputed this characterization, noting that even without strong centralized government society did not collapse, but found other ways instead to resolve disputes and establish or re-establish the peace. The Peace of God movement gained its success through moral suasion; lords and knights invited to the Peace coun-cils were persuaded to swear great oaths not to harm the defenceless. Although such methods did not of course end attacks on the weak—and the very lords who had promised to protect the defenceless turned on them if they seemed to be taking self-defence into their own hands—they were sufficiently successful that by the second half of the eleventh century bishops were proposing the Truce of God, attempts to make armed men promise not even to attack each other on holy days. Disputes were often resolved by mediated compromise, as both sides in a quarrel recognized the value of returning to some sort of stability, a return often assisted by an offer to engage in trial by ordeal. Although such ordeals were once seen as indicative of barbaric crudeness, it is now understood that they were proposed far more often than they were ever carried out—the proposal itself could serve to move the disputing parties past a stalemate toward compromise.

Accompanying the appearance of castles and fiefs was a marked emphasis on the male line of descent, on those who would inherit the castle or hope to take up the fief in the next generation. This emphasis should not, however, be seen as a radical change from some earlier, more amorphous form of family structure. Counts and lords in the tenth century had also tried regularly and assiduously to estab-lish inheritances they could then pass on to their sons. In the tumul-tuous late Carolingian period, however, it had proved very difficult to establish any sort of rule that would last more than a generation or two, because of the frequent extinction of ruling lineages through acts of war. In the eleventh century, in contrast, once castellans were established in their castles, they had at least a somewhat better chance of establishing male-line inheritances, linked to these castles, which might endure through many generations of heirs.

Even this emphasis on the male line, of course, did not mean that succession normally passed smoothly from father to son. It did in fact do so among the Capetian kings, but they were considered very unusual even at the time, and Kings Louis VII (1137–80) and Philip Augustus (1180–1223) both contracted repeated marriages in search of male heirs. Among the contemporary kings of England/dukes of Normandy, even though one would have to consider the crown hereditary, with preference given to the male line, in most cases in the late eleventh and twelfth centuries the succession did not pass from father to son. Indeed, on the death of William the Conqueror in 1087, the English crown went to one son and the duchy of Normandy to another; but there was not another case of father–son inheritance for either the kingdom or the duchy for an entire century, until Henry II was succeeded by his son Richard the Lionheart in 1189. In the intervening century, both the crown and the duchy were taken up in turn by a brother, a nephew (a sister's son), and a cousin (again, someone related through women).

This emphasis on the male line, furthermore, should not suggest that women were becoming marginalized or less important. Women could and did inherit in the absence of brothers, including taking up counties or castellanies, even being granted fiefs. Indeed, women's ability to command in their own right seems to have increased rather than decreased in the supposedly more patriarchal twelfth century. Powerful countesses and duchesses, of whom Eleanor of Aquitaine is only the most outstanding example, commanded large stretches of territory, sometimes for decades, in some cases as regents for minor sons, but often in their own right—or, as in the example of the redoubtable Countess Blanche of Champagne, as regent for years after her son had achieved his majority.

Knights and castles continued to spread during the twelfth century. Anyone with a castle felt compelled to upgrade it at least once a generation, to incorporate the latest defensive technologies. By the twelfth century castles were almost always built of stone rather than wood, and the expense of that much masonry and the skilled craftsmen required to shape it began to cut into nobles' disposable incomes. The French fighters on the crusades took their military architecture and architects with them, and the Middle East is still scattered with the ruins of powerfully built twelfth-century castles. By the end of the century a castle in France might be very large: still dominated by its grim eleventh-century keep, it could spread over several acres, with round towers, well-lit sitting rooms, stables, kitchens, mews, barracks, weapons shops, and storage facilities all built out of stone, all encircled by massive stone walls.

Such castles were virtually impregnable. If they were captured, it was only after long siege. The only quick alternatives to a siege were treachery or, as at Château-Gaillard in Normandy, having someone crawl up inside the drains. Not until the invention of cannons in the fourteenth century was there any really viable way to attack a well-manned castle. Although the ravages first of the Hundred Years War, then of the Wars of Religion, then of Vauban's attacks on renegade castles during the time of Louis XIV, and finally of the French Revolution have substantially reduced the number of surviving castles, in much of France in the twelfth century every major hill would have been crowned by castle walls.

Not surprisingly, the castellans who commanded these castles made them an important part of their own self-image. Starting in the second half of the eleventh century, French nobles began attaching the names of their castles to their own names, so that someone who might, for example, have previously been known simply as Milo would now be referred to in the charters as Milo of Noyers. At the same time, they also began identifying themselves with the other major image of military might at the time, the horseback fighting of their service knights. When nobles first began adopting seals in the middle of the twelfth century, they most commonly depicted themselves on horseback, a sword in the fist. From the late eleventh century on, a noble might be referred to as *miles*. Thus, somewhat paradoxically, while knights were originally not nobles, by the twelfth century nobles could be knights.

During the twelfth century, then, knights and nobles slowly moved toward each other, as nobles increasingly adopted military attributes, and as knights attempted to imitate their lords. This gradual melding was made easier by the tendency of knights to marry wives from the lower fringes of the nobility. Although they could not ennoble themselves by these marriages, they thereby gave noble blood to their children. The noble lords were willing to give their daughters to these relatively low-born partners for several reasons, including the need to provide properly for excess daughters. In a period when many more men than women entered the Church, or died of knightly adventuring before marriage, there were more prospective brides than bridegrooms within any given cohort of the aristocracy. This was especially true because aristocratic men tended to marry older than did the women at the time, at perhaps twice their age: thus, even postulating stable generational size, men had had more opportunities to die before marriage from violence, disease, or accident than had their prospective brides. In addition, and even more importantly, the lords of castles found such marriages a useful way to bind their service knights to them. At a time when consanguinity was taken seriously, when parents actively sought to find spouses for their children to whom they were not related too closely, knights without noble blood but with strongly established positions made attractive choices as spouses for unattached young women of the lower nobility. Of course, with such marriages knights entered the web of blood relations that bound nobles together, and in the next generation their sons and daughters too become part of the group that was too closely related to make intermarriage possible.

One of the crucial elements in the slow movement of knights and nobles toward each other's status was the development of an ethos of chivalry. Chivalry (*chevalerie* in Old French) originally denoted nothing more than rough-and-ready battlefield virtues, such as bravery and loyalty. The service knights of the eleventh century practised nothing like the courtesy and determinedly Christian virtue which were considered chivalrous a century and a half later. Indeed, the Peace of God, with its emphasis on knights not attacking the unarmed, was a rather startling innovation at the time. The roots of a chivalric ethos cannot therefore be found simply in the eleventh-century appearance and spread of *milites*.

A central aspect of the formation of an ideal of chivalry was the incorporation of the concept of a holy war at the very end of the eleventh century. Knights who had never particularly considered fighting as Christian seem to have seized upon the idea, enunciated by Pope Urban II at Clermont in 1095 and quickly spread by others, that in going to fight the infidel they could save their souls. This Christianization of warfare, soon expanded from fighting the infidel to fighting the enemies of the defenceless everywhere, was always the least convincing aspect of chivalry, but all literary accounts from the twelfth century attempted to make their glorious heroes pious Christians at the same time as being the slayers of dozens of foes.

Courtliness constituted another element which fused with the fighting abilities originally meant by chivalry. The term meant the correct way to behave at court, and had evolved separately from battlefield ideals of loyalty and bravery. Courtliness was at the beginning of the twelfth century a separate and much more sophisticated idea of correct behaviour, one that owed much to the Roman Stoics—as mediated through Christianity. Tenth- and eleventh-century bishops received good classical educations in the empire and much of France, educations that by the twelfth century were given also to the chaplains and priests who served the powerful. Indeed, by the first decades of the twelfth century many noble youths were receiving substantial classical educations themselves, of the sort that allowed the Cistercian order to recruit prominent young men and, after a year, make them choir monks, with the ease in Latin required for the liturgy. Young nobles who received a training in fighting and warfare were also imbued with ideals that included personal restraint and gentleness toward the weak.

By the end of the twelfth century all these elements—courage and ability in battle, Christian virtue, and courtly behaviour—had fused into a rather uneasy amalgam, called 'chivalry' in contemporary literature. The ideal of chivalry was thus shot through with fundamental conflicts, which both the fiction writers who glorified it and the nobles who enjoyed stories about it fully recognized. The French nobility at the end of the twelfth century was in fact in a very difficult position, threatened from below by the independence and power of knights and peasants—and even, unthinkable as it might be, townsmen—and from above by the king. Their literature reflected their recognition that they lived in a time without good answers, but where ideals of conduct and deportment could at least afford some kind of basis to face the challenges of an uncertain world.

The peasantry

The eleventh and twelfth centuries were a period of rapidly improving agricultural production, which made possible the cultivation of new lands, the amassing of new money, the growth of cities to a size they had not reached for 500 years, and the development of important new relationships between landlords and peasants. The principal crop continued to be wheat, as it had been in France since the

Romans arrived, but this wheat was grown more efficiently and successfully.

At its base the agricultural expansion of the central Middle Ages was the result of changes in the climate. Pollen and tree-ring studies have indicated that, starting in the late Carolingian period, France became both a few degrees warmer on average and, even more importantly, somewhat drier. Even a few degrees rise in average temperature resulted in an appreciably longer growing season, important in an age before modern fast-ripening hybrid crops; and the drier climate made it possible for the first time to cultivate the richer bottom lands along the rivers, without worrying that the seed would be washed away or simply rot in the field.

These climatic changes meant that crops could be brought in more reliably, making more food available and thus resulting in population growth. The French peasantry also adopted technological improvements that assisted in the increase in the harvest. The most important of these was the adoption of the heavy iron plough, the *carruca*. This plough, only possible with the greater level of iron-working that has already been noted in connection with improvements in weaponry and horseshoes, was generally wheeled because it was so much heavier than the scratch-plough that had been used for centuries. Its most important feature was not its weight, however, but the mould-board, an attachment that turned the soil over as the plough cut into it, meaning that land did not have to be cross-ploughed as it had been previously, and that the soil would dry more quickly. The *carruca* seems to have first been used in the tenth century, and it spread rapidly in the eleventh and twelfth centuries. The only parts of France where it was not widely adopted were the Mediterranean littoral and the higher mountains, where the thinner, drier soil meant that the peasants preferred not to use a plough that cut deeply and encouraged soil drying. The use of the *carruca* meant that heavy, rich soils which earlier generations had not been able to cultivate were now available.

During the course of the eleventh and twelfth centuries, several other technological improvements were also adopted, at least in some areas. Sometimes horses rather than oxen were used for ploughing; their greater speed, meaning that more land could be cultivated in the same amount of time, could make up for the higher cost of their upkeep. In richer areas, a 'three-field system' of crop rotation was often adopted, where only one-third of the arable land lay fallow each year, rather than the one-half that had earlier been the norm, and two separate grain crops could be grown on the remaining two-thirds, such as wheat and oats. These two crops would require the work of planting and of harvesting at different seasons. Medieval wheat was generally planted in the autumn for early summer harvest, whereas oats were planted in the spring and harvested in early autumn. Thus the three-field system spread the year's agricultural work out more, and also provided a crop (like oats) that could serve as a backup if the main wheat crop failed. Some of the crops grown in addition to grain, once the three-field system was adopted, included lentils and other legumes, which helped restore nitrogen to the soil; it was recognized at the time that incorporation of these crops into the rotation was beneficial, even though the mechanism was not understood.

Many of these improvements worked together: because horses could pull a plough faster, more land could be cultivated in the same amount of time, even if part of that land had to be set aside for oats to feed the horses. Ploughing with a mould-board plough also increased the amount of land that could be cultivated in the same amount of time because one did not have to cross-plough, and the spreading out of the labour for different kinds of crops also meant that a single family could, during the course of the year, cultivate more land. More agricultural land, especially more of the rich soils for which a *carruca* was best suited, resulted in substantially improved yields.

Expansion of arable land led, naturally, to a rapid decrease in wooded and waste land. The large and forbidding forests that had stretched across much of France in the Carolingian era were substantially cut down to make more fields available for farming. Early in the twelfth century, when Abbot Suger of Saint-Denis was looking for long timbers for his new abbey-church, it was considered miraculous that he was able to find a sufficient number of suitably tall trees still standing.

Another important technological innovation was the mill. Water-mills had in fact been known to the Romans, but they considered them little more than toys, and had slaves grind most of their flour in handmills. But while the Romans had wanted to ensure that their slaves had plenty of exhausting work to do, to keep them from having time or energy to rebel, the relatively underpopulated early and central Middle Ages were much more interested in labour-saving devices.

Watermills were built wherever there was enough force in a river to run a wheel; a map of mills in England in 1087, as constructed from the information in Domesday Book, is a thick series of dots along most watercourses. This pattern is also found in the French landscape.

In the twelfth century mechanical milling became possible even in areas away from the rivers, with the adoption of the windmill. Windmills reached western Europe from the East, but new improvements were quickly added, and the windmill itself spread across France in less than a generation. The great advantage of mills, whatever their source of power, was that families no longer had to have a household member essentially do little else all day but grind grain in a handmill, just to have enough flour for the day's food—although this had been normal in the heyday of Rome. Half an hour at the mill would turn a big bag of grain into a big bag of flour, and although millers of course would grind only for a fee, generally a share of the flour, most peasant families found the freeing up of labour for other agricultural chores well worth this expense.

These technological changes, coupled with widespread land clearance, led to the development in northern France of what is usually termed the 'open-field' system of agriculture. Rather than having each family's plot of land fenced off from the rest, as had been the case in the early Middle Ages and indeed continued to be in the southern regions, all arable land ran together. The village was now a cluster of houses, surrounded by long, unfenced fields. The dividing line between those regions that adopted the open-field system and those that did not is the same as the line dividing those areas where the *carruca* predominated from where it was little used. Because the *carruca* was heavy and hard to turn, it made sense to have each furrow as long as possible. Because of its expense and the manpower needed to manoeuvre it, peasant families would share in the cost and the labour, and thus they also shared in the extra production it afforded. Arable lands were not owned in common, but the strips belonging to one family or to another were remembered as theirs from generation to generation even without fences. The pattern of ridges in the soil—some of which are still visible even today—was enough to make clear where one person's land stopped and another's started.

Even if the peasants of a village did not own their property collectively, the decision to adopt open-field cultivation, where the same plough and plough-team would be used to cultivate first one person's land and then another's, meant that decisions had to be made collectively. That is, because they worked together, village members would all have to agree on when it was time to start ploughing, when to harvest, and when to turn the animals out on the stubble. By the first decades of the twelfth century, many villages were demanding—and getting—charters of liberties, which gave them the legal right to create assemblies to decide such matters. These 'communes', as they were called, were one of the clearest indicators of the new liberties enjoyed by the French peasantry in the twelfth century. Their escape from servitude was relatively recent. In contrast to both England and Germany, where serfdom lingered for the rest of the Middle Ages, legal servitude was essentially gone in France by the end of the first quarter of the twelfth century.

There had of course been free peasants throughout the early Middle Ages, some of whom were allodists, owning outright the lands that they cultivated. But the great mass of early medieval peasants had been subjected to some sort of servitude. The great Roman agricultural slave-gangs had disappeared in the sixth century, with the end of the wars of conquest that had brought constant waves of new slaves into the empire for close to a millennium, even though household slaves continued to appear intermittently for the next two or three centuries. Those who worked the fields for the great lords in the early Middle Ages were normally serfs rather than slaves, men and women who could have their own houses and families as earlier agricultural slaves had not, and who, although subjected to heavy dues, were still not subject to their lord's arbitrary commands, as are slaves. Still, being born into servitude, serfs were considered less than free, and could not become clerics or give testimony in court. They also owed their 'lords of the body' various dues, such as inheritance taxes, not assessed on free peasants, and were restricted in where they could live, and even whom they could marry.

Not surprisingly, serfs quickly sought to free themselves once the economy had improved enough to make social mobility possible. Beginning in the eleventh century, French peasants gradually worked their way out of servitude. Several factors made this transition easier, including the first conceptualization of society as divided into 'three orders', and the rise of banal lordship. Although historians once assumed that medieval society was strictly divided into three 'orders', three groups of people each of whom had their own responsibilities and functions, it is now understood that this idealized picture is not an accurate description of how people actually lived and interacted. Rather, it was a model, first created in the tenth and eleventh centuries, of how some theorists thought society ought to be structured.

During the eleventh and twelfth centuries, this model gradually replaced the older forms of social categorization, such as that between servile and free, or sometimes between laymen, monks, and clerics, as the predominant theory of social organization. Not until the creation of the Estates General at the beginning of the fourteenth century, however, was this vision made into any sort of concrete structure. Even in the eleventh century, a division of society into those who worked, those who fought, and those who prayed was highly problematic, as many people could be seen as belonging to two different groups (for example, the bishops), and townspeople never really belonged to any of them. Nonetheless, the creation of a unitary category, those who worked, for all peasants, both serfs and free, by de-emphasizing the distinctions between them, at least prepared the way for the serfs to try to achieve the same freedoms as some of their neighbours.

Another, contemporary development which also tended to break down the serf/free division was the development of banal lordship in the first half of the eleventh century. This was a new form of exaction demanded by the lords of castles within the *bannum*, the area they controlled which stretched for some distance around their castles. Some of their exactions took the form of monopolies—that only the lord could have toll-bridges, or that all local peasants were required to grind their grain at their banal lord's mill. Others were essentially the extortion of protection money, *consuetudines* as these payments were called in the records, with an arbitrariness which, not surprisingly, intensely irritated both peasants and rural monasteries. But the significance of these banal dues lay in the way that they were assessed on everyone who lived in a certain region, whether serf or free, whether or not the castellan was their landlord. By removing the distinctions that had long been drawn between those who were servile and those who were not, banal dues, doubtless unintentionally, helped break down those distinctions.

There has been some scholarly debate about the process of French peasants freeing themselves from servitude. Although it is generally agreed that the last remnants of Roman slavery had disappeared in the tenth century, and that in the early twelfth century servitude had disappeared as well, the question has arisen whether the servitude that came to an end then was the remains of the serfdom that had first been found in the sixth century, or whether it was something relatively recent which had first made its appearance during the 'feudal revolution' of the eleventh century. The well-documented violence of some knights and castellans against peasants in the eleventh century has been taken as symptomatic of a period of feudal anarchy in which this new servitude could be forced upon the peasantry.

However, this model has not gained wide acceptance. It seems much more likely that the servitude of the late eleventh century, described in exactly the same terms as had been that of the late tenth century, was indeed a continuation of the same set of restrictions. One need not, therefore, attempt to create a golden if exceedingly brief first period of peasant freedoms around the year 1000, after they had finished freeing themselves from the slavery of antiquity and before they fell under 'feudal' servitude, only to free themselves yet again a century later. Certainly there were some free peasants at the very end of the tenth century—there had been free peasants in the preceding centuries as there were also in the eleventh—but servile status was still the norm. The violence in the chronicles was in fact normally exercised not by a lord against his own tenants but against another's, and thus cannot be considered some novel form of rule: rather, it was simply an attack on the source of a rival's wealth and power. Moreover, the fact that monks as well as peasants were forced to pay banal dues—without thereby becoming in any way a castellan's serfs—indicates that banal lordship per se should not be interpreted as a new imposition of servitude. Thus, while the biggest social change for the aristocracy came at the end of the tenth century and beginning of the eleventh, with the first appearance of knights and castles, the biggest change for the peasantry came only a century later, as they managed to shake off the bonds of serfdom.

There were several ways that peasants could escape from servitude. The simplest was to move away and neglect to mention to one's new neighbours that one had been born a serf. In the rapid agricultural expansion of the central Middle Ages, there were always new lands being cleared where one could settle, and in an era without either good communication or identification methods, no one was likely to pursue a serf and force him to come home. The cities that began to grow rapidly in France in the first decades of the twelfth century were especially good places for serfs to find freedom. Here, in fact, the astute and hard-working could amass a fair amount of wealth and autonomy. When Count Charles the Good of Flanders was murdered in 1127, it was said that those who plotted against him feared that their shameful servile origins were about to be revealed. A generation later, note, the issue of servile status would not even have come up.

But there were distinct disadvantages to moving away in order to escape from servitude, especially that of having to leave one's land. Even in the early Middle Ages, serfs could not legally be put off their land by a capricious lord, and late eleventh-century serfs would have preferred to stay on what they considered their hereditary property, among the people they had always known. Hence, the most common way for French peasants to escape from servitude was to buy their way out. The greater agricultural productivity meant that it was possible for families painstakingly to accumulate enough pennies to attract their lord's attention, especially in a time when the greater availability of luxury goods—and his need to upgrade his castle—had increased his appetite for money. Since the peasants would still be paying the traditional combination of coin, produce, and labour dues for their land-rents, the lords felt that they were losing little, other than a few specifically servile dues, which were quite trivial in economic value but considered highly degrading by the serfs themselves. The burgeoning agrarian economy also created new avenues to attain freedom. A lord attempting to open up a new area for cultivation at the beginning of the twelfth century would often negotiate with a whole group of peasants on the conditions of their settlement, and freedom from servitude was almost invariably specified.

Nobles and peasants in partnership

As the above remarks suggest, much of the economic development of the central Middle Ages was due to a partnership, or at least shared goals, between the landowners and those who worked the land. It is doubtful that many nobles had peasants' best interests closely at heart, or that peasants conscientiously sought benefits for those from whom they rented. And of course nobles in competition with each other would quite unconcernedly attack each other's tenants. But both the powerful and wealthy and those behind the plough recognized the rewards of economic expansion, and both realized that they needed the other's cooperation to achieve it.

The adoption of the mould-board plough was one of the first areas in which noble landlords, through investing money in technology, helped to increase agricultural yields. Heavy iron ploughs were expensive enough that peasant families or even groups of families initially could not afford them—and, quite understandably, would have been reluctant to pay, even if they had the money, for something untested which would require a whole new approach to basic farming. It appears to have been the wealthy landlords in the tenth and eleventh century who first paid for these ploughs, using them on their own demesne lands. Here their peasant tenants who were required to work on the lord's demesne land for a day or more a week—as were most serfs—would have come into contact with the plough and seen its advantages. Similarly, the wealthy, rather than the peasants themselves, were usually the ones who paid for building a mill and collected the milling fees, even though the peasants too gained great benefit from a mill once it was in place.

Even more fundamentally, nobles helped make agricultural expansion possible by taking the lead in opening up new lands. Sometimes these were swampy areas where the lords hired men specifically to come and drain them, to make crop-growing possible. In other cases a lord paid to have the location for a village cleared and laid out, so that he could then tell his would-be tenants that a place was ready for them. By renting out land that had been unproductive, even if, as was generally the case, a landlord attracted new tenants by offering them lower rents than they would have been paying elsewhere, someone who controlled a large amount of territory could increase his own income while making more food production possible.

More specifically, if a lord wanted to establish a new vineyard, which was especially attractive in the good grape-producing regions where the wine could be floated down-river to the expanding cities, he generally established some sort of share system with the workers. In an arrangement called *complante*, the lord provided the land, the tools, and the rootstocks. The peasant in turn provided the labour. For the first few years, during which the vines were becoming established, the peasant would pay nothing. Once the vines were producing, lord and worker would share equally in the proceeds.

Freeing peasants could also be seen as a form of investment. Any-one will work harder for himself than for a master, and by granting their peasants juridical freedom lords were able to ensure their hard labour—which, because the lords were still receiving rents, would help their own financial condition. Although it may be doubted that many lords were cunning enough to foresee how their own revenues might be enhanced by agreeing to free their peasants from servitude, they could certainly appreciate the success other lords were having in the early twelfth century, luring the tenants of their neighbours to their own lands by promising them freedom and relatively low rents. Loosening the burdens of servitude thus became for many lords a way to increase—or at least not lose—their most vital sources of income.

Originally, when lords freed their peasants from serfdom, the latter continued to pay the same mix of rents, in coin, in produce, and in work on the lord's demesne lands, which they and their ancestors had always paid. But by the middle decades of the twelfth century many French landlords decided to turn the work-days their tenants had owed them into monetary payments, from a similar motivation to their previous freeing of the peasants from servitude. Moreover, it was always difficult to force the tenants to work a day or two a week on one's land, especially if they lived some distance away, so they could not start work until well into the morning, demanded to be fed at midday, and had to leave early enough to be home before dark. But if these tenants paid an extra rent rather than performing the labour dues, then the lord could hire men who would be more than willing to put in a hard day's work—knowing that they would not be paid if they did not.

Thus in France many labour dues were 'commuted' into monetary payments during the twelfth century. Peasant tenants were willing to come up with more coins than they had previously been paying, to avoid having to leave their own lands every week to work on the lord's. This arrangement not only helped the lord, who could hire willing labour, but also provided a source of employment for young men without land of their own. For a generation or so, then, both lords and peasants felt that they had gained from a commutation of labour rents. By the late twelfth century, however, lords were discovering the fundamental flaw in this arrangement. Because everyone agreed that rents should be fixed, that someone should not pay more for the same piece of land than his ancestors had paid, the monetary payments that had replaced the labour dues remained stable. But at the same time, prices were gradually rising, as they will always do in a growing economy, and thus the wages the lords had to pay to hire labourers were rising as well. Feeling pinched between a fixed income and rising labour expenses, some lords tried to reimpose labour dues. But these attempts were rarely successful, at a time when *villeneuves*, 'new towns', where the peasants were attracted by promises of no labour dues, were constantly being established. In England some landlords were able to reimpose labour dues, and in Germany they had only infrequently been abolished, but in France by the thirteenth century they constituted only a small fraction of most lords' rents.

It was not merely the rising wages they had to pay the peasants who worked their demesne lands which pinched many French nobles. Noble families that had been making generous gifts to the Church and providing at least some inheritance to the children of every generation found themselves without the apparently unrestricted resources of their ancestors. And at the same time as their sources of income were becoming restricted, the number of things on which a noble was expected to spend money increased dramatically.

The most expensive enterprises were those connected with war. Castle technology was advancing so fast that most castellans rebuilt at least once a generation, with a stunning outlay of funds for the material and the masons. Going on crusade, getting together the equipment, armour, weapons, and supplies for an expedition that might last several years, was sufficiently expensive that by the middle of the twelfth century many members of the lower aristocracy were pawning at least some of their property to the local monks—or, increasingly, to moneylenders in town. Since very few came back from crusade richer than when they had left, pawned property was generally forfeited. And the increase in luxury trade at the same time meant that no self-respecting lord could do without the expensive silks and spices that were now available.

This increase in expenses provided an incentive to lords to try to wring more income from their lands through clearance and settlement, as already suggested. It also encouraged them constantly to try to find new sources of income, whether by taking the lead in new, more efficient forms of crop rotation, by enforcing banal monopolies, or, as did the counts of Champagne, by establishing lucrative sales taxes on markets in their regions. Thus, landlords and peasants assisted each other, even if not always intentionally; the development of the agricultural surplus and the flourishing of the market economy required the participation of both.

Rural monasteries

The monasteries of the French countryside were very much a part of the society and economy of the central Middle Ages. Between the sixth and eleventh centuries most monasteries served the function of landlords. They owned land, had peasant serfs, and collected revenues from their tenants. Indeed, most scholarly information on peasant conditions during these centuries comes from monastic archives. With the collapse of Roman urban civilization in the fifth and sixth centuries, monasteries had to become self-sustaining, and the monks' daily liturgical round meant that they needed peasants to do the farming for them. Pious donors who gave their land to a monastery generally gave with it the peasants who worked it; these now paid their rents to their new landlord.

In the tenth and eleventh centuries, most monks were members of noble families, put into the monastery by their relatives while still boys. In the monastery they would pray for these relatives as well as for the rest of society. Although scholars once thought that making sons monks was a way for noble families to 'dispose' of an excess number of children, in fact all donations of a child to a monastery were expected to be accompanied by a substantial gift, which would not be returned even if the child died, thus making it difficult to see the offering of these children as a purely economic activity. In addition, most noble families had a harder time placing their girls than their boys (as discussed above), yet very few girls became nuns; instead the nunneries (always outnumbered by male monasteries) were primarily refuges for well-to-do widows.

Monasteries needed secular nobles—as sources of new members and as sources of land and revenue. When new monasteries began to be established in large numbers in France in the eleventh century, after over 300 years during which very few new monastic houses had been founded, the monks needed the powerful to give them the land they needed to become established; they could not very well go where they were not wanted. But the nobles also needed the monasteries. With an increasingly Christian education, great lords began to feel uneasy, at least intermittently, about the state of their souls, and gifts to monks believed to have the ear of the saints could assuage this uneasiness. The pious generosity of some noble families was such that by the eleventh century a number of heirs felt the pinch when they came into a reduced estate, and began their rule by attempting (generally not successfully) to regain what their ancestors had granted the monasteries.

In the twelfth century, the Cistercian monks in particular became a much more active force in the rural economy, making agricultural innovations as well as acting as landlords. From obscure origins as a small group of monks who settled at Cîteaux in the woods of Burgundy in 1098, the Cistercian order developed by the later twelfth century into a flourishing affiliation of monasteries scattered across France—and indeed much of the rest of Europe. With an austerity of life unmatched by any other Benedictine monks of the time, they attracted the attention—and the gifts—of an aristocratic society that was increasingly beginning to see a life of voluntary poverty, a life that contrasted markedly with their own, as a life of holiness. But the Cistercians did not merely wait for gifts. They actively acquired new property, through purchase, through lease, through exchange, and through advancing cash to crusaders, who forfeited the land they left as surety when they came home poorer rather than richer, if at all. The Cistercians also made active efforts to consolidate their holdings, trading away some gifts for property that lay closer to their other lands, and created an efficient system of agricultural granges.

These granges were primarily worked by *conversi*, peasants who wished to enjoy the spiritual benefits of the Cistercian life but who did not have the education to become choir monks—since the Cistercians, unlike earlier Benedictine monks, took only adult converts, to become a full member of the community one already had to have had a classical education. Unlike other Benedictine monks, the Cistercians preferred not to have tenants, instead adopting a more hands-on approach to agriculture; indeed, they were accused at the time of wantonly ejecting peasants from their long-time lands. Although the first generation of Cistercian monks cultivated their fields personally, an activity very foreign to the young knights and nobles who made up most of the community, from the 1130s onward the bulk of their agricultural labour was done by *conversi*. Thus the order provided a way for peasants to escape from the involuntary poverty of being a lord's tenant into the voluntary poverty and spiritual wealth, as they saw it, of being an active member of a religious community.

Grain was the principal crop for the Cistercians, as it was for all farmers of the time, but the monks also practised pasturage on a large scale, particularly the raising of sheep. Those monasteries where the soil was really not suitable for grain, both within France and in such areas as Yorkshire, became major centres of wool production. In France, the sheep were also needed for the raw material (parchment) for book production, as the monks became important copiers of bibles and biblical commentaries.

The Cistercians, both the choir monks themselves and their *conversi*, were economic innovators, taking the lead in new methods of agriculture and rural industry. Because the first Cistercian houses were founded by preference in areas far from human habitation, which generally meant in wooded and marshy locations, the early monks had to become proficient in drainage and in channelling streams. Even today, the ruins of Cistercian monasteries are surrounded by elaborate networks of canals and drainage systems. The waters were generally routed in such a way as to pass successively through the kitchens, the workshops, and finally the latrines.

The workshops were powered by water-driven mills. The Cistercians appear to have been pioneers in realizing the potential for mills to do much more than to grind flour. They geared power from the wheel to hammers, to beat wool cloth as part of the fulling, or finishing, process, and especially they used mill power in forging. By the end of the twelfth century a number of Cistercian monasteries were running both the bellows and the forge hammers off waterpower, thus making iron working much more efficient. If the image of ethereal monks working at the forge appears incongruous to the modern idea of the Middle Ages, it is because present-day sensibilities tend to separate religion and manual labour, whereas in twelfth-century thought the former was aided by the latter. The Cistercians were more actively involved in the agricultural and industrial developments of their time than any other group of monks, but this trait was cause not for criticism but for admiration.

Conclusion

The central Middle Ages in France saw rapid change in both the economy and the society of the countryside. The appearance and spread of knights and castles, accompanied by the creation of fief-holding, changed relations among all sectors of society, as society's leaders increasingly defined themselves in military terms and as the wealthiest, those able to become banal lords, imposed new exactions on their neighbours. Castles were generally stabilizing forces; they were not the symbols of anarchy, contrary to the image which the tired word 'feudalism' incorrectly evokes. Shifts in aristocratic family structure, as revealed by the adoption of place names and by marriage patterns, point to important changes in group identity and consciousness, as does the emergence of the concept of chivalry. At the same time, the efforts of peasants, mostly unrecorded and unappreciated, led to their own freedom from servitude and, with an impact affecting the rest of society, much greater agricultural productivity. Increased demand, significant and sustained population growth, the opening up of new lands for exploitation, and new technologies all interacted with one another in complex patterns of cause and effect to bring about profound changes in the rural economy. Monks were very much part of this evolving society, functioning both as landlords, as did their secular cousins, and as innovators in agriculture and industry. The activities of the Cistercians in particular throw light on contemporary understandings of the value of careful investment and sound management. The greatly improved crop yield, a development that required the engagement of both lords and peasants in ways that belie the old-fashioned image of conflict between the two groups, made possible the economic growth which in turn led to a revival of urban society and the flourishing of high medieval culture.

4

The south

Linda Paterson

At the beginning of the twelfth century, King Louis VI's rule beyond the borders of the royal domain of the Île-de-France was nominal. Even if Philip Augustus had succeeded in gaining control over much of modern-day France by the end of it, many areas, such as Aquitaine and Montpellier, long remained outside it, and both north and south comprised a considerable diversity of smaller regions. The most marked division was the distinction between north and south, between what those sensitive to twenty-first-century regionalism prefer to call 'France' and 'Occitania'. But in what sense is it valid to think of Occitania as a separate entity? This question will be explored through Occitan self-perception and the perception of Occitans by others; through southern social structures; through courtly culture; and through the rise of the Cathar heresy. Since it is these last two above all which characterize the south, and since both emerge in the twelfth century, this is where the emphasis of this chapter will inevitably lie.

Occitan identity

To many people of the Midi today the idea of Occitan identity, while problematic, is meaningful and important. Resistant to metropolitan domination, many still work to preserve an 800-year-old cultural heritage that often seems to enjoy greater prestige outside France than within it. In the Middle Ages there certainly was never an Occitania consisting of a coherent political unit; rather, a multiplicity of disparate, competing, and often semi-autonomous regions and towns with complex and shifting allegiances. The vast duchy of Aquitaine, nominally subject to the king of France, in reality exceeded the power and wealth of his domain until the mid-twelfth century, when it passed into the effective control of the king of England through Eleanor's marriage to Henry Plantagenet in 1152. What by 1300 comes to be called 'Languedoc' was dominated by the counts of Toulouse but was also claimed in the late eleventh and early twelfth century by Duke William IX of Aquitaine, who occupied Toulouse between 1096 and 1099, and again between c.1111/14 and 1121. Provence, part of the kingdom of Burgundy from the tenth century and owing fealty to the German emperor, was disputed throughout the twelfth century by the counts of Toulouse and the count-kings of Aragon and Catalonia, united in 1137 under Ramon Berenguer IV. Roussillon and enclaves in the upper Languedoc also fell under Catalan control, as did the wealthy city of Montpellier. 'Occitania' also contained many other semi-autonomous areas such as the Auvergne and the Pyrenean baronies of Béarn, Bigorre, Comminges, and Foix, and many cities fell outside the dominance of the main territorial lords: Toulouse was well on its way, by the end of the twelfth century, to becoming a republic independent of its count.

While signs of regional awareness flash intermittently throughout the period before 1200, Occitan self-perception only coalesces in the face of the Albigensian Crusade (1208–29)—in other words, just after the chronological limit of this volume. That is not to say, however, that a retrospective sense of Occitan identity is wholly unfounded. First notions about southerners come from outside observers. Though residents of southern Gaul may have been regarded as cultivated and urbane in the time of the late empire, from the eighth century non-Occitan authors sporadically labelled them as unreliable, prone to garrulousness and gluttony, and ignoramuses at Latin. By the eleventh century, ecclesiastical fulminations held southerners responsible for importing scandalous fashions and conduct into northern France:

In about the year 1000 of the incarnate Word, when King Robert married Queen Constance of the region of Aquitaine, thanks to the queen men of all the vainest frivolity began to stream from the Auvergne and Aquitaine into France and Burgundy. Perverted in their customs and dress, with their armour and horse trappings badly put together, they shaved their hair from half-way down their heads, went beardless like jongleurs, wore the most disgusting yellow boots and leggings, and were entirely devoid of any law of faith or peace. And so, alas, the whole of the French people, until recently the most decent of all, together with the Burgundians, seized avidly on their abominable example, till at length everyone came to conform to their wickedness and infamy.[1]

Such denigrations suggest a sense of southerners being out of the control of the northern regions. They also categorize them in terms not of a homogeneous 'south', but of smaller territories— unsurprisingly, given the fragmentation of powers that followed the break-up of the Carolingian empire. Such conceptualization persists well into the twelfth century, and not only in Occitania. Thomas Bisson argues that although there are some signs of Catalan geo-political awareness from the eleventh century, it is only after 1175 that regional identity based on counties or blocs of counties gives way to a firm sense of pan-comital identity. Reports of Urban II's preaching of the First Crusade in 1095 do, admittedly, show signs of appealing to what could be called national pride, especially to emotional notions of Frankishness, and a sense of cohesion in the face of non-Latin people:

Peoples of the French, peoples living beyond the Alps, peoples chosen and beloved by God, as is radiantly shown by your many deeds, distinguished from all other nations as much by the situation of your lands and your Catholic faith as by the honour you show to Holy Church . . .[2]

—a sense reflected in Occitan lyric and epic poetry. Nevertheless, there is still a strong emphasis in crusading texts on regional attach-ments, with crusading appeals probably being pitched at this level. The First Crusade did spawn some sense of north/south difference arising from rivalries between different contingents: the Norman Ralph of Caen praised the military prowess of the Normans, by con-trast with the Provençals, who were reputed to be more interested in eating. The Normans, he declared,

have a haughty eye and a fierce spirit, and are prompt to spring to arms. They also spend extravagantly and hoard with reluctance. In customs, attitudes,

---

[1] Rodulfus Glaber, *Opera*, ed. and trans. J. France, N. Bulst, and P. Reynolds (Oxford, 1989), 164–6. Translation by Linda Paterson.
[2] Robert of Reims, 'Historia Iherosolimitana', *Recueil des historiens des croisades: Historiens occidentaux*, ed. Académie des Inscriptions et Belles-Lettres (5 vols., Paris, 1844–95), iii.727.

dress and diet the Provençals were as different from them as hens from ducks. These people had a frugal, circumspect, laborious way of life; but frankly, they were less warlike.[3]

Yet it is noticeable that the term chosen for southerners here should be 'Provençals', no global term being available: the choice perhaps arose from the fact that Raymond of Saint-Gilles, one of the leaders of the crusade, laid claim to Provence. If identity appears to centre principally on regions such as counties, this does not mean there is much evidence of regional stereotyping during our period. As Matthew Bennett has shown, vernacular literature similarly provides a less than clear picture of Norman-ness or different types of 'Frenchmen'.

Occitan self-awareness is eventually—and too late—precipitated by French aggression. At the time of the Albigensian Crusade, negative feelings of opposition to France give rise, among formerly rival southern groups, to a positive attitude to a cultural community which clearly distinguishes itself from the invaders. This finds its most articulate expression in a dialogue poem between the troubadours Albertet and Monge ('Monk'), which debates the relative merits and defects of the French and the southerners. Monge vaunts the liberality, fine clothes, cuisine, and military skills of the French. Southerners he reviles as poverty-stricken courtly fools, repeatedly accusing them of brigandage—a theme common in northern circles, which reproached the south with an inability to maintain public order. Albertet in return praises southern hospitality, gaiety, and sociability, as well as a concern to compete for a high reputation through speech and action, deriding French surliness and lack of courtesy to guests. Albertet's geographical notion of the south embraces Gascony, Provence, the Limousin, the Auvergne, and the Viennois, as opposed to the French regions ruled by the kings of France and England; what is striking, however, is that the term by which he designates the people of all these regions is 'Catalans'. So there is apparently still no pan-Occitan term for southerners, and while there may exist in Albertet's mind a southern geographical, cultural, and probably political whole, the people in it seem to take

[3] Ralph of Caen, 'Gesta Tancredi in expeditione Hierosolymitana', *Recueil des historiens des croisades: Historiens occidentaux*, ed. Académie des Inscriptions et Belles-Lettres (5 vols., Paris, 1844–95), iii.651; cf. *ibid.* 617.

their identity from the only leadership powerful enough to lend it any hope of political cohesion.

For twenty-first-century observers, the identity of Occitania lies not in its political boundaries but in its language and culture. A Romance, or neo-Latin, language like French, Catalan, or Italian, Occitan was the language of approximately a third of present-day France. Whether southerners conceptualized this language as distinct from French before the thirteenth century is uncertain. Twelfth-century troubadours sometimes refer to their vernacular as *lengua romana* as opposed to Latin. By the thirteenth century some municipal documents distinguish between *roman* and the *langue du roi*; the Catalan Raimon Vidal calls these *lemosi* and *parladura francesca*, while Italians prefer for Occitan the term *proensal*, Dante opposing the languages of *oco*, *oïl*, and *si* ('yes' in Occitan, French, and Italian respectively). The term *occitan* emerges in fourteenth-century administrative documents, and has been adopted by modern medievalists as preferable to the more geographically narrow 'Provençal'. Although both the *langue d'oc* and the *langue d'oïl* include several dialects, Occitania alone has a unifying literary *koîné*; in France, literary dialects compete for supremacy. Above all, of course, Occitania is the birthplace of courtly love and the land of the troubadours. But before we consider this more closely, let us ask what features, if any, distinguish Occitan society from that of its neighbours.

Social structures

As in France and Catalonia, power in post-Carolingian Occitania progressively fragmented, with centralized authority becoming concentrated in the hands of counts, viscounts, and lesser lords. Catalonia seems to have undergone an acute and violent upheaval during a process which may have been more gradual and drawn out elsewhere; but despite differences in the pattern and chronology of change, the general drift seems to have been similar, and by the end of the tenth century the real focus of power was the local castle. This period saw the rise of the knight, initially as a relatively humble retainer employed by the local castellan to impose his authority in the neighbourhood and engage in raids on neighbouring territories. The extent to which it also saw the rise of 'feudalism' in the sense of a well-ordered system of vassalic ties remains a thorny question. There is much to be said for the avoidance of slippery terms such as 'feudalism' and 'feudal' (often employed as a slack synonym for 'medieval') in favour of a sharper focus on various different forms of lordship, subjection, service, reward, and property-owning arrangements.

Of these, Occitania manifests a considerable diversity, as does France. Even by the twelfth century, Occitania as a whole is far from dominated by a strict system of vassalage, if by this one understands a pyramidal social structure with free men and sometimes women entering into a personal tie of dependence with an overlord and receiving a fief in exchange for military and court service. It is arguable that the upper aristocracy was not enclosed within such a vassalic network in Catalonia or France either. Certainly, in several Occitan regions aristocrats enjoyed considerable independence as property-owners, owing little if anything in the way of services. This situation is mirrored in twelfth-century Occitan epic poems, where landowners' inherited patrimony is little burdened by explicitly active obligations towards a suzerain: perhaps a reflection of contemporary reality, or perhaps a sign of resistance to the efforts of contemporary rulers to impose greater control on their nominal but powerful subjects.

The allodial (freehold) status of much of the land in pre-thirteenth-century Occitan regions such as the south-west and the Auvergne may be a further indicator of the absence of personal vassalic ties, though identifying allods is problematic and they may be even more prevalent in non-Occitan regions. Free fiefs were also widespread in Occitania, as in Catalonia; while it may be argued that the conversion of allods to free fiefs, or *fiefs de reprise*, signals increasing control on the part of rulers, the free fief still implies less dependence and less of a personal tie than one owing military and court service. Documents such as Fulbert of Chartres' famous letter of about 1020/1 to Duke William V of Aquitaine and the *conventum* between William and Hugh IV of Lusignan, often cited as evidence of close personal ties of vassalage in Poitou and northern Aquitaine, are still very much the subject of debate among historians, and may suggest efforts on the part of rulers to impose obedience rather than the obligations associated with such personal ties, let alone the reality of what was actually done.

Resistance to homage seems a particular feature of the south: at the time of the First Crusade, Raymond of Saint-Gilles was the only western leader to refuse it to the Byzantine emperor, even though his relations with Alexius Comnenus were particularly cordial. A special oath of non-belligerent fidelity was drawn up between them along the lines of the *convenientiae*, or egalitarian compacts characteristic of the Midi, which involved no personal tie or the subordination of one man to another. Two flurries of acts of homage in Provence in 1113 and 1144 correspond to its brutal imposition by Barcelona during military campaigns, and may well have reinforced a southern dislike of homage as a humiliating form of subjection. In some areas, such as the Toulousain, it was a common sign of serfdom, which again may have militated against its acceptance by those of higher rank.

Moreover, many lesser knights seem to have been employed on the basis of ad hoc cash payment rather than personal ties or the exchange of fief for services. The knight whom a late tenth-century castellan employed as a mounted retainer to garrison his castle and impose his will on the surrounding countryside was likely to be a man of little more social prestige than the peasant stock from which he may have sprung. As time went on, as knightly equipment and training became more costly and sophisticated, this professional horseback warrior gradually became further removed from his humble origins. Northern France by the second half of the twelfth century had developed complex chivalric codes and ideologies, accompanied in the early thirteenth by the formation of an exclusive caste where, in theory at least, only men showing knightly ancestry could accede to the noble order of knighthood. There is much less evidence in Occitania of many of these developments, at least by the end of our period. In the twelfth century knights in France, Occitania, and Catalonia were in fact a highly heterogeneous group of men, from great magnates such as dukes or counts to a considerable diversity of fief-holding knights—where a fief might be anything from a viscounty to an olive grove—and to part-time farmers, garrison knights, household knights, and mercenaries.

Literary sources reinforce other evidence that mercenary knights were a common, even typical, feature of Occitan military life: such combatants emerge only as a shadowy presence in Old French literature before 1180, whereas in Occitan literature they form an important group of knights fighting for gain in the form of maintenance in cash or kind, permanently or regularly attached to a lord, or recruited for a particular campaign. Whether knights or sergeants, men serving for pay alone were a significant and visible part of southern armies, and the counts of Toulouse relied heavily on them, rather than on men bound by personal ties of vassalage.

Urban knights were an even more prominent feature of Occitania, or more precisely, the Languedoc, Rouergue, and Provence, along with Catalonia. As Martin Aurell has argued, before the thirteenth century the southern town remained much more of a fortress than a market, warriors having long been its masters. Together with their relatives they constituted about a tenth of the city populations. In many ways they can be said to have formed part of a vassalic network. Often ensconced in rebuilt Roman remains, such as the arenas of Nîmes or Arles or the theatre in Orange, these eleventh- and twelfth-century knights held their fortified, turreted houses from lay or ecclesiastical lords in return for aid and counsel in the military, judicial, and policing spheres: guard and cavalcade duties, military service at times of disturbance, attendance at the law courts, the provision of guarantees and hostages, and performance as champions in duels. But until the second half of the twelfth century, their agreements with their lords involved the negative promise not to harm the lord, to guarantee his physical safety, and to help to recover his property, with little evidence of homage or personal dependence. Since they often owed fidelity to not one lord but several, there was an opportunity to play one off against another to pursue their own agendas. If their military activities were their prime occupation, urban knights were also bankers and tax collectors, commercial and political entrepreneurs. In some towns, especially Toulouse and those of western Provence, they took over the burgeoning consulates and on occasion their powers of the ban, which Martin Aurell sees as a kind of co-lordship, to control high justice, judging such serious crimes as homicide, wounding, adultery, and *raptus* (rape or abduction).

The epic poem *Aigar et Maurin* (second half of the twelfth century) presents a literary image of powerful urban knights who, while representing a military resource for their lord, have been waging war on each other for over a century from their respective fortified cities. The text emphasizes that they cannot be *ordered* to aid the king, having no obligation of *ost* or *servitium*, but that they readily do so if they hear he is in trouble, apparently of their own free will and from a sense of honour or moral obligation:

He was the king's pledged and sworn man, but he would never be summoned by command in the king's hour of need; he owed him neither host nor requisitioned services, but if he learned that the king had been defeated or shamed or had lost in battle or was put to flight, the king was avenged the next day; or if these men heard a proclamation issued on account of a forthcoming battle, or a message that battle lines should be drawn up, they would arm themselves in the great hall and bring aid swiftly, effectively, and at the drop of a hat.[4]

This expresses a view of fidelity based on honour and loyalty rather than legal obligation. The text probably arose from the Plantagenet sphere of influence rather than the Mediterranean; if it reflects the spirit of meridional *convenientiae*, it no doubt also articulates a more widespread desire for autonomy and respect.

Occitan Mediterranean towns may have lagged behind those of northern Italy in their overseas trade, but they were expanding dynamically by the twelfth century, some regenerating themselves from former Roman cities, others spreading outwards from castles or monasteries. When consulates, the southern counterparts of northern French communes, began to emerge in the second quarter of the century—the first was Avignon's in 1129—municipal power was already strong and confident enough to make itself felt. These southern consulates by and large acquired their powers peaceably, by contrast with some northern communes which took control through revolt against local lordship.

The consulates were oligarchies elected by a restricted group of the towns' inhabitants. While freedom-seeking peasants may have gravitated towards the towns, the growing collective liberties of towns during the consular period did not necessarily lead to an increase in the political participation of the ordinary citizen. Towns were nevertheless the site of relative social mobility, entrepreneurial opportunity, and a relative tolerance of foreigners and people of different faiths. The status of knights and burghers, for instance, was sometimes indistinguishable. Anti-Semitism was by no means absent, but religious and ethnic tolerance was comparatively greater than in the north: Jewish communities thrived in many Occitan towns, pursuing

---

[4] *Aigar et Maurin*, ed. A. Brossmer (Erlangen, 1901), vv. 1349–58.

a considerable variety of occupations, and playing a crucial part in southern public administration, banking, and commerce. To encourage the discipline and practice of medicine, which flourished early in Occitania, William VIII, lord of Montpellier, issued an edict in 1180 granting freedom to people of all origins to teach this 'excellent science'. Mediterranean artisans began to form trade associations with an earlier and more pronounced corporate spirit than towns further north. Along with the rise of the consulates, the increasing complexity of administrative and legal business in twelfth-century Occitan towns, and the earlier revival of Roman law in the south, there proliferated an expanding body of trained lawyers, from notaries to judges, judicial officers such as vicars and bailiffs, and experts in technical or learned law.

In the countryside Occitan peasants were generally poor. Forests were in retreat, and land under pressure from an inability to develop a system of triennial crop rotation and the conflicting needs of agriculture and a huge-scale livestock industry dominated by the capital of rich lords and townspeople. Peasants were subject to tithes, customary dues, and other more or less occasional payments to their lords, to obligations such as the provision of lodging, and to arbitrary requisitions relating to military service, enforced by the lord's agents. They were sometimes required to serve as foot soldiers, or pay money to be let off, and fined for defective equipment. They could also be at the mercy of brigands such as roving mercenaries or feuding local lords. In some ways, however, the hand of an oppressive lord fell on them less heavily than in the north. They were not generally required to carry out labour services, and punishments inflicted for violations of seigneurial reserves lacked the ferocity of northern French sanctions. Many of the Occitan regions were mountainous, ever the site of 'liberty, democracy, and peasant "republics"',[5] or at any rate out of the easy reach of seigneurial control. The fragmentation of much of the land meant the relative autonomy and individualism of the small farmer, in contrast to the community organization in the open fields of northern France. Labour was in short supply in parts of the south, with large numbers from the south-west emigrating to *reconquista* lands in Spain, or moving to newly created villages in the grouped

---

[5] F. Braudel, *The Mediterranean and the Mediterranean World in the Age of Philip II*, trans. S. Reynolds (2 vols., London, 1972–3), i.40.

habitats typical of Mediterranean countries in the Middle Ages: the eleventh- and early twelfth-century *salvetats* which offered ecclesiastical protection and freedom in return for land clearance; and *castelnaux*, fortified villages attached to castles and providing protection against bandits. For those with the energy and resources, the livestock industry provided opportunities for entrepreneurial activity and freedom from ties to the soil. Some peasants successfully challenged tax demands in court, and a few actively revolted.

The Peace and subsequent Truce of God arose in the south-west in the late tenth and early eleventh centuries as a way of limiting private wars, pillage, and the disturbances caused by 'bad customs'. Some historians stress the popular nature of these movements, which they see arising primarily from the collaboration of Church and peasantry; others, the initiatives of powerful laymen such as Duke William V of Aquitaine (d. 1030). Some judge the primary goal to have been the protection of the peasantry, while others focus on the concern to defend ecclesiastical rights and property. For monastic and clerical writers, the instigators of violence targeted by the Peace movement were *milites*, and their victims primarily churches, the clergy, and those working on ecclesiastical lands—though some of this violence may well have resulted from the pursuit of claims to lands or dues that laymen honestly believed were theirs. But Peace protection was also extended to other unarmed people—travelling merchants and peasants labouring on lay territory. While the movement seems to have lost impetus in the later eleventh century, it revived with the preaching of the First Crusade, and was extended at various intervals during the twelfth century throughout Occitania, with its own system of taxes, levies, and militias. Thomas Bisson has argued that the organized Peace was a considerable institutional success, providing a viable alternative to a system of vassalic fidelities and obligations, and that contrary to a commonly held view of the south as institutionally weak through its alleged incomplete feudalization, southern governments were not weaker than the Angevin or Capetian monarchies, but simply different. The setbacks of Occitan and Catalan rulers in the thirteenth century, he maintains, were the result of political, personal, and dynastic failures, not of institutional ones, and moreover aspects of meridional institutions were to survive and prosper in the new regalian order in some parts of the south, as well as in French forms of justice.

Lay culture: courtliness and courtly love

In contrast to northern France and Anglo-Norman England, twelfth-century Occitania was not a chivalrous society. In a series of articles published in the 1970s, Jean Flori argued that chivalry as 'an ethos in which martial, aristocratic, and Christian elements were fused together' in a 'veritable social and juridical elite, with its ethos, its ideology, its rites, and its customs' only came into being in France in about 1180.[6] While he seems more recently to have nuanced his chronology, especially with respect to a professional code of honour in existence from the late eleventh century, and while recent attention to Gaimar's *Estoire des Engleis* points to chivalric ideals and practices in Anglo-Norman England in the 1130s, the twelfth century can nevertheless still be seen as the period in which chivalry came into full flower with its varied and sometimes conflicting connotations of vassalic duty, courtly love service, and religious ideology. Occitan evidence, however, reflects little of this. In literary sources the word *chevalier* retains its professional, functional sense throughout the century, with few ethical or ideological overtones. There is no clear link between the idea of vassalic loyalty and knighthood, nor any indication of a code of professional honour that accords courtesy or mercy to a knightly opponent. If eloquence is praised as an asset to a knight needing to speak at court assemblies, only a few late twelfth-century examples link knights with courtly or religious ideals, with no marked turning point such as we find in the north in the chivalric romances from the time of Chrétien de Troyes (writing in the 1170s and 1180s). Indications of the tournament as a force generalizing the standards and rituals of European chivalry are weak, and clear evocations of dubbing ceremonies rare and late. To be sure, there are non-literary records of the arming of knights and this must have always been a rite of passage, but it is questionable whether these point to a notion of chivalry as Flori defines it. If northern ideals of chivalry made only a slight impact on the Occitan mentality, this may well be

---

[6] M. H. Keen, *Chivalry* (New Haven, Conn., 1984), 1–2, 16; J. Flori, 'Les origines de l'adoubement chevaleresque: Étude des remises d'armes et du vocabulaire qui les exprime dans les sources historiques latines jusqu'au début du XIIIe siècle', *Traditio*, 35 (1979), 209–72 (236).

because, by the thirteenth century, Occitan lands were facing the impact of a more brutal side of French militarism.

If Occitania largely failed to embrace the new chivalry, it produced an equally far-reaching cultural innovation: courtly love. 'Everyone has heard of courtly love,' wrote C. S. Lewis, 'and every one knows that it appears quite suddenly at the end of the eleventh century in Languedoc . . . Real changes in human sentiment are very rare—there are perhaps three or four on record—but I believe that they occur, and that this is one of them.'[7] Despite ensuing debate in which some have denied that courtly love ever existed, a recent authority has felt able to reiterate this in its essentials: 'The invention of Western love by southern French troubadours in the late eleventh or early twelfth century is rightly seen as momentous, a phenomenon in comparison with which "the Renaissance is a mere ripple on the surface of literature"; although it would be more accurate if less dramatic (since erotic texts of some kind or other are found in most cultures) to speak not of invention but, as Auerbach does, of "the elevation of love to a theme worthy of the sublime style, indeed, to its principal theme".'[8]

Although Lewis claimed that it had a 'systematic coherence throughout the love poetry of the troubadours as a whole',[9] there was no single, monolithic code of courtly love, or what the troubadours called *fin'amor*, any more than there was a single set of rules for chivalry. Each embraced both diversity and debate. Troubadour poetry spanned more than two centuries, including the social and ideological upheavals of the Albigensian Crusade. It comprised a great many inventive individual poet-musicians interacting with each other in a continuing dialectic, assimilating but also disputing and competing with each other's ideas and style. The first known troubadour, Duke William IX of Aquitaine (1086–1126), presents his own code of courtesy founded upon patient submission to the demands of love, an accommodating manner to others, willingness to perform services for them, and polite speech at court: a code bound up with the artistic excellence of well-crafted songs

---

[7] C. S. Lewis, *The Allegory of Love* (Oxford, 1936), 2, 11.

[8] S. Kay, 'The Contradictions of Courtly Love and the Origins of Courtly Poetry: The Evidence of the *Lauzengiers*', *Journal of Medieval and Early Modern Studies*, 26 (1996), 209.

[9] Lewis, *Allegory of Love*, 3.

appreciated by connoisseurs who praise the concomitant merit of the courtly lover.

This social formulation of *fin'amor* with its emphasis on courtesy, while anticipating much of the later tradition, lacks one key element: the notion that love for a courtly lady or *domna* is an ethical force. To repeat a much-quoted passage from Father Denomy, 'Courtly Love is a type of sensual love and what distinguished it from other forms of sexual love, from mere passion, from so-called Platonic love, from married love is its purpose or motive, its formal object, namely the lover's progress and growth in natural goodness, merit and worth.'[10] The principal catalyst for change whereby *fin'amor* becomes marked by an ethical dimension is the troubadour Marcabru, who began his known poetic career at the court of Poitiers in the 1130s under the first troubadour's son, Duke William X of Aquitaine (1126–37). A composer of satirical and moralizing songs and a man of extensive clerical education, Marcabru excoriated love lyricists who, as he saw it, fostered an atmosphere of sexual excitement among the upper classes all too eager to dress up adultery as fashionable manners, with the consequent corruption of the pure bloodline of the aristocracy. His sermonizing line must have encountered stiff resistance, which was what no doubt led him to formulate a distinction between false and true love (*fals'* and *fin'amor*). The former sprang from either wanton greed and lechery or else dangerous foolishness; the latter from joy, patience, self-control in speech and behaviour, mutuality of desire, trust, purity, honesty, freedom from greed, courtesy, personal worth, liberality, and monogamy. Marcabru's formulations of these virtues are often abstract and vague, but in as far as they involve the love between man and woman, they approximate twelfth-century canonists' ideas on the place of affection in marriage. If his audiences did not always like what they heard, they listened to him, for he is the earliest troubadour whose songs survive in some numbers in the troubadour songbooks, and his successors generally make serious claims for the moral virtues of love.

Bernart de Ventadorn in particular, who is generally regarded as marking the crystallization of the key elements of troubadour love poetry, inscribes Marcabru's ethical definitions into a concept of love which is clearly not that of monogamous marriage. In ways which

---

[10] A. J. Denomy, 'Courtly Love and Courtliness', *Speculum*, 28 (1953), 44.

would have no doubt been anathema to Marcabru, he insists like him on the importance of sincerity, mutuality of desire, and freedom from greed and selfishness, while endowing love and the *domna* with an aura of spirituality. His invocation of God's creation of female beauty and sympathetic aid to lovers avoids awkward questions about a love that is illicit from a Christian viewpoint, and henceforth, with a few exceptions, troubadours defend *fin'amor* as a source of moral or social benefit to the individual or the court. Its hallmarks are joy, whether the elation felt by the lover or a social atmosphere; youth, involving the essential quality of generosity and referring also to an association of those endowed with it; courtliness, meaning the civilized qualities and refined manners appropriate to life at court, including eloquence and polite speech and willingness to serve others; liberality on the part of the rich who give freely to uphold the courtly way of life; personal merit and reputation; self-control; educated manners and discriminating judgement; good sense, wisdom, and knowledge; and the composition and/or appreciation of the art of *trobar* (poetic and musical composition). *Fin'amor* inspired the artistic brilliance of the troubadour *canso*, or courtly love song, and created a social and moral code fostering the cohesion and self-esteem of the court: a code which proved not only powerfully innovative but also remarkably durable in the history of European literature and manners. Its more gifted and subtle exponents could be well aware of its contradictions and questionable premises, sometimes wilfully accepting them, sometimes ironically subverting them within the *canso* itself, or else opening them up to discussion through the many other genres of *trobar*, notably debate poems and moralizing and satirical verse.

Lay culture: courts

What were these Occitan courts that fostered the rise of the new lay culture? Medieval courts in general were movable entities consisting essentially of a lord's household: sometimes itinerant; sometimes located at his or her residences, whether the lord was present or not; sometimes assemblies specifically arranged as a special festival for the display of the lord's prestige, or with some particular political agenda in mind. The first known troubadour courts appear in Poitou and the Limousin, in the entourage of the first troubadour, William IX of Aquitaine, and his neighbour and rival Viscount Eble II, 'the Singer', of Ventadour, whose compositions have not survived. Initially the number of courts known to have been associated with troubadour activity was small and their distribution limited: in William's day, the only other one was at Narbonne. Among the second generation of troubadours, Marcabru appears to have begun his poetic career in Poitiers under William X, and on William's death in 1137 he sought patronage at the court of Alfonso VII of Castile-Leon and possibly of Peter, viscount of Béarn and Gabaret, subsequently moving between northern Spain and south-west France. Gévaudan in the Auvergne saw some troubadour activity among minor noble families by the 1150s, and by the 1160s this was evident further north at Le Puy, in Provence at the court of the troubadour Raimbaut of Orange, and in the Toulousain at that of Count Raymond V. Thereafter it spread more dramatically to include Catalonia, Foix, Comminges, the Rouergue, numerous small courts of the Limousin and lower Languedoc, and northern Italy.

Geoffrey of Vigeois, a chronicler keen to promote the cultural credentials of his native Limousin, describes how at the early courts of Poitou and the Limousin William IX and the viscounts of Ventadour engaged in tussles of courtly one-upmanship, each striving to make the other look like a country bumpkin. One method was to put a host on the spot by unexpectedly turning up with a large retinue: the trick was instantly to produce a feast of lavish food. On one occasion during a visit by the Poitevins, the Limousins put on a display of the ostentatious waste of wax. On another, Adhemar III, viscount of Limoges (c.1090–1139), managed to outdo his richer rival William IX in both prodigal hospitality and ingenious extravagance:

The Adhemar who later became a monk at Cluny was, according to custom, entertaining William, father of William the Toulousain, when he was visiting Limoges. So the steward asked Constantine of La Sana for some pepper. The latter led him into a house where priceless pepper was lying about on the floor like acorns ready to be fed to pigs. 'Here,' he said, 'take some pepper for the count's condiments [also: to match the count's wit].' And seizing a common spade he spilled more pepper than he proffered. This episode was favourably reported in the hall; but the duke considered it in silence. It happened sometime that Viscount Adhemar was visiting the Poitevins. So the count forbade anyone to sell wood to the viscount. Adhemar's retainers then bought huge piles of nuts and lit a large fire with them. When this became known, the duke suitably applauded the Limousins after previously endeavouring in various ways to discredit them with rusticity.[11]

For later troubadours the ideal court was one where gifts were freely dispensed in an atmosphere of smooth, harmonious social intercourse, cultured conversation, music, and female company, where leaders of society welcomed their inferiors without aloofness and handled awkward people with discrimination and tact. In the twelfth century, however, seriousness was seasoned with *foudat*, the jocular wit and capers of the jester. The Anglo-Norman historian William of Malmesbury, who disapproved, said that William IX made his audience roar with ribald laughter, and Raimbaut of Orange professed to skip and tumble like a *joglar* and outdo the star minstrel Mita at singing. The famous court festival which Geoffrey of Vigeois describes as taking place in Beaucaire in 1174 also reflects the spirit of *foudat*, combined with extravagant spending and conspicuous waste:

During the summer days a multitude of Provençal lords and barons flocked to zany festivities. These were occasioned by the proclaimed day of reconciliation, brought about by the king of the English, between Raymond, duke of Narbonne [Raymond V, count of Toulouse, 1148–94], and Alfonso, king of Aragon [Alfonso II, 1162–96]. But for some reason the kings were not present: the lords honoured their name in a madcap fashion. The count of Toulouse gave 100,000 sous to Raymond of Agoult, a liberal knight, who at once divided the thousands by a hundred and distributed single thousands to a hundred individual knights. Bertran Raimbaut had the castle grounds ploughed by twelve pairs of oxen, and then coins up to the value of 30,000 sous sown into them. William the Fat of Martello, who had 300 knights with him (the court in fact comprised about 10,000 knights) is reported to have cooked all the food from the kitchens with wax and pitchpine torches. At the same time the countess of Urgel sent a crown worth 40,000 sous; they arranged for William Mita to be called king of all the minstrels lest he have any reason to absent himself. Raymond of Vernoul burned thirty horses in a fire with everyone watching, because of a boast.[12]

As Bertran de Born sang in 1182, 'A court where no one laughs or

---

[11] Geoffrey of Vigeois, 'Chronica', in P. Labbe (ed.), *Novae Bibliothecae Manuscriptorum Librorum* (2 vols., Paris, 1657), ii.322.

[12] Geoffrey of Vigeois, 'Chronica', 321–2.

jokes is never complete; a court without gifts is just a paddock-full of nobles.'[13]

Great court festivals marking special events such as receptions for visiting diplomats, aristocratic betrothals, or weddings, or the high feasts of the Christian calendar such as Whitsun and Christmas, were a particular draw for entertainers who hoped to profit from customary displays of liberality. More usual were smaller gatherings in seigneurial residences. These might take the form of fortified town houses, places which Martin Aurell has described as the privileged habitat of troubadours, the workshop in which their poetry was created, and the centre for the diffusion of their songs—places embellished with Saracen slaves, musicians and singers, and luxury objects brought back from crusades and pilgrimages or acquired through the growing trade with the East. On the other hand they could include more isolated, rural castles such as Ventadour, home to Eble the Singer and to the celebrated troubadour Bernart de Ventadorn, situated at the end of a granite spur overlooking two steep-sided valleys. Yet more modest centres of social activity may have included the dower houses of noble widows, marginalized at the edge of family estates.

The composition of the court varied according to time, scale, and circumstances. The troubadours themselves included some great lords such as William IX and King Alfonso II of Aragon, less powerful nobles such as Raimbaut of Orange and Bertran de Born, and a townsman and abbot, Fulk of Marseilles, who became bishop of Toulouse in 1206. For many we have to rely on the insecure testimony of the *vidas*, or troubadour biographies, written in the songbooks of the thirteenth century or later: according to these, troubadours could be poor knights, sons of the bourgeoisie, errant minstrels, the occasional monk, and men who had begun their careers as clerks, canons, or students and had abandoned the Church for a secular life. The troubadour Giraut de Borneil, referred to as *maestre* (*magister*), was said to travel from court during the summer, accompanied by two singers to perform his songs, and to spend the winter teaching 'letters' in a school. While some troubadours may have depended on their art for a livelihood, it is likely that many combined their function as

---

[13] *L'amour et la guerre: L'œuvre de Bertran de Born*, ed. G. Gouiran (Aix-en-Provence, 1985), poem iii, 60–1.

entertainers with other jobs, whether menial or, in the case of the better educated men such as Marcabru and Cercamon, serving as administrators or bureaucrats in a seigneurial household. These two remained attached to the single court of William X of Aquitaine until his death and clearly hoped for a long-term appointment afterwards, though Cercamon disappears from view and Marcabru was disappointed in his hopes of the Castilian court. But the late twelfth century seems to have offered good hospitality to itinerant *joglars* on a bed-and-breakfast tour of the Carcassès, or the trip from Auvergne to Provence, Toulouse, the Sabarthès, Castillon, and Mataplana, if the lord was at home.

The distinction between troubadour and *joglar* is problematic. The term *joglar*, sometimes pejorative, covered a vast range of entertainers including acrobats, jugglers, imitators of bird-songs, musicians and performers of narratives, and lewd contortionists and dabblers in sorcery condemned by the Church. It may have been used of individual troubadours when they were envisaged primarily as performers.

William IX's court included high-ranking clergy and laity, household and local officials or servants, and *milites de curia*, apparently knights of relatively modest status, though one held the important post of steward. Baronial residences were home to the lord's family, ladies and their female companions, and noble children entrusted to him for their upbringing. William IX's bawdier songs addressed to male companions or knights suggest that women were not always present at social gatherings. All residential courts would have been enlarged from time to time by members of the extended family, allies, and passing guests and travellers.

Courts were a place of tension and rivalry as well as the site of development of courtly manners and values. Men competed for the lord's favour, gifts, and promotion. In troubadour poetry, the hated rival often takes the form of the *lauzengier*, the back-biter and spy who poisons the lord's ear. This figure might be a man of the same class and situation as the speaker: another troubadour, another poor younger son of a knightly family. But tensions also occurred between the upper and lower nobility, between clergy and laity, between troubadours and court officials: 'surly gastalds (stewards)', 'squatters with their combed-out hair, who are always demanding perks', favoured at the expense of more legitimate claimants, or the 'forked-tongues', smooth-talking hypocrites rewarded with cash, luxury clothing, and status symbols, venal judicial agents who corrupt the legal system and abuse their power to order the seizure of other people's property.

Lay culture: women

What was the role of women in the development of courtly culture? It used to be a commonplace among literary historians that the invention of courtly love marked a significant advance in the status of women, who were supposedly its happy, if passive, beneficiaries. According to this perspective, the cult of love and the *domna* reflected a new-found respect for woman as the civilizing inspiration of men, though women could hardly be credited with any creative input into this new 'great spiritual value' and its poetic manifestations. Subsequent accounts of women's marginal relevance to courtly love have interpreted it as a front for masculine social tensions. According to Erich Köhler, the lyric expression of unfulfilled desire for the *domna* sprang from strains in relations between the lower and upper nobility. The former's frustrated longing to be fully integrated into the life of the latter was sublimated in an imaginary world of classless social harmony where the excellence of the lover took precedence over wealth and rank. For the wealthier nobles, the advantage of collaborating in this fantasy lay in the defusion of social conflict and the containment of discontent. According to Georges Duby, who has pronounced the period resolutely male, tensions arose rather between young men and their elders. The nobility, whose estates were threatened by ever-increasing partitions, began to restrict the inheritance rights of younger sons, sending them off elsewhere to find heiresses and lands. Their patrons used courtly love as a game and their wives as a pawn with which to contain the turbulence of the young men in their household. Excited by the flouting of a taboo against adultery, these unmarried youths would compete for the potential, but withheld, favours of the lord's wife, who would thereby help her husband to gain a stronger hold over them so that he could use them for military purposes.

As Fredric Cheyette has argued, these views are attractive in many ways, yet questions remain. Not the least of them is the presence of *marit drut*, married men who become lovers, as a target of early troubadour satire: from the outset married and established noblemen such as William IX were clearly involved in the manners of courtly love. But another is the suspicion that to write out romantic sentiment and explain it away in terms of something else is somewhat perverse. Would it not be more reasonable and down-to-earth to see the veneration of the courtly *domna* as a mirror and product of the real power, patronage, prestige, and attractions of Occitan noblewomen? Alternatively, as Howard Bloch has asserted, could it be that *fin'amor* was not so much a celebration of their power as a misogynistic reaction against it, at a time when their freedoms and property rights were allegedly undergoing a significant advance?

There can be no doubt that powerful Occitan noblewomen existed. Many ruled lands in their own right or on behalf of absent husbands or minor children. Agnes of Burgundy, grandmother of the first troubadour William IX of Aquitaine, was an ambitious player on the political stage; Guillemette, viscountess of Nîmes, ruled on behalf of her son Bernard Atto; Adelaide of Toulouse ran the estates of her son Viscount Raymond Roger of Carcassonne in conjunction with Bertrand of Saissac. Eleanor of Aquitaine governed the duchy from 1152, after her marriage to Henry Plantagenet, until 1154, then in the name of her chosen heir, Richard the Lionheart, between 1170 and 1173, and finally after 1189 and Henry's death. Viscountess Ermengard governed Béziers and Carcassonne for twenty-five years, after not only the death of her husband but also her son's majority. Ermengard of Narbonne ruled her city for nearly sixty years, despite being married and having to defend herself against rebellious vassals and her own suzerain, Alphonse Jordan of Toulouse. Beatrice of Mauguio associated both her husbands in her rule, and although both were entitled count of Mauguio, neither acted independently within her lands; when her son began to act independently in defiance of her, she disinherited him. Several aristocratic women took over from their husbands when they went on pilgrimage or crusade. Some female rulers used seals to conceptualize their relation to power, representing themselves as armed equestrians ready to fulfil any military obligations inherent in their landholdings. This was not simply symbolic: Ermengard of Narbonne, for example, took part in the reconquest of Tortosa (1148) and the sieges of Les Baux (1162) and Puy-Saint-Front (1183), and at another moment promised King Louis VII to lead her army in aid of the count of Toulouse. Women also held castles under obligations of fidelity and service: a number have been identified from the twelfth century, and six of the castles held by the lords of Montpellier had a woman castellan during this time. According to Fredric Cheyette's analysis of archival evidence, women were expected to participate in political life, 'in waging feuds and calming disputes, in pressing and defending claims to property and rights';[14] legal formulas were designed to take account of the fact that women as well as men might attempt to break or circumvent property agreements.

It should not be forgotten, however, that such women were in the minority. Women are present in the archival records, but their numbers are limited. Women were vulnerable to, if not invariably repressed by, male coercion. Maria of Montpellier (d. 1213), lord of that city, recorded with insistent vehemence how she was 'crucified' and forced to consent to her husband Peter of Aragon's arrangements for their infant daughter's marriage:

King Peter, my husband, seeing that I was unwilling in any way to agree to these things, told me that if I did not consent, he would no longer lend any help to the town of Montpellier or its dependencies . . . What is more he would abandon them all forever, because he did not want to have any land, estate, wife, or anything else which he could not dispose of as he chose. Then I raised my voice to him and repeated several times: why do you want to defraud me? But he replied angrily that he wished me to agree to these arrangements, because he had promised firmly that he would make me consent to them, and if I refused, I would be doing him great harm. And on these words the king withdrew angrily.[15]

Here the pressure point was her need for military support in defending her inheritance, in a context of political struggles and intrigues in which women could be bandied about on the marriage market. Her own mother, Eudoxia, brought from Greece to marry Ramon Berenguer IV, count of Provence, had been dropped under pressure from Ramon's suzerain, the German emperor Frederick Barbarossa, and hastily married off to William VIII of Montpellier. William later repudiated her, whence she retired to a convent. From the age of eleven Maria was the target of various attempts to prevent her from

---

[14] F. L. Cheyette, 'Women, Poets, and Politics in Occitania', in T. Evergates (ed.), *Aristocratic Women in Medieval France* (Philadelphia, 1999), 160.

[15] *Histoire générale de Languedoc*, ed. C. Devic and J. Vaissete (16 vols., Toulouse, 1872–1904), viii.533–4, no. 132.

inheriting lordship over the town, first being married off with a cash dowry in exchange for the renunciation of her rights to the city. Widowed at twelve, she was married again at fifteen, when once more she was obliged to renounce her claim, only to be repudiated on the expedient grounds of consanguinity. She became lord of Montpellier when the pope refused to acknowledge the legitimacy of William VIII's second marriage, but married Peter of Aragon two months later, whereupon he set about wresting the seigneurial rights from his wife in violation of their marriage contract. With the support of the people of Montpellier, the pope, and her own strength of character, she succeeded in ensuring the succession of her son, the future James the Conqueror of Aragon, though she died in the process at the age of thirty-two. Occitan noblewomen certainly had rights and powers; but they were likely to be vulnerable and less free than a comparable man. Even Ermengard of Narbonne, with her exceptional record, was edged out of power, exiled and isolated, at the end of her life.

And if such women did wield power, was this greater than that enjoyed by their northern French counterparts? A recent volume edited by Theodore Evergates including studies of aristocratic women in Blois, the Chartrain, Champagne, and Flanders, as well as Occitania, suggests that this was not so. While outlining the diversity of experiences of such women, the contributors return emphatically to the conviction that women exercised more acknowledged power than has been generally assumed. Though the extent of their rights varied according to regional customs and family circumstances, northern Frenchwomen too inherited both titles and properties, including fiefs, which they transmitted to their children. In their capacity as lords, they settled disputes among their subjects, garrisoned and fortified castles, raised and commanded troops, and sometimes led them into battle. As in the case of Occitan noblewomen, they could exercise the same powers as men, but did so less frequently. Some historians have suggested that from the ninth to the eleventh centuries, Occitan (and Catalan) women seem to have enjoyed property rights unknown in northern France. If so, this difference seems to have disappeared by the twelfth and thirteenth centuries.

Georges Duby's picture of a 'male Middle Ages' where women were simple objects of exchange, confined to inner chambers except for ceremonial purposes, can therefore be set aside. Neither is it tenable to argue, as Howard Bloch has done, that a significant improvement at the end of the eleventh century in Occitan women's power to control and dispose of property provoked a misogynistic reaction in the peculiar form of courtly love. His argument runs broadly as follows. Occitan women's power was embodied in the so-called 'feminist movement' represented by Robert of Arbrissel (d. 1116) and the founding in 1101 of the double monastery of Fontevraud, which was subsequently headed by a young abbess. This movement supposedly coincided with two other phenomena: first, an increase in women's control over property and second, their acquisition of the right to refuse to consent to marriage. These marked a serious ideological, if not practical, threat to men and the future of the family fortune: women could in theory choose their own marriage partners, and also dispose of property as they wished. Whereas previously woman had, he claims, been denigrated as the root of all evil, once she was capable of disposing of property she was idealized in terms of courtly love—an ideal which nevertheless cloaked an equally profound misogyny. This process of idealization supposedly sprang from William IX of Aquitaine's rivalry with the charismatic Robert of Arbrissel, whose attractions as a so-called great liberator of women in the Middle Ages lured noblewomen, including William's wife, to take spiritual refuge from secular life.

Bloch's arguments flowing from the southern use of matronymics, the supposed prevalence of allods in the south, and his analysis of inheritance practices, are flawed in various ways. It is highly questionable whether Occitan women's control of property was increasing at the end of the eleventh century. Moreover, Robert of Arbrissel was no particular protector of women and guardian of their interests, and both William's matrimonial situation and his relations with Robert have been clouded in myth. The idea that he invented courtly love as a response to Robert's rival attractions melts away in the face of analysis of the sources. The idea that the Church's doctrine of consent raised the spectre of female freedom to marry and hence dispose of property in a way inimical to family interests is an interesting one, but it is far from clear that this had any impact on actual practice (widows had long been able to dispose of property anyway, and marriages continued to be arranged by families with little attention to the personal preferences of their daughters or indeed their sons), and it is hard to see how it could relate to *fin'amor*, which was essentially extramarital.

So should we return to the idea that in the troubadour courtly *canso*, the power of the *domna* faithfully mirrors and enlarges the power that a minority of Occitan noblewomen wielded in real life? It is certainly true that metaphors of the *domna* as lord have their counterparts in a number of legal documents where subjects, male or female, acknowledge the authority of women lords. It is also striking that the language of political allegiance in such terms as *drut*, found in Occitan documents as early as 1065 in the sense of a trusted friend and ally and appearing also in this sense in Old French and Occitan *chansons de geste*, becomes eroticized in courtly literature. As Cheyette perceptively observes, relations of power and status thus become projected onto a world of intimacy, and at the same time the force of sexual longing is reflected back into the world of power. His argument that this could only serve to promote the legitimacy of the *domna* is less persuasive as a generalization. The *domna's* power in the *canso* is frequently undermined: by the fact that she has no voice; by her appearing only as an abstract projection of the male speaker's feelings; by the way in which the male speaker speaks more to other men (patrons, friends, and rivals) than to the alleged object of his desire; or by a gender system that divides the feminine between the *domna*, the lady admired but desexualized and circumscribed by a strict code of conduct, including an implied obligation to conform to the speaker's wishes, and the *femna*, the difficult, dangerous, and despised woman dragging the heavy baggage of overt medieval misogyny.

What we do know is that Occitan women were widely involved in the patronage of troubadour poetry. Some 600 women, designated by proper names or pseudonyms, are addressed in their songs. It is not clear what proportion of these was involved in any tangible reward of payment or promotion, which is more demonstrably the domain of male patrons. It is also certain that women collaborated in the game of courtly love by contributing to a sociable and flirtatious atmosphere in the courts, and in composing poems or songs themselves. By contrast with the two known female poets of Old French for our period, some twenty-three *trobairitz* are known by name, with some further twenty-five surviving poems by anonymous women. A third of the manuscripts have preserved poems by women. Nevertheless, *trobairitz* are outnumbered by male troubadours by twenty to one; about forty-six female-authored poems have survived, in comparison with 2,500 by men.

Women may well have encouraged poetry of encomium in their honour. The most tangible evidence for this comes from a non-Occitan woman, Adela of Blois. William IX's declaration that if his lady is willing to grant him her love, he is ready to promote her praises may suggest corroboration. However, it is also clear from the surviving record that from the outset it is men who claim authority and leadership in the development of courtly values. Women may have been an important part of the social rituals of courtliness and courtly love, and exploited them for their own ends; their poetry shows that they were sometimes able to speak out with authority, and often with wit and artistic accomplishment; but they were only one set of players in the game, and a secondary one at that.

Religious life and the rise of Catharism

If courtly love is one of the key markers of Occitan culture, the other is the Cathar heresy. In the eleventh-century south, as everywhere in Europe, men and women yearned for spiritual purity. Their religious impulses took many forms: the veneration of saints and holy relics, pilgrimages, the foundation of new parishes and monasteries, the creative profusion of Romanesque art and architecture, pious donations, and the renunciation of the world in a quest for the apostolic way of life, whether in the cloister or in the enthusiastic following of charismatic itinerant preachers.

Orthodox spirituality included participation in early crusading movements. The First Crusade attracted a sizeable Occitan contingent under the leadership of Raymond of Saint-Gilles, count of Toulouse, its efforts being chronicled by the Latin history of Raymond of Aguilers and the Occitan *Canso d'Antioca* composed by Gregory Bechada. The count was respected by the Byzantines for his cultured manners, in contrast to those of the northern leaders, though there was friction between the different western groups, and the northerners made disparaging comments about the southern lack of warlike spirit and fondness for food. With the Poitevin Raymond of Antioch subsequently occupying a position of power and influence in the

Holy Land, the latter continued to be a draw for Occitan crusaders, but in serious contention was the Spanish *reconquista*, which many perceived as an equally valid spiritual (not to mention temporal) goal. Indeed, after the failure of the French contribution to the Second Crusade (1147–9) under Louis VII, southern disillusionment was palpable and the troubadour Marcabru, in his famous *Vers del lavador*, urged his compatriots to cleanse their souls in the washing-place of nearby Spain, with the support of the Templars and the Catalan leader Ramon Berenguer IV of Barcelona, rather than in the eastern crusade led by French 'broken failures, weary of valour'.[16]

Eleventh-century spiritual excitement also inspired the so-called 'Gregorian Reform'. The state of the Occitan Church before this upheaval is a matter of controversy. The traditional papal perspective has condemned it as materially, institutionally, and spiritually stagnant, with a morally lax and ignorant clergy neglecting worship and religious buildings, and ecclesiastical lands and offices extensively controlled by lay nobles. On the other hand, others have argued that from 900 to 1050 a largely healthy Occitan and Catalan Church represented the most important single force for law and order in many otherwise anarchic regions, developing as it did the Peace and Truce of God to combat the depredations of the *milites*. Elisabeth Magnou-Nortier in particular has energetically contested the value of the 'reform', which she prefers to refer to as the Gregorian 'crisis'. For her, although real abuses, much exaggerated, did exist in the Occitan Church, Gregorian policy failed to diagnose the real problem, namely a split between the high Church of the aristocracy and the prelates on the one hand, and the low Church of the rural priests, peasants, and ordinary townspeople on the other. Its repressive interventions succeeded only in creating a gulf between itself and the laity, generating a climate of antagonism and fear, undermining lay people's confidence of their place in the Church, dismantling an effective system of government, and, in its ambition to separate the temporal and spiritual, rather too visibly annexing the temporal for itself. Magnou-Nortier argues that during this time of spiritual fervour the Church's policy in the south was a disaster, creating a vacuum in which the manifest

---

[16] *Marcabru: A Critical Edition*, ed. S. Gaunt, R. Harvey, and L. M. Paterson with J. Marshall and M. Florence (Woodbridge, 2000), poem xxxv, 62.

asceticism of heretical leaders was able to inspire a laity cut off from its traditional links to the Church.

The institutional framework of the Occitan Church suffered mixed fortunes after the Gregorian reforms. Before it took place, Occitan bishops often experienced considerable independence, enjoying hereditary office under the control of a local aristocratic family and being subordinate only to a distant pope who rarely intervened in their affairs. After the reforms, the papacy intruded much more into the everyday life of the diocese, while monasteries and even whole religious orders were removed from the bishop's jurisdiction. It is true that the expansion of European society led to an increase of business in matters of his jurisdiction over the clergy, ecclesiastical property, wills, debts, usury, and all forms of moral and doctrinal offences; and materially bishops were much better off, since papal support vastly improved their ability to recover or acquire ecclesiastical property and tithes. However, the episcopate of Narbonne in particular must have lost its previous cohesiveness as the province languished for a quarter of century with the loss of its southern dioceses and two of its archbishops deposed and excommunicated. When heresy began to take root, the bishops seem to have been either too weak, too busy, or too lacking in contact with the people to mount an effective opposition.

What of the monasteries? While few Occitan convents for women existed before the thirteenth century, male spiritual life found varied forms of expression in the proliferation of monasteries for men. In the twelfth century many new foundations arose in response to a desire for renewal and a return to the primitive purity and austerity of the early Church: from eremitical movements such as those associated with Grandmont, La Sauve-Majeure, Fontevraud, and the order of the Carthusians, to that of the Cistercians, with twenty-nine abbeys being founded in twelfth-century Occitania, and the Military Orders of the Templars and Hospitallers. The Cistercians were most active in attempting to combat heresy in the twelfth century, but without much success. Despite the asceticism of their original inspiration, the Cistercians' pioneering land clearance in deserted and uncultivated sites led to enormous wealth and a perception of their greed, aggressiveness, and arrogance on the part of the general Occitan population. The Military Orders, too, became wealthy landowners and powerful lords, competing with each other and the

Cistercians over the control of land. Monastic communities in the south also handled money to an extent unknown in other regions. They were hard-bitten about material matters, and an easy target for dissidents who revered the manifest austerity of the 'good men', or Cathar Perfects.

Catharism probably arose as a combination of the indigenous development of contemporary conditions in the West and Bogomil ideas imported from the Balkans by missionaries, merchants, or crusaders. It made its first securely attested appearance in western Europe in Cologne in 1143, surfacing in Liège, Périgord, and the Albigeois from 1147. But as early as 1119, heretics allegedly condemning the sacrament of the Eucharist, infant baptism, priestly office, other ecclesiastical orders, and marriage had previously been denounced by Pope Calixtus II, apparently with the support of William IX of Aquitaine. In c.1140 a priest from the Dauphiné, Peter of Bruis, was burnt at the stake for heresy, though not Catharism; subsequently the heretical preaching of Henry of Lausanne in Toulouse and the Albigeois provoked an unsuccessful mission to the south on the part of St Bernard. Church councils from 1148 to 1162 condemned protectors of heresy in Gascony, Provence, and Toulouse, and in 1165 a meeting took place at Lombers where a certain Olivier and his sect, generally thought to have been Cathars, debated publicly with Occitan prelates. By the mid-1170s the Cathar heresy was firmly established in Occitania, when Occitan, French, and Lombard Cathars and Nicetas, Cathar bishop of Constantinople, assembled at Saint-Félix-de-Caraman and established dioceses in France, Toulouse, Carcassonne (which included the whole of Catalonia), Albi, Agen, and Lombardy, to join the seven churches of Asia.

Sources for Cathar doctrine are suspect in that most of them were written by Catholics. However, most historians agree that Catharism was a dualistic religion, distinct from other Christian sects in its belief that the material world was the creation of the Devil or evil principle, corresponding to the God of the Old Testament. It held that Lucifer, son of the evil principle, had succeeded in seducing certain angels who were expelled from heaven and imprisoned in earthbound, material bodies. Through reincarnation they passed from one body to another until, by means of the ritual of the *consolamentum*, they could be freed to re-enter heaven. Cathars believed that they were the true Church of God, a Church consisting of the life of its members and not buildings of wood and stone. The Church of Rome, along with its institutions and sacraments, they saw as the work of the Devil. They rejected much of the Old Testament, and the doctrine of the Incarnation: Jesus could not have been embodied in evil flesh or matter, and was seen as a pure spirit who brought God's message of salvation. The Virgin represented for some a symbol of the Church, for others a woman through whom Jesus passed in order to appear in spiritual form on earth.

Christ had given the true Church the power to remit sins through prayer and the *consolamentum* or baptism of the Holy Spirit. This spiritual baptism was opposed to the baptism by water of the Roman Church, and was granted to believers, so not generally to children unless they were in peril of death. This form of baptism followed a period of instruction, ascetic discipline, and tests of doctrine. After the ceremony the consoled man or woman became a Perfect, who was then committed to a life of extreme austerity, avoiding all fleshly indulgence and thought of sin. Physical contact with the opposite sex was taboo, as was food produced by sexual generation such as meat, milk, eggs, or cheese, though fish was allowed as it was thought to be generated spontaneously. On certain days of the week and for three forty-day periods a year Perfects fasted on bread and water. In theory the *consolamentum* could not be repeated, so it was vital not to lapse into sin; as a result most believers waited until their deathbed before receiving it. However, in practice a repeat did occur if a Perfect had changed allegiance between different groups of Cathars, or if there were doubts about the quality of the Perfect who had conducted the ceremony. Ordinary believers were not obliged to follow their life of austerity, but supported them with gifts of food and clothing, gave them lodging, listened to their preaching, attended their ceremonies, and practised a ritual greeting known as the *melioramentum* which expressed reverence for the Perfect and a commitment to seek the *consolamentum* before death.

The appeal of Catharism, which in its extreme form logically aimed at the end of human life on earth, lay above all in the manifest commitment and asceticism of its leaders and its contrast with the perceived worldliness of the established Church. Catharism offered a guarantee of salvation to those who received the *consolamentum*, more securely so in a faith which placed great emphasis on the purity of the officiating Perfect, at a time when Catholic priests were often seen as unworthy to transmit the sacraments and hence possibly (if not doctrinally) unreliable mediators of grace and protectors from hell. Other factors were the social services provided by the Cathars, their provision of places for girls in their hospices in regions where nunneries were very few and far between, and perhaps the fact that, unlike the Catholic Church, the Cathars did not impose on believers the pressures of the confessional or penitential system. Catharism may also have been attractive to women, who could attain the full status of Perfects, whereas the Catholic priesthood was closed to them: however, analysis of available data has cast doubt on the previously advanced idea that women were attracted to the heresy in disproportionate numbers.

Until the end of the twelfth century, heresy flourished unchecked in the south. Lay leaders such as Raymond V of Toulouse were either unable to combat it as a result of political weakness or unwilling once their families and friends were involved. Bishops were busy and distant, and if they did engage in public debate they lent credence to their opponents. Monasteries were often visible symbols of the materialism rejected by the heretics, who were seen to live up to their spiritual ideals; on a more worldly level, many resented the Church's increasing pressure on the laity to pay tithes. Southerners were used to a number of freedoms, including the freedom to question authority. This was soon to change. The thirteenth century was to see heresy pursued by means of a crusade against Christians, and the founding of the Inquisition. Repression was to prove effective, and to set dark institutions in place for the future.

Conclusion

As a consequence of the invasions occasioned by the Albigensian Crusade, the south acquired a retrospective identity. This was constructed partly through a new sense of social solidarity and hostility to the French enemy, expressed in lyric and epic poetry, partly through the compilation of troubadour *chansonniers*, particularly in Italy. William Burgwinkle has argued that the authors and scribes of these anthologies, by listing the songs under the names of particular poets who are further individualized by the addition of 'biographies' (*vidas* and *razos*), created a new form of cultural and literary history that advocated a political identity founded on cultural practices rather than geography or ethnicity. Their retrospective view has of course mediated our own reception of troubadour poetry. This new political identity hardly existed before the Albigensian Crusade. Until this watershed, Occitania consisted in a multiplicity of shifting regional groupings characterized, as was northern France, by political and social diversity. That there existed some awareness of the differences between north and south is suggested by the criticisms that northern writers occasionally made of southerners' appearance, customs, and morals. But we should not overestimate the amount or significance of regional stereotyping in our period, and the absence of a generally recognized term for 'southerners' is noteworthy. In some respects, such as in the roles and opportunities available to aristocratic women, Occitania's experience closely resembled that of other parts of France. And the old caricature of a corrupt, unreformed Occitan Church, out of step with the progressive north and bringing Catharism down upon itself, is difficult to sustain. This is not, however, to deny the existence of features more typical of the south than the north. These included a dislike of homage; a preference for cash transactions and egalitarian non-aggression pacts rather than the exchange of fiefs for services; the proliferation of mercenaries and urban knights; a relative tolerance of ethnic diversity and freedom of religious belief; the early development of medicine and Roman law; the relative autonomy of the small farmer; and the importance of the institutionalized Peace. Patterns of urban government point to a region that was open to influences from the Mediterranean world. Comparatively unmarked by, and eventually sceptical of, the rise of chivalry in the north, the south made its principal impact on history through the momentous invention of courtly love and the poetic and musical brilliance of the troubadours.

5

The Church

Marcus Bull

> When Our Lord heard him [the Good Thief] he turned towards him:
> 'Friend,' he said, 'the people are not yet born
> Who will come to avenge me with their steel lances. . . .
> Holy Christianity will be honoured by them
> And my land conquered and my country freed.
> A thousand years from today they will be baptized and raised
> And will cause the Holy Sepulchre to be regained and adored.
> And they will serve me as though they were my offspring.
> They will all be my sons, I promise them that.' . . .
> 'Friend,' said Our Lord, 'know certainly
> That from over the sea will come a new race
> Which will take revenge on the death of its father.
> Thenceforward there will be pagans only in the Far East.
> The French will deliver all that land . . .'[1]

These remarkable sentiments are attributed to Christ on the Cross in the *Chanson d'Antioche*, a late twelfth-century epic account, in Old French, of the events of the First Crusade. The author, Graindor of Douai, saw the success of the crusade as nothing less than the playing out of a divine plan; God's instrument were *li Franc*, the Franks who took up arms in response to Pope Urban II's appeal and captured Jerusalem in July 1099. Crusading reintroduced a measure of ambiguity into the vocabulary of Frankishness, which had been in the process of becoming appropriated by the kings and inhabitants of western Francia, France. Such was the wide geographical spread of enthusiasm for the crusade that it revived memories of the broader

---

[1] *La Chanson d'Antioche*, ed. S. Duparc-Quioc, Documents relatifs à l'histoire des croisades 11 (2 vols., Paris, 1976–8), i.26–7; trans. L and J. S. C. Riley-Smith, *The Crusades: Idea and Reality 1095–1274* (London, 1981), 72–3.

range of the Latin word *Franci* and its vernacular derivatives, which could denote all those living in what had been Charlemagne's old empire, including the Germans. But even though *Franc* could technically refer to those from beyond France itself when one was talking about crusaders, there can be little doubt that, as far as Graindor and his audience were concerned, it must have been the French in particular that Christ had in mind when he foretold the appearance of a vengeful *novele gent*.

Graindor was being daring in introducing this scene into an evocation of such a charged moment in the Christian story. He must have been confident that this would not jar with his listeners and readers, and this was confidence born of the expectation that the audience would unproblematically share his assessment of the special place that the French enjoyed in God's scheme for mankind. By extension, the assumption that underlies this passage is that there was a place, France, that was particularly favoured by the Church, for this was understood as the continuation of Christ's presence on earth. The Church, in other words, necessarily sustained and bore witness to Christ's love of France and its people. To understand France and the French in our period, therefore, it is important to understand something of the place of the Church in French society, thought, culture, and politics. In short, what was the background to the sort of confidence in the close connection between Frenchness and religion that is so apparent in the speech attributed to Christ?

Basic premises

In order to understand the workings and importance of the Church in central medieval France, it is useful to stand back and gain an overview of the Church in general, for the French experience was one (often very important) part of a wider picture. A good way to begin thinking about the Church is to remember that historians who study the Middle Ages must constantly be on their guard against anachronisms. One of the most misleading and persistent is the couplet 'Church and State' when used to denote discrete entities that were potentially, and often actually, in some form of conflict. The usual way to demolish the term is to attack it at its weakest point, which means pointing out that the word 'State' introduces modern-day associations about nationhood and political institutions that would have been quite alien to the aims and methods of medieval governments. This is an effective approach—so effective, indeed, that it tends to obscure the fact that the use of the word 'Church' as a counterpoise to the domain of secular government, and by extension to the wider world in which that government functions, is also very problematic.

Part of the problem is that the word itself has a wide range of possible meanings when applied to medieval conditions. To modern-day observers, the most obvious sense of 'Church' is a form of institution, and certainly this corresponds to an important part of the medieval scene: there was a more or less clearly defined group within society—clergy, monks, and nuns—who had formally separated themselves from the lay majority by rituals of ordination or the taking of solemn vows, as well as in their physical appearance; these people operated in structured ways that were governed by hierarchical chains of command and numerous regulations; and in the form of churches and monasteries, they had their own designated spaces in which to live and perform the rituals that were reserved for them. Basic binary divisions—orthodox and heretical, clergy and laity, monastery and outside world, consecrated and unconsecrated space—were a central part of how the Church understood itself. But even within the institutional context, it should be noted that there was scope for enormous variations that were as great as any to be found in society more generally. The clergy ranged from a rich and powerful elite of prelates (cardinals, archbishops, bishops, and abbots) to an often impoverished and chronically under-resourced rural 'proletariat' of parish priests; and from the beneficiaries of the most demanding and prestigious forms of education that were available at any given time, to semi-literates who simply served a form of apprenticeship on the job, knew little or no Latin, and had no developed understanding of the meanings behind the various rituals that they were called on to perform. Furthermore, while ordination into the 'major' orders (sub-deacon, deacon, and priest) did constitute a line of fairly clear demarcation, at least in theory, at the lower end of the scale those in 'minor' orders (acolyte, exorcist, lector, and porter) were often young boys or married men who simply worked for a church and blended in with the lay world around them.

Moreover, any understanding of what the word 'Church' meant in the medieval period must extend beyond the institutional framework to take account of two dimensions which can usefully be termed the 'longitudinal' and the 'latitudinal'. The longitudinal, or historical, dimension relates to the Church's sense of its place in time. If we were able to travel back to, say, a French cathedral or abbey church in the twelfth century, our reaction would doubtless be to interpret every-thing that we encountered—ceremonies, music, art, architecture, lan-guage, dress, even the style of handwriting in books—as culturally specific expressions of a particular time and place set within patterns of historical change. While alive to the notion of change, which they often perceived as the manifestation of inexorable decline, medieval clerics would have argued that our modern perspective is false. They would have claimed that they, their roles, and their environment were not the result of the countless contingencies of historical develop-ment, but expressions of a divine plan: a mandate that Christ had communicated to the Apostles and had been handed down to every succeeding generation of clergy. In sharp contrast to the later Protest-ant churches, which can be described as 'gathered' in the sense that they are believed to be created by and for their congregations and have ministers whose authority derives from below, the 'apostolic' quality of the medieval Church, and by extension the nature of the authority that its clergy exercised, amounted to the single most important aspect of its belief system. Each facet of the Church's oper-ations, however small, expressed this fundamental notion, in the same sort of way that each tiny fragment of a holographic plate can project the whole of the image recorded on it.

This, at least, is how educated clerics, monks, and nuns, who had direct access to the Church's biblical foundation texts and accumu-lated body of learning, would have conceived matters. It is difficult to know exactly what ordinary lay men and women believed, although the basic fact of the Church's authority would have been constantly present to them in many facets of their day-to-day lives. It is also reasonable to suppose that many people shared with the clergy a sense of the Church's uniquely long chronological reach and con-nectedness to a past that was simultaneously distant and close— through, for example, the veneration of saints who dated from the early Christian centuries, through witnessing Christ's 'presence' in the consecrated bread and wine of the Eucharist, and through the impression of permanence generated by ecclesiastical buildings that dominated the human landscape in which they were set. People would have been aware that the Church had a uniquely long memory. And it provided answers, though not necessarily the only answers, to fundamental questions about the nature of human existence, moral choices, and death.

The latitudinal, or social, dimension was likewise related to the belief in the Church's divinely mandated quality. Unlike modern-day congregations in pluralistic societies, which are exclusive in the sense that people join one of them as a matter of more or less free choice, the medieval Church was effectively inclusive, meaning that in those areas such as France where there was a widespread and deeply rooted ecclesiastical presence, everyone was assumed to be a member unless certain limited exceptions applied—essentially being a Jew or a heretic. Baptism, in the early Christian centuries a ritual designed for adults but by our period almost always performed on infants, was the basic criterion for inclusion. Perhaps more people slipped through the net than is sometimes supposed, for instance in areas disrupted by invasions in the ninth and tenth centuries, and in more remote regions where the system of parish churches was slowest to develop. But as a shared and ritually conferred status, baptism was the nearest thing to a universal point of reference that the Church, and thus society as a whole, possessed. It means that when we speak of the medieval Church, we should understand by it a collectivity that was nearly coterminous with society, which is why it was implicated in a very wide range of social operations, from the blessing of a peasant's seeds to the solemn consecration of kings.

The French Church or the Church in France?

To what extent, then, can we speak of a specifically 'French' Church that was anything more than simply one part of the greater whole? It must be noted that there were no national churches along the lines of those that emerged after the Reformation. As well as seeing the Church as an international organization, moreover, it is important to remember that at the opposite extreme the actual experience of most people most of the time was extremely localized: symptoms of this include the many saints' cults with a modest geographical spread, the fact that the parish church was effectively the 'face' of the Church as a whole for the majority of the faithful, and the persistence of regional variations in the liturgy. One of the aims of ecclesiastical reformers in this period was to introduce greater consistency into the workings of the Church at its grass roots. To this end, they often found it useful to work with secular rulers. But this did not mean that the reformers' vision was of an ecclesiastical order that was simply derived from, or that functioned as an extension of, kingdoms and other political units. To that extent, then, they would have seen no virtue in there being a sub-division of the Church that simply corresponded to the French kingdom. In addition, the organization of the Church did not match linguistic or other cultural divisions. There was, therefore, no portion of the Church marked out specifically by the Frenchness of its members.

The central point to note is that Christianity as an organized religion pre-dated the emergence of the Germanic kingdoms that succeeded the Roman empire in western Europe. By our period, many of the Church's basic institutions still bore the heavy imprint of the Roman past. The most obvious indication of this is the fact that Latin remained a living language as the Church's medium of communication even as the vernaculars descended from it—including the various French dialects, of course—were moving further away from their Latin ancestor. On the other hand, the Church in the central Middle Ages was far from being its late classical predecessor frozen in time. It had adapted to momentous changes in order to survive. In southern and eastern Britain, for instance, Christianity had to be reintroduced virtually from scratch after the end of Roman rule and the settlement of pagan Anglo-Saxon migrants. In the Carolingian period large parts of northern Germany had been Christianized by the Franks (or at least subordinated to the religion of the region's new masters), and by our period the northern Germans were themselves extending their Christian culture into the lands of their pagan Slav neighbours. In the Iberian peninsula, Christian rulers and prelates were forced to make slow and often very difficult readjustments after the Muslim invasions of the eighth century had completely overturned the late Roman/Visigothic order. Generally speaking, the area that was to become the French kingdom and the French-speaking regions bordering it did not face convulsions on the same scale, with the result that a sense of continuity developed early and took firm root. The Germanic peoples who had settled in Gaul, the Franks, Visigoths, and Burgundians, had in most areas formed a small minority within the Christian Gallo-Roman population. The newcomers converted early. And, significantly, the form of Christianity that the Franks adopted after *c.*500 was orthodox Catholicism rather the heretical variant, Arianism, to which other Germanic groups had been exposed. These Catholic origins were to be an important part of the French myth in later centuries: there is a distant but direct connection between the baptism of the Frankish king Clovis (traditionally but insecurely dated to 496) and the sort of French self-confidence, the potent mix of religious and national identity, that is so evident in the passage from the *Chanson d'Antioche* that was quoted above.

It was not the case, however, that the Church in France was unscathed at the beginning of our period. The ninth-century invasions, particularly those by the Vikings, had hit it hard. In the area of densest Viking settlement, in what was to become Normandy, ecclesiastical organization was destroyed for about a century. Elsewhere in France churches were looted, resources were lost, and monastic communities were scattered. Internal political conflicts compounded the Church's difficulties. But the key point to note is that when the Viking threat eased and the late Carolingian political reordering achieved some level of stability, a revival of ecclesiastical life was possible precisely because it was *re*-vival, the reactivation of pre-existing frameworks. So, for example, the Norman counts/dukes and their clerical allies rebuilt ecclesiastical life in their region on two foundations: monasticism, which had had a successful history in the area before the Vikings arrived, and the seven bishoprics in the province of Rouen, which had been severely disrupted but had not been forgotten.

The value that the Norman rebuilders attached to the restoration of bishops' sees is particularly revealing. The significance of bishops generally needs to be stressed. They are figures who sometimes get downplayed in discussions of the medieval Church: topics such as changes in monastic fashion, the political struggles of the popes, and popular religious movements lend a dynamic quality to the story, whereas bishops can seem like unexciting embodiments of conservatism. But this is unfair. The continuity and stability that they represented were their greatest assets. In most of France, bishops' sees were based on former Roman *civitates*, regional urban centres and their hinterlands which were themselves often based on even older tribal units. The boundaries of bishoprics were in many instances based on the circumscriptions of late Roman government (and some in turn are preserved by modern-day units of local and regional government). This was where the Roman legacy was most deeply felt, for the result was a quite even distribution, especially in northern and western France, of episcopal cities between fifty and a hundred kilometres apart. There were exceptions to the overall pattern. For example, there was a tighter cluster of smaller bishoprics in the south-east of the kingdom and across the Rhône in Provence, a consequence of the earlier and concentrated urbanization of that area in the classical period. At the other extreme, bishops' sees on the fringes of the mountainous Massif Central were further apart than in the lower-lying regions to the north and west. In the deep south-west, bishoprics were small, but not because of precocious urbanization. On the contrary, the Basques of Gascony had resisted or reversed Romanization. A network of Gascon bishoprics on the basic model only emerged around the middle of the eleventh century, after a period in which several sees had been so impoverished that they had been amalgamated into a single bishopric of Gascony. These exceptions apart, however, the main point to note is the remarkable potential that bishoprics created for consistency and the flow of information and ideas both up and down the chains of command.

Bishops, then, were the key to the Church's ambitions to achieve 'coverage'. How they interacted with those above and below them in the ecclesiastical hierarchy, therefore, throws a good deal of light on the problem of whether there was a discrete and distinctively French Church. The immediate superiors to whom bishops theoretically answered were their metropolitans; these were the senior bishops within a cluster of bishoprics, from the tenth century often known by the now familiar term 'archbishop'. Archbishops exercised jurisdiction over the bishops whose sees lay within their 'province', though the extent to which they did so over the bishops' own clergy and flocks was a grey area until the thirteenth century. As with so much else, their origins were late Roman, the provinces survivals of Roman administrative units enshrined in a text known as the *Notitia Provinciarum*. The pattern inherited by the west Frankish kingdom, therefore, did not correspond with the new political ordering. Seven provinces were wholly or overwhelmingly within the kingdom. Tours, Sens, Rouen, Bourges, and Bordeaux were solely inside France. The Gascon metropolitan see of Eauze, relocated to Auch before the beginning of our period, may have periodically extended its jurisdiction over the Pyrenees into Navarre and Aragon. The seventh archbishopric, Narbonne, had been granted supervision of the Catalan sees when the Carolingians created the Spanish March in the northeast of the Iberian peninsula. As the Spanish Church reorganized itself in the wake of Christian territorial expansion, the influence of the archbishops of Narbonne came to an end, especially after the restoration of the Catalan archbishopric of Tarragona in the early decades of the twelfth century. Two very important provinces, Reims and Lyon, were mostly within the French kingdom. The city of Lyon itself, however, was in imperial territory, and its own diocese straddled France and the Empire. This liminal status was one reason why the Capetian kings tended to resist Lyon's claim to the largely honorific 'primacy of the Gauls' (effectively the right to a senior ranking among the northern French metropolitans), favouring instead the claims of Sens. One of Reims's suffragan sees, Cambrai, was in imperial territory; a new (or rather, revived) 'French' diocese of Arras was detached from it in 1093, interestingly with the support of King Philip I. Speakers of northern French, Franco-Provençal, or Occitan living beyond the kingdom's eastern borders formed all or virtually all of the populations of the provinces of Arles, Aix-en-Provence, Vienne, and Embrun, the majority of those in the provinces of Besançon and Tarentaise, and a substantial portion of those in the provinces of Cologne and Trier.

Given this varied picture, it is not surprising to find that the fit between political and ecclesiastical structures was seldom close. One of the exceptions was the duchy of Normandy, the boundaries of which corresponded closely to those of the province of Rouen (which was slightly the larger). It is often argued that this was of great benefit to the dukes, who were able to exercise control over 'their' Church in close cooperation with churchmen who could see the value of ducal patronage and protection. The efforts of rulers who were not so favoured to effect a similar conjunction suggest that there is some merit in this argument. For example, in their capacity as dukes of Aquitaine and Gascony, the counts of Poitiers ruled over an area that corresponded quite closely to the provinces of Bordeaux and Auch.

But the important city of Limoges was the centre of a diocese within the province of Bourges. The dukes' efforts to detach Limoges from Bourges and bring it under the archbishops of Bordeaux never met with success; the bishops of Limoges regularly operated *de facto* as part of an Aquitanian episcopal network—in many of the Peace of God councils, for example—but the old formal structures could not be removed.

The history of the ill-starred archdiocese of Dol in Brittany provides another example of the Church's resistance to any organizational adaptation that was driven by current political needs. The idea of a Breton grouping of dioceses with Dol as the metropolitan emerged in the ninth century in the aspirations of the rulers of Brittany to achieve the sort of situation that would later benefit the Norman dukes. But the bishops of Dol were fated to live in a state of near-permanent uncertainty. The archbishops of Tours, within whose province the breakaway dioceses were located, vigorously resisted any loss of their authority and status. Popes vacillated: Gregory VII (1073–85) permitted the bishop of Dol to wear the *pallium*, the shouldercloth that was an archbishop's distinctive symbol of office, but Urban II removed that right in 1094. At the Council of Nantes in 1127, the archbishopric of Dol was recognized, but with only two suffragan bishops; the archbishop of Tours was to keep the other five Breton sees, and retained some power over the new province. In 1148 the archbishop of Dol was actually excommunicated for resisting the authority of Tours. The English Pope Hadrian IV (1154–9) reasserted Dol's metropolitan status in deference to Henry II, who claimed overlordship over Brittany. But the dispute rumbled on, Pope Innocent III finally ruling in favour of Tours in 1199.

Dol's vicissitudes as an archbishopric with a distinctively Breton identity reveal in microcosm some of the problems involved in identifying a distinctively French Church in this period. It was perhaps only in the reign of St Louis (1226–70) that the notion took root of a Church that was 'French' by virtue of its comprising those parts of the Church Universal that were located within the kingdom of France, were staffed by the king's subjects, and were answerable in some way to the king. Before the thirteenth century, the political resources of the monarchy were too geographically restricted for this sort of equation to have been possible. True, the late Carolingians' and Capetians' ecclesiastical domain—the rights of hospitality, powers of patronage and appointment, and various incomes—was always a substantial part of their political and economic resources, giving them a reach beyond the areas where they exercised temporal lordship. Archbishops and bishops from northern and north-eastern sees were among the Capetians' most important supporters. And the kings' theoretical protection over many of the kingdom's churches, *garde*, gave them opportunities to extend their power into areas that would otherwise have been closed to them, as when, for example, Louis VI backed the bishops of Clermont in their dispute with the counts of Auvergne in the 1120s. On the other hand, the French kings of our period never enjoyed the benefits of the close integration of Church and kingdom that was found in Germany and England. Historians nowadays debate whether the 'imperial church system' in Germany was as orderly, and indeed systematic, as the term implies. But it is clear that in the tenth and earlier eleventh centuries the German rulers were able to rely closely on a network of bishoprics and abbeys in ways that had a national dimension. Similarly, the kings of Wessex, who copied a good deal from German models, bequeathed to their Anglo-Norman successors a tradition of close supervision over and cooperation with the English Church, aided by having to deal with only two archbishops, of whom one, Canterbury, was much the more powerful. In France, paradoxically the kingdom where ecclesiastical reinforcement of the ideology and ceremonial of rulership had emerged earliest, this sort of situation was impossible. The kings thereby avoided many of the tensions that beset other monarchs. Louis VII, for example, got a good deal of mileage out of Henry II's discomfiture during his dispute with Archbishop Thomas Becket and after Becket's murder in 1170. But the truth was that this sort of conflict, which by pitting the king of England against the archbishop of Canterbury necessarily engaged England's secular and ecclesiastical political elites in general, could not have been fought out for such high stakes in the more fragmented political and ecclesiastical landscape of France.

The French Church and papal reform

If a central fact of the French Church, therefore, was the frequent discordance between ecclesiastical and political units at local, regional, and national levels, a further complication was introduced by the papacy, which claimed to be the head of the Christian community everywhere and could entertain realistic hopes of exercising authority over at least the western, Latin part of Christendom. A consideration of the papacy's relationship with the French Church in this period must obviously focus on the papal reform movement, which turned the popes from nominal to proactive superiors, with enormous implications for all parts of Europe. The papal reform movement began in the 1040s. It therefore neatly bisects our period, but creates problems of perspective in the process. It is important not to judge the pre-reform Church on the basis of what reformers said and did. This leads to an artificially stark contrast between 'before' and 'after' that downplays the importance of numerous continuities and slow evolutions. Reformers' rhetoric always tends towards the hyperbolic and selective. Moreover, it is important to note that many of the reform ideas that the papacy came to champion had already been articulated in France and elsewhere for many years. It is generally agreed, for example, that the papal reformers, many of whom were monks, were heavily influenced by the ideal of *libertas*, the freedom from secular interference that was espoused by the abbey of Cluny and other French monasteries. Other issues that exercised the reformers, such as clerical discipline and lay morality, had been addressed in various French diocesan and provincial councils in the tenth and early eleventh centuries, in many instances inspired by ninth-century Carolingian legislation. Concerns about whether married priests were sufficiently 'clean' to perform the sacraments, about the problem of laymen choosing who filled ecclesiastical positions and siphoning off churches' incomes as part of their lordships, and about simony, the buying and selling of ecclesiastical office that were symptomatic of the immersion of churchmen in family and clientage networks, were all raised before *c*.1050. In addition, much of the impetus for reform came from below, from the grass-roots sentiments and initiatives of pious aristocrats and townspeople, monks and nuns, and educated clergy.

Nonetheless, it was very significant that a group of reformers chose to activate the latent power and prestige of the papacy in order to pursue its goals—to some extent inverting the normal pattern in ecclesiastical history of a conservative hierarchy dealing with reform pressures from below. This galvanized the energies of supporters and opponents across western Europe. And, even more significantly, it entailed administrative changes that had enormous implications for how the Church in an area such as France was able to function. From the middle of the eleventh century a real change in tone and direction is evident. The first major papal reform council to be held outside Italy took place at Reims in 1049 under Leo IX (1049–54). Papal legates, emissaries with wide-ranging powers to inspect and judge who hitherto had been used only intermittently, began to penetrate France and other parts of Europe on a regular basis. An early sign of things to come is provided by the legate Hildebrand (the future Pope Gregory VII), who deposed several bishops at a council at Chalon in 1056. In addition to legates sent from Rome, the papacy relied on 'viceroy' legates, local prelates such as Bishops Amatus of Oloron (later archbishop of Bordeaux) and Hugh of Die (later archbishop of Lyon) in the final quarter of the eleventh century, and Gerard of Angoulême in the first third of the twelfth. After Gerard backed the 'wrong' pope, Anacletus II, in the papal schism of 1130–8, this system fell out of favour, though some archbishops continued to be granted legatine powers. On the other hand, *legati a latere*, usually cardinals sent from the papal curia, continued to be highly influential in the French Church's affairs: men such as Matthew of Albano, a vigorous advocate of Anacletus's rival Innocent II, Hyacinth of S. Maria in Cosmedin, who had studied in France under Peter Abelard, Peter of S. Grisogono, who became archbishop of Bourges, and Henry of Albano, who had been abbot of Clairvaux and was active against heretics and as a crusade preacher. Legates brought papal power, or at least acknowledgement of its existence and potential, to the regions. But traffic was both ways. Like most medieval rulers, popes projected their authority principally by functioning as judges. Cases brought by French litigants account for a major part of the enormous growth in judicial business that characterizes the late eleventh and twelfth centuries.

The popes grew to rely on France and to derive considerable bene-fits from close relations with it. The French kings sometimes incurred papal censure. But after the easing of the tensions caused by the marital adventures of Philip I (1060–1108) and the formal resolution at Troyes in 1107 of the thorny problem of royal control over the appointment and investiture of bishops and abbots within the kings' sphere of influence, they succeeded in cultivating a favourable image as the papacy's reliable friend. In this they were enormously aided by being able to cast themselves as different from the German emperors and other troublesome monarchs. From the papal perspective this must sometimes have amounted to the Capetians appearing no more than the best of a bad lot: Louis VI (1108–37), Louis VII (1137–80), and Philip Augustus (1180–1223) all had serious disputes with the popes at various points in their reigns. But overall the monarchy and the kingdom derived added prestige from the papal connection. Unsurprisingly, France became the principal refuge for popes when-ever German emperors, antipopes, Norman Italian kings, or Roman aristocrats made their situation in Italy too perilous. This explains why the late eleventh and twelfth centuries are punctuated by papal councils held in French cities: Troyes (1107), Reims (1119, 1131, 1148), Clermont (1095, 1130), Toulouse (1119), and Tours (1163). Significantly, when the popes were exiled in France, they spent most of their time based in churches that had close connections to the kings; the south-ern French Church already had a long tradition of support for the papacy, but now the north took the lead, in large measure because of royal initiative. In addition, the wealth of French churches was vital to the papacy in hours of need. Suger of Saint-Denis remarked that when Innocent II was driven from Rome by Anacletus II's supporters, he chose 'the very noble kingdom of the French as the most reliable and safe refuge after God', and 'then spent some time travelling about the land, visiting the churches of the Gauls, supplying his wants from their wealth'.[2]

Important as France was to the papacy, however, it is important to enter some qualifications. The principal orientation of the papacy after c.1050 remained what it had been since the mid-tenth century, that is to say, its relations with the German kings/emperors and the

---

[2] Suger, *Vie de Louis VI le Gros*, ed. H. Waquet, Les classiques de l'histoire de France au moyen âge 11 (Paris, 1929), 258, 264–6; trans. R. C. Cusimano and J. Moorhead, *The Deeds of Louis the Fat* (Washington, DC, 1992), 146, 149.

connected issue of the distribution of power among the various competing parties within Italy, of which the popes were one. France's value was principally as an accessible resource and communication centre that was close to, but safely outside, the central axis stretching from Germany down to southern Italy; it was more central than the peripheral polities whose rulers were sometimes vassals of the popes, closer than the most obvious point of comparison, England, and more securely Christianized than areas that had been converted in recent times. France was seldom the popes' sole or principal interest. Similarly, one can detect a considerable but not dominant French influence on the papacy in terms of key personnel. Important figures in papal administration and politics such as the influential Haimeric of S. Maria Nuova, papal chancellor between 1123 and 1141, were from France. Many cardinals in the twelfth century had studied in the northern French schools. But once again the picture is of France as the single most important element outside the central Italo-imperial nexus. Italians substantially outnumbered Frenchmen in the college of cardinals. Pope Innocent II (1130–43) spent two periods of exile in France and largely had the support of French ecclesiastics, galvanized by Bernard of Clairvaux, to thank for his eventual victory over Anacletus II. But only about one-fifth of the cardinals he appointed were French. Alexander III (1159–81) likewise spent time in France and was sufficiently impressed by the quality of French churchmen to headhunt some as possible cardinals in 1178, but the actual composition of the college remained overwhelmingly Italian during his pontificate.

From the mid-eleventh century, it was almost always from the ranks of the cardinals that popes were chosen, so an important corollary of the limited French recruitment to the college was the small number of French-born popes. In the pre-reform period, when the choice of pope was a matter for the German emperors or Roman nobility and the papacy was a generally distant presence, it is unlikely that French prelates regarded elevation to the papal throne as a meaningful pinnacle of achievement to which to aspire. The first French-born pope was the polymath and career ecclesiastic Gerbert of Aurillac, who reigned as Silvester II between 999 and 1003. It is possible that Nicholas II (1059–61) came from Burgundy, although he is more likely to have been a Lotharingian. Urban II (1088–99) was born into the Champagne aristocracy. He was a canon at Reims and a monk at Cluny, where he rose to become grand prior, before becoming cardinal bishop of Ostia in 1080. Some contemporaries disregarded Gerbert of Aurillac, who developed an oddly lurid and fantastical reputation after his death, to describe Urban as the first 'French' pope. Calixtus II (1119–24), formerly Archbishop Guy of Vienne, was a son of the count of (imperial) Burgundy with family connections across the frontier with the dukes of (French) Burgundy and the Capetian kings. The antipope Gregory (VIII) (1118–21) was formerly Maurice Burdinus, a monk from southern France. For the next French-born pope we have to wait until Urban IV (1261–4). This patchy picture compares favourably with other western and northern countries: there was only one English pope in this period (Hadrian IV), for example. But it is important to remember that it was not these men's Frenchness that secured their elections, some of which took place in exceptional circumstances. Gerbert of Aurillac owed his election to the fact that he had become part of the imperial ecclesiastical elite—he was archbishop of Ravenna when elected—and was a close adviser of Emperor Otto III. Urban II was a long-serving senior cardinal, an expert in German affairs, and a loyal disciple of Gregory VII; these factors, more than his French connections, were what commended him as choice of pope to the papal reformers. Calixtus II owed much of his rise to the fact that his predecessor, Gelasius II, happened to die at Cluny, close to Calixtus' own familial and ecclesiastical power bases and away from most of the cardinals back in Italy. Maurice Burdinus made his career in Spain rather than France, becoming archbishop of Braga; he owed his elevation as antipope to the chance fact that he came to the attention of Emperor Henry V on a diplomatic mission. Overall, then, the picture that emerges is of a significant but not pivotal French role in the western Church as viewed from its centre.

Monasticism

Monasticism was a facet of the Church's operations in which the contribution of the French-speaking lands was considerable and at times decisive. As with other features of ecclesiastical organization and religious life, differences that can be identified seldom if ever map neatly onto secular units such as kingdoms, which means that we cannot speak of distinctively or uniquely 'French' monastic forms in this period. The twelfth-century orders of Savigny and Tiron, for example, were 'French' to the extent that their points of origin and main areas of expansion were within the kingdom. But to some degree this was only a consequence of their relatively limited appeal compared to other, more renowned orders. The most prestigious abbey in tenth- and eleventh-century Europe, Cluny, was located in the portion of Burgundy that lay within the French kingdom, but in a liminal space close to the border with the Empire. Most of Cluny's dependencies and satellites were in southern and south-western France, as well as in the north, but its influence also spread into southern Germany, Italy, Spain, and England. The order of Grand-mont was based in central and western France, but it spread into other places such as England, being favoured by King Henry II (1154–89). The Cistercians, the most visible products of the boom in monastic life in the twelfth century, originated in French Burgundy, but rapidly expanded into virtually all parts of the Latin world. Similarly, the Military Orders of the Temple and Hospital recruited mainly from francophone areas, and France was where the greatest number of their European properties came to be located. But they were, and were perceived to be, truly international enterprises. The Premonstratensian canons were founded by Norbert of Xanten, a Rhinelander, who was given important assistance by Bishop Bartholomew of Laon. The originator of the Carthusian order, Bruno, was a German who taught at the school at Reims before founding La Grande Chartreuse in what is now the French Alps but was then imperial Burgundy. Italian hermits were a source of inspiration for several French monastic reformers. The picture that emerges, then, is complex, and the flow of influences was varied. Overall, the French role in monastic history in this period was substantial, even formative in many instances, but not unique or self-contained.

As is the case with the issue of papal reform, the development of monasticism in the first half of our period must not be judged according to the rhetoric of later critics. What looks like a monastic monoculture in the tenth and eleventh centuries can appear conservative and homogeneous compared to the experimentation and variety that characterize religious life after c.1100, but this perspective misses the enormous social, economic, political, and devotional impact made by monks in the earlier period. A major reason for this impact was the effectiveness of the basic blueprint for monastic life, the Rule of St Benedict, which had been written in the sixth century and was later propagated by the Carolingian kings and their ecclesiastical advisers. The Rule, supplemented by Carolingian additions, was the basis of the first major monastic innovation in our period, the foundation in 909 of the abbey of Cluny by Abbot Berno of Baume and Duke William I of Aquitaine. William famously surrendered all his rights to interfere in the running of the monastery, contrary to what lay benefactors would normally have expected from their foundations, and placed the monks directly under the protection of SS Peter and Paul in the person of the pope. By the first half of the eleventh century, Cluny had succeeded in attaining an effective degree of independence from both secular and episcopal jurisdiction, while the originally notional papal protection gradually acquired some substance.

Historians in the past tended to overestimate the importance of Cluny's influence, making it virtually the leitmotif for all monastic life in France and those areas influenced by it in the tenth and eleventh centuries. A scholarly reaction has placed more emphasis on the variegated nature of Cluny's network, which ranged from houses in close subordination to the abbot of Cluny to monasteries that simply imitated aspects of Cluniac observance or entered into prayer unions with Cluniac communities. In addition, the achievements and reputations of houses that were Benedictine but not Cluniac are now more fully appreciated. But it is also fair to say that Cluny was the pre-eminent French monastery, achieving unparallelled success under a succession of long-lived and active abbots, and in its liturgical elaboration and emphasis upon intercession striking a chord with contemporaries' spiritual and penitential sensibilities. Thanks in large part to the offerings made by the kings of Leon-Castile, who were recirculating tribute money paid to them by Muslim client states, Cluny was able to build what was the largest church in western Christendom at that time, what is today known as Cluny III. (Most of it was unfortunately destroyed in the nineteenth century.) When a Cluniac 'old boy', Pope Urban II, returned there in October 1095 to consecrate the new main altar, Abbot Hugh (1049–1109) and the many thousands of monks in the Cluniac network could have been forgiven for believing that theirs was a secure and enduring dominance of the monastic world.

But change was already beginning and would soon accelerate, as new forms of religious life began to emerge. It is important to be wary of the effects of hindsight: many initiatives came to nothing or had to be rescued by more successful institutions, and even those movements which did eventually succeed led precarious existences in their formative years. For example, the future of Cîteaux, which began as a breakaway movement of monks from the Burgundian abbey of Molesme in 1098, was in doubt for about a decade. The first Alpine hermitage created by Bruno of Cologne was swept away by an avalanche, forcing the survivors to relocate to a less heroic but more realistic choice of site. For all the tentative beginnings, however, there are numerous indications of a new mood and tempo in religious life beginning to emerge in the 1080s and 1090s and then gathering momentum in the first quarter of the twelfth century—a period in which there was room for experimentation, with people's energies only gradually being channelled into rigid institutional forms.

The reasons for this remarkable expansion of religious life are many and complex. On one level it was the result of economic growth that created greater amounts of surplus to provide for more professed religious. In part, too, the proliferation of new orders was a consequence of a heightened historical consciousness that found expression in appeals to the original way of life that was supposed to have been followed by the early Church, the *vita apostolica*. Paradoxically, diversity was the complement of greater unity, for many of the new orders were favoured and protected by the papacy. Individual personality also played a part: the personal historical significance of figures such as Bernard of Clairvaux, who is often portrayed as the main reason for the Cistercians' success, has tended to be exaggerated, but the more important point is that the widespread cult of the founding father or second-generation animating genius, based on the assumption that individuals *could* make a big difference, was a powerful force for identification and cohesion among the new orders and their supporters.

In considering the many reasons for the expansion of religious life, however, it is important not to lose sight of the significant continuities between the old and the new. Historians of the thirteenth-century Church sometimes claim that the truly decisive shift in religious life in the medieval West only took place after 1200 with the appearance of the mendicant friars; before then, monastic and eremitical revivals had been in the nature of new variations on old themes. While this argument severely underestimates how much the friars owed to earlier types of vocation, it still makes a lot of sense. Certainly, the once common view that the old monastic establishment went into steep decline after *c.*1100 is ño longer tenable: Cluniac and similar forms of monasticism continued to attract high-quality recruits in substantial numbers until the mid-twelfth century, and Abbot Peter the Venerable of Cluny (1122–56) was able both to enact reforms that borrowed from the new monasticism and to defend his order's traditionalism in polemical disputes with spokesmen of the avant-garde. The appeal of the new orders, moreover, was substantially an endorsement of the enduring appeal of the Rule of St Benedict even as it was read in new lights. A good illustration of the importance of this link to an earlier monastic legacy is provided by the relative numbers of recruits attracted to various of the new orders in their early, expansionist decades. The Carthusians, the order that pursued the ideal of extreme individual asceticism the furthest, gained dozens of recruits (although they enjoyed great prestige out of proportion to their numbers); the Grandmontines, whose vocation was an attempt to combine eremitical and coenobitical (community-based) ideals, numbered many hundreds; the Cistercians, who made great play of their returning to the Rule 'to the last dot' (even though they in fact introduced numerous innovations), attracted many thousands of recruits.

A rather schematic but useful way of understanding monastic movements in the Middle Ages is to plot the points that each, at any given time, occupied on two intersecting axes. These represent the range of choices that was available within the developing monastic tradition. The first axis extends between, on the one hand, the attractions of experimentation and renewal, and on the other, the value attached to organization, consistency, and stability. Cutting across this is a second axis running between the opposing ideals of retreat from the world and engagement with it. Further variables were introduced by the different emphases placed on the aspirations of the individual monk or nun in relation to the needs of the monastic community as a whole. By the twelfth century, variety was in the ascendant, a fact noted by the author, a canon from Liège, of the *Libellus de diversis ordinibus et professionibus qui sunt in aecclesia* (A Short Book about the Various Orders and Professions in the Church).

This variety appears all the greater if one includes, as did the author of the *Libellus*, not just monks but also canons regular, often known as Augustinian canons. Though not strictly speaking monks, the canons regular ('regular' in that they followed a Rule) drew much of their inspiration from monastic ideals and practices. Some of their communities became virtually indistinguishable from monasteries, but others interacted fully with the outside world, for example in running pilgrim hospices and hospitals. Much of the pastoral work that canons undertook in towns foreshadowed the ministry of the thirteenth-century friars. The origins of the canons regular are usually seen in the establishment of Saint-Ruf, Avignon, in 1039, though the foundations of the movement had been laid in the ninth-century Carolingian reforms. By the 1060s communities of canons regular were appearing in the French kingdom, for example at Saint-Denis, Reims. Often appealing to richer townspeople and the lower levels of the aristocracy, because their communities were generally cheaper to endow than monasteries, the canons became an important element of ecclesiastical life from *c.*1100.

For all the Augustinians' internal variety and their new forms of ministry, however, it is important to remember the debt that they owed to contemporary monasticism. They are, therefore, one special indication of the broad and enduring appeal that monastic life and spirituality exercised in our period. Certainly there were many differences between the various forms of the religious life; and monasteries functioned in diverse social environments, some situated in urban centres, others located in settled rural areas, and still others created in the 'wilderness'. But transcending these differences were powerful continuities rooted in a shared respect for tradition. This tradition ultimately fed back to the Desert Fathers of the late Roman period, and was thus not something containable within the boundaries of latter-day circumscriptions like France. France, therefore, cannot be seen in isolation; its monastic history is tied up with larger developments in the rest of Latin Christendom and beyond. On the other hand, monasticism is a subject that nicely demonstrates France's potential for innovation, leadership, and adaptation within the wider context of the Christian world.

Education and learning

An important element of the divine mandate that the Church was believed to be obeying was the duty to teach the faith. By the beginning of our period, ecclesiastical institutions had long dominated the provision of teaching, especially north of the Alps. The late Roman system of secular schools had collapsed in what was to become western Francia, with a few possible exceptions in some southern towns. Teaching at both basic and more advanced levels was conducted by monks and clergy; and its content, methods, and aims duly reflected that central fact. We have seen that the history of the Church in our period is cut through by various 'fault lines' such as papal reform and the new monasticism; the development of education and learning likewise breaks down into two phases, though again it is important to avoid judging the earlier period by the standards of the latter, and to be wary of exaggerating change at the expense of significant continuities.

The earlier phase, up to the turn of the twelfth century, was dominated by monasticism. The ninth-century Carolingian reformers had placed great emphasis on monasteries as centres of education and learning, and the momentum that they generated carried over into the tenth and eleventh centuries despite the many difficulties that monasticism had to face in that time. Monastic schools focused on teaching child-oblates (young boys and girls given to monasteries by their families) the skills that they would need for a lifetime in the cloister. A good command of Latin was a functional necessity for performing the liturgy, and when taken further it was the means to engage in meditative and prayerful reflection on a body of key works which included the Bible, the writings of the Latin Fathers (authoritative early Christian thinkers), saints' Lives, and some pagan Roman classics. Most monastic schools were solely concerned with in-house training for their own recruits. But some also offered opportunities to boys destined for a career in the world. The future Louis VI, for example, spent part of his boyhood at Saint-Denis, though the attractive story that he was a classmate of his future collaborator Suger is unfortunately untrue.

The later phase is the period of dominance exercised after c.1100 by schools that grew up in and around cathedrals—establishments that are often described as the forerunners of the thirteenth-century universities, though in fact only a small proportion of them went on to achieve that status. Cathedral schools were not themselves new: they had been operating in parallel with monastic schools for centuries, similarly geared towards a form of 'professional' training. The central medieval Church had inherited from its Carolingian predecessor the Roman liberal arts curriculum, comprising the *trivium* (grammar, rhetoric, and logic) and the *quadrivium* (arithmetic, geometry, astronomy, and music). Like monastic schools, cathedral schools mostly focused on the teaching of the first two elements of the *trivium*, essentially how to read and write Latin correctly and how to express oneself clearly in it. But the cathedral schools, provided they had a particularly learned and effective *scholasticus* (schoolmaster) and an above-average library, were better placed to push on into the other strands of the curriculum, especially logic, that is, how to analyse and argue systematically. By about 1100 certain cathedrals (a minority of the total, it must be emphasized) were developing reputations as centres of learning, with northern French towns such as Laon and Chartres taking a lead.

It is against this background that we should place the emergence of Paris as the foremost centre of education and scholarship in twelfth-century Europe. An excellent source for the growth of the Paris schools is the autobiographical *Historia Calamitatum* (History of my Troubles) by Peter Abelard (1079–1142), the most brilliant figure in the new wave of learning. As Abelard's account of his peregrinations in and around Paris reveals, the careers of both teachers and the students they wanted to attract were initially characterized by a remarkable degree of mobility. But to be fully effective, schools needed stable environments in order to provide the full apparatus of teaching and learning: libraries, spaces in which to lecture, accommodation, and support services. So a cluster of institutions developed, including the school of the cathedral of Notre-Dame itself, the community of canons regular of Saint-Victor (founded c.1113 with an express emphasis on scholarship), and various groupings on what is now the Left Bank. By the middle decades of the twelfth century, what had emerged was a sense of Paris as the hub of northern Europe's learned community. The (all-male) alumni of its schools represented only a very small percentage of the population, of course, but they enjoyed a disproportionate degree of importance in the upper levels of the Church and in the growing bureaucracies that served lay rulers. Significantly, Paris created an 'old boys' network' that included many leading figures from outside the kingdom: men such as Otto of Freising, bishop, historian, and close kinsman of Emperor Frederick Barbarossa; John of Salisbury, probably the foremost Anglo-Norman figure in the so-called 'Twelfth-Century Renaissance'; and William of Tyre, the chronicler of the Latin East. Many cardinals had studied at Paris.

In the tenth and earlier eleventh centuries, the court circles of the German kings had been the cultural pace-setter of western Europe; northern France, centred on Paris, assumed this role in the twelfth. It is important not to exaggerate the exclusiveness of this change: the Midi made an important contribution to the study of medicine and law; and there were major centres outside France, including Bologna, renowned for its legal teaching. In addition, we have been concentrating on the elitist end of an educational spectrum that was becoming more variegated and complex; the growth of vernacular literature in twelfth-century France, for example, reveals that the traditional distinction between the 'literate' (Latinate) and the 'illiterate' (non-Latinate) can mask the existence of a lively vernacular textual culture—something that had to be taught and learned. But that said, the development of the Parisian schools was of major significance, and represents one facet of the Church's operations in which we can readily isolate a distinctive French contribution within the wider context of Latin Christendom.

Women

The rescue from historiographical neglect of the experience of women has been one of the most significant developments in medieval scholarship since the 1970s. A greater understanding of women's economic and political roles, and of the gendering of social structures and identities, has led to re-examinations of the place of women in the institutions of the Church and in religious culture more generally. The inescapable problem, of course, is that men dominate the sources. And individual women who have a clear surviving 'voice', such as the remarkable Héloïse (c.1100–64), pupil, lover, and wife of Peter Abelard, abbess of the Paraclete, and erudite writer of letters, are very few. Nonetheless, historians are piecing together a striking picture.

A major difficulty is that the Church's love of binary oppositions that was noted earlier found particularly effective expression in its attitudes towards women. This explains the stark contrast between two exemplars: Eve, the evil temptress and embodiment of sin; and the Virgin Mary, whose cult was growing in importance in our period, taking off in popularity in the twelfth century. Given this polarization, it is unsurprising that medieval writers regularly resorted to glib generalizations when describing women, or else fashioned images of individual women that were projections of male assumptions and needs. Suspecting the worse came easy. For example, Bishop Burchard of Worms's *Corrector*, an early eleventh-century penitential handbook that was written in Germany but was much copied in France, includes a long list of questions that a priest should ask of someone making confession. It is striking how many of Burchard's questions relate to superstitious practices, pagan survivals, sorcery, and witchcraft that supposedly involved women. They made incantations while weaving; they could make men fall in love or extinguish sexual urges; they rode with demons on certain nights; and they conducted bizarre rituals to murder their husbands.

This fascinated abhorrence was part of the stock-in-trade of the sort of clerical attitudes which one would be tempted to label misogynistic if that term did not introduce anachronistic value judgements. Yet it is important to note that clerical and monastic writers also described favoured women in unrealistically stark terms that seldom offer clear insights into how they really lived and thought. For example, the Anglo-Norman chronicler Orderic Vitalis has a positive description of Odeline, the wife of the lord Ansold of Maule (d. 1118). But her value, in Orderic's estimation, resided in her obedience to her husband's and the Church's commands, and in her moral influence over her son. She is as much a caricature as someone like Orderic's *bête noire*, Mabel of Bellême (d. c.1077), 'a forceful and worldly woman, cunning, garrulous, and extremely cruel' 'who had shed the blood of many'.[3]

---

[3] Orderic Vitalis, *The Ecclesiastical History*, ed. and trans. M. Chibnall (6 vols., Oxford, 1969–80), ii.48; iii.134.

Within the institutions of the Church, women were of course handicapped by the inescapable fact that they could not be ordained as priests and were thus wholly reliant on men to perform spiritual services such as hearing confession and performing the mass. In addition, female monasteries tended to have larger administrative staffs than equivalent male monasteries because monks could take on many of the duties that nuns had to leave to others. This made female convents relatively expensive to found and maintain, which is one reason why female monasticism was an often significant but never dominant part of the wider monastic scene. Unlike the situation in the modern Catholic Church, in which female religious significantly outnumber their male counterparts, medieval nuns made up a small minority of the total numbers of professed religious, and the geographical distribution of nunneries was uneven. Even in the late Carolingian 'Dark Ages' of female monasticism there were some important foundations such as Sainte-Trinité, Poitiers, created by the widow of Duke William III of Aquitaine. On the other hand, the first Cluniac nunnery, Marcigny, was not founded until 1055, nearly 150 years after Cluny itself. And the Cistercians, though inspiring the foundation of a number of nunneries by their example, such as Tart l'Abbaye not far from Cîteaux itself, remained ambivalent at best about the place of women within their order. Orders such as the Premonstratensians and the congregation of Obazine, which started out favourable to women's religious aspirations and needs, tended to retreat from that position over the course of the twelfth century. Nunneries sat uncomfortably within the more systematic and orderly administrative regimens that new orders usually favoured. Where nunneries achieved the most success, therefore, they tended to do so in ways that were similar to the reasons for the growth of their Carolingian and even Merovingian predecessors—as modest centres drawing on accumulated traditions of support among an urban elite or a local aristocratic network which valued the nuns' prayers alongside those provided by male religious.

Within France, there was one important exception to this broad pattern—the remarkable growth of the order of Fontevraud. Its origins lay in the inspirational preaching and asceticism of a Breton holy man named Robert of Arbrissel, who abandoned a promising clerical career to lead a call to penance. Various religious experiments emerged from the group of followers that he attracted—the orders of

Savigny and Tiron were products of his network—but the most noteworthy dimension of his ministry was its appeal to women, both young and unmarried virgins and more mature widows. Under pressure from local bishops to make proper provision for the women who had joined him in the forest of Craon, on the borders of Brittany and Anjou, in 1101 Robert founded the monastery of Fontevraud, within the diocese of Poitiers. The most distinctive feature of this establishment was that its community comprised both nuns and male canons, who provided spiritual and administrative services. The Fontevrist order grew rapidly, acquiring dependencies in much of south-west and central France and securing the support of important lay benefactors, most notably King Henry II, who chose to be buried at Fontevraud. Fontevraud was not a unique experiment—a similar English community was created at Sempringham later in the twelfth century, for example, and some Premonstratensian foundations were double communities—but it was the most conspicuous and distinctive attempt to find an institutional framework for the role of women religious within the Church.

Lay religious culture

For all its variety and internal inequalities, the institutional Church at least had a more or less clear identity—a sense of history and self-hood that reformers, for example, could exploit. When we broaden the perspective to examine the 'Church' in the sense of the whole community of the faithful, the focus inevitably becomes much more blurred. Given the many categories that can be used to break down the medieval population into its constituent elements—gender, age, education, language, status, family, wealth, health, mobility—is it possible to speak of something as uniform as lay religious culture? And, if so, were there aspects of that culture that were distinctively French?

On the face of it, religious beliefs and practices mirrored social divisions and may even have entrenched them by providing yet more opportunities for underlying economic and cultural differences to be made visible and ritualized. For example, a great gulf seems to separate the religious experience of the isolated and low-status rural communities envisaged in much of Burchard of Worms's *Corrector* from the rather austere and self-absorbed piety that Guibert of Nogent, writing his so-called 'autobiography' in 1115, described in his aristocratic mother. An imbalance is introduced by the fact that we are far better informed about the religious lives of the upper levels of society because of their dominance of the written record. In this connection, it is significant that the single most abundant type of source material from this period is the charter. Many thousands still survive (a small proportion of what once existed). They record the grants of property and rights by lay men and women to religious institutions such as monasteries or collegiate churches in return for the intercessory prayers that were so highly valued. The point to note is that this sort of evidence does not overwhelmingly feature the wealthiest, landowning classes simply because they were the elite; the property that aristocratic families gave was conceived as an extension of themselves. It thereby became the means to forge particularly close bonds with the saints represented by the recipient church, and with that church's monks, nuns, or canons—people who were mostly from the same social levels as the lay aristocracy and, very often, related. Young children given to monasteries as oblates were believed to forge a similar link—perhaps more intense given the human dimension but, significantly, of the same basic order as the ties created by property. In the absence of equivalent written evidence for lower-status people, it is impossible to assess the emotional and social investments that underpinned the material support that they gave to churches, in the form of tithes, the fees paid to parish clergy for certain services, offerings, and exvotos. Overall, peasants and poorer townspeople probably gave a greater proportion of their disposable wealth to the Church than did aristocrats and rich burgesses, and they had less freedom of choice about what, when, and where to give. But their feelings are largely lost to us. The Church esteemed heroic sacrifice, and it was therefore richer people with most to lose who tended to be most conspicuous.

On the other hand, there are indications that the Church was alive to the issue of inclusion and attempted to provide some form of 'coverage' which, if scarcely a solvent of social distinctions, at least offered the poor majority of the population both institutional and affective channels for their religious experiences. The key to the institutional provision was a network of parish churches, the growth of which falls largely within the three centuries covered by this volume. Early Christian organization had reflected the urban character of late Roman government and culture: churches were located in or near towns, and there was little infrastructure to serve rural populations. By the beginning of our period this had begun to change, but the picture was still very uneven. As the upheavals caused by invasions began to ease in the tenth century, and with the first stirrings of economic growth, it became possible to invest more resources and effort into the building and staffing of rural churches. The Burgundian chronicler Ralph Glaber famously described the 'white robe' of new churches that was covering the French countryside in the first half of the eleventh century. This metaphor was partly inspired by large and high-status building projects involving monasteries and cathedrals. But much of the robe also consisted of numerous parish churches—very modest affairs, of course, compared to, say, Cluny III or the abbey church of Saint-Denis built by Abbot Suger in the mid-twelfth century, but typically much the largest buildings within the small communities that they dominated. Many of the churches were built through the initiative of landowners, who saw them as useful adjuncts of their lordships. Indeed, these accounted for much of the lay control of churches that so exercised reformers, who were in effect reacting to a building boom that they feared was not properly under their control. Later on, more churches were founded through partnerships between aristocratic kindreds and religious communities, increasingly the canons regular who were better equipped than monks (and more entitled in canon law) to supervise parish clergy, their churches, and their flocks. The key to the parish system was its inclusiveness. Services that had originally been performed in urban centres were devolved onto dispersed locations. Everyone should belong to a parish, and there should be a parish for everyone—at least in theory. The priest's remit, the *cura animarum* (cure of souls), engaged with numerous aspects of the faithful's individual and communal identities, taking them through life from baptism to burial.

The principal channel for affective religious experience in this period was the cult of the saints. Numerous churches claimed possession of prestigious relics that became the focal point of pilgrimage. France could not boast any of the three major international pilgrimage centres, Rome, Jerusalem, and Santiago de Compostela. But large numbers of pilgrims travelling to these places passed through or began their journeys in France. Compostela in particular, which grew in popularity from the eleventh century, had a large impact on the organization of pilgrimage and the provision made for pilgrims in France. By the mid-twelfth century, four key pilgrim routes were recognized that passed through central and southern France and converged in the Pyrenees. In addition, both along these pilgrimage roads and in many other places, numerous French churches were significant pilgrimage sites in their own right. Important cult centres included those of St Faith at Conques in the Rouergue, Mary Magdalene at Vézelay in Burgundy, St Martin at Tours, St Martial at Limoges, and St Hilary at Poitiers. The point about this list is that it could easily be multiplied many times over: France and the French-speaking imperial territories were far from unique in their possession of numerous cult centres, but they had the greatest concentration of prestigious pilgrimage sites in western Europe, certainly north of the Alps. In large part this reflected the continuity with the late Roman past that was noted earlier. Indeed, many saints' cults were effectively the oldest locus of historical memory in a locality or region, giving the inhabitants a sense of rootedness and stimulating a form of local patriotism. The manner in which a saint brought prestige and lustre to a shrine, its church, and its hinterland is thrown into sharp relief by the vogue, particularly evident in the tenth and eleventh centuries, for pushing what were believed to be a saint's biographical details as far back as possible into the early Christian era. The result was some remarkable 'rewritings' of history that turned figures with no historical connection to first-century Palestine into people who knew Christ or the Apostles. But there were also relative newcomers in the saintly cast, adding to the rich layering of cults with localized, regional, or pan-regional followings.

One common view of the cult of the saints and of its apparatus of holy sites and objects is that these represented the survival of a sub-stratum of pre-Christian religious practice that had been accommodated by the Church. Saints, in effect, were the continuations by other means of pagan deities. Yet while there is some evidence to suggest that some pagan cults did metamorphose into new forms in the early Christian centuries, it is doubtful whether French people in our period, living in a long-Christianized part of the world, would routinely have been aware of the connection. In any event, by 900 there were already many Christian holy sites that were the products of centuries of specifically Christian history and did not reach back into a forgotten pagan past. Another popular view, connected to the first, is that the cult of saints was by way of a concession to the uneducated majority on the part of the clerical elites, who themselves stood apart from it even as many of them served as the impresarios who staged the rituals around saints' shrines. In other words, the cult of saints and relics was an outlet made available to people who could not think beyond the literal and whose capacity for religious expression revolved around the tangible, visible, and immediate. Again, this view is unfair. It relies on an unfavourably one-dimensional caricature of what lay men and women were capable of thinking and believing. And it creates an unrealistic gap between the value systems of the clergy and the laity.

It is true that evidence can be found for a measure of distance on the part of some educated observers. A commonly cited example is that of Bernard of Angers, a northern French schoolmaster who travelled to southern France in the second decade of the eleventh century and expressed learned contempt for the 'idolatry' he witnessed when the faithful venerated statue-reliquaries of the sort that were common in that area. But the oppositions that can be detected were as much rhetorical as cultural: Bernard himself wrote about his initial reaction to the statue-reliquaries in order to set up his subsequent 'conversion' to their value. Similarly, Guibert of Nogent, writing a century after Bernard, is sometimes supposed to have been a spokesman for learned detachment from the cult of relics. His treatise *De pignoribus sanctorum* (On the Relics of the Saints) is believed to be an attack on the manner in which the Church had compromised itself by exploiting the appeal of relics to the faithful. But in fact Guibert was commending the basic principle; his attack was on unscrupulous or uncritical excesses that led, for example, to the duplication of relics and to the sort of strained thinking that flew in the face of doctrine by believing in the authenticity of corporeal relics that had supposedly been left behind on earth by Christ or the Virgin Mary. Numerous examples can be cited of members of the educated elite immersing themselves in saints' cults in ways that were far removed from simply keeping up appearances. Hugh of Lincoln, for example, who hailed from imperial Burgundy, was a Carthusian and a bishop—a bishop, moreover, who could stand up to Henry II. A figure further removed from the popular mainstream would be hard to find. Yet Hugh was a great collector of relics. His devotion to Mary Magdalene dissolved into near-comedy when he bit into the saint's arm during a visit to the Norman monastery of Fécamp, which housed this prized object. The numerous collections of miracle stories compiled at saints' shrines—a genre that was in vogue during our period and was particularly common in the French-speaking regions—attest to the broad social range of devotion to saints' cults. When the twelfth-century *Miracles of Our Lady of Rocamadour*, for example, describe the duke of Lower Lorraine helping a poor and crippled pilgrim up the steep climb to the church, there is probably a strong element of stylization, if not wishful thinking. But the cumulative message of the thousands of surviving miracle stories is of the cult of saints and pilgrimage as a broad and inclusive form of religious expression. Alongside baptism and the few basic formulas that people were expected to know such as the Creed and Pater Noster, the cult of the saints was one of the relatively few common points of cultural convergence. As with many other facets of the Church's life, the contribution of the French Church in this sphere can be characterized as important but not unique.

Conclusion

In 1081 Pope Gregory VII had what on the face of it looked like an excellent idea. The papacy would tap into the wealth of the churches of France by demanding the payment of Peter's Pence, something already familiar in several other parts of Latin Christendom, most notably England. This was essentially a levy on churches which was channelled through royal coffers and passed on as a gift of alms to the popes. It had often proved a valuable asset. But the plan to extend it to France in fact came to nothing. In part this was because the French kings, unlike their English counterparts, lacked the apparatus to enforce and collect payment throughout their kingdom (just as, a century later, the French return on the so-called 'Saladin Tithe', the tax levied to fund the Third Crusade, was much more modest than that in England). But at a deeper level, the frustration of Gregory's scheme was rooted in the nature of the Church in France, for it lacked a clear sense of identity as the 'French Church'. France was important in ecclesiastical terms because it was one large, relatively populous, and (sometimes) peaceful part of the larger Latin world. Trends and changes that were initiated within France did not stop at its borders, nor was it immune to forces from outside. Several developments in our period, such as the growth of Cluniac monasticism, the foundation in France of many of the new orders of the twelfth century, and the emergence of the northern French schools, add up to what looks like a distinctive French contribution. But in all these instances the differences with other parts of Europe were ones of degree, not of kind. The sort of confidence in France's place in the world that Graindor of Douai put into Christ's mouth was born of a sense of pre-eminence rather than out-and-out uniqueness. Once the pagan Vikings had turned into Christian Normans, and after the destruction of the last Saracen base in Provence in 972, France and the francophone regions to the east did not have to contend with a religious frontier of the sort that so influenced the destinies of contemporary Germany, Spain, and, for a time, southern Italy. Over the course of our period, this encouraged a sense of security and historical continuity, and the notion that France was a major part—*the* major part—of Latin Christendom's inner heartland, a place whose role was to be a net exporter of ideas, institutions, and people to more peripheral areas. This was why, according to the *Chanson d'Antioche*, when Christ turned to look to the west and into the future, it was the French whom he saw coming.

6

The French overseas

Jonathan Phillips

Of all the peoples of the Latin West there is a strong case for arguing that it was the French who made the greatest impact outside their own lands in this period. It is true that the Germans made substantial territorial gains to the east, but theirs was a slow and progressive landward expansion. Perhaps Italian traders travelled further afield, or the reform papacy exerted the most widespread influence, but the French were the most dynamic of all. Their involvement ranged from conquest and settlement, through participation in military campaigns, to contact via trade and diplomacy. This chapter will examine why, where, and how the French made their mark. It will also consider how the French overseas viewed relations with their homeland and, in turn, how their homeland regarded them. These relationships operated and overlapped on religious, familial, political, and economic levels. The extent of influence exerted by the French obviously varied according to circumstance, time, and place. We must also note that some episodes concerning the 'French' actually refer to the activities of a particular regional group such as the Normans or the Poitevins.

In terms of territorial expansion the principal achievements of this period were the Norman conquests of England and of southern Italy and Sicily, and the French-led occupation of the Levant which followed the success of the First Crusade (1095–99). By reason of geographical proximity, the relationship between France and the Anglo-Norman realm was intense, all-involving, and often antagonistic. From the start, there was relatively little sense of rupture on the conquerors' part because their new territory, although markedly different from their homelands in many respects, still seemed to represent an extension of their French lands. Moreover, for part of this period the Anglo-Norman realm was controlled by the same family that had initiated the conquest, and by related families thereafter. This was a very different process from the establishment of completely new political entities, as happened in francophone Sicily and the Levant. Consequently, this chapter will concentrate more on these areas rather than the familiar events of Anglo-Norman England. It should also be indicated that in Sicily and the Levant the French were simply one of a series of influences (albeit often the most dominant) on areas with complex cultural, political, and religious histories.

In the first half of our period there was little French activity overseas. Individuals and groups travelled, traded, and settled, but from the latter half of the eleventh century onwards there was a significant step forward in the scale, intensity, and permanence of the French presence outside their homeland. This reflected a general European trend of expansion and advance and, through the Norman conquests of England and Sicily, and the First Crusade, the French can be seen in the vanguard of such a movement. But the eleventh and twelfth centuries also witnessed a more widespread growth of Christendom; thus the extension of the Latin West was not the exclusive preserve of the French. First, as the *reconquista* gathered pace (and, as we shall see, featured some French involvement) the Christian lordships of northern Spain pushed deeper into the Iberian peninsula. Secondly, the Church and the secular rulers of the German empire led the settlement and conversion of the pagan lands in eastern Europe throughout this period.

The conquest of southern Italy and Sicily

The first large-scale French expansion overseas took place in southern Italy. The dominant element comprised Normans, who from the early 1040s conquered a region of great cultural, linguistic, and religious diversity. Much of what they encountered was outside their previous experiences: southern Italy was inhabited mainly by Greek Orthodox Christians, and much of the eastern side of the peninsula was ruled by the Byzantine empire. There was also a large population of Lombards (both Catholic and Greek Orthodox), whose Germanic descendants had reached the south by the eighth century. Sicily, by contrast, was mainly Muslim, with an Orthodox enclave in the north-east of the island. The Normans were never dominant in terms of numbers because the bulk of immigrants were of the ruling class and, in contrast to the later settlements in the Levant and England, few farmers or traders came to live. Yet, through military strength, coupled to some extent with religious change, the Normans created a new power structure to cover the whole region. They established a series of lordships and principalities, and by 1130 had created a fully functioning and vigorous kingdom.

The establishment of Norman rule in southern Italy and Sicily was a relatively slow and convoluted process. Normans are first recorded in southern Italy at the very end of the tenth century, taking part, as people from all over Christian Europe did, in pilgrimages. In 999 a group of pilgrims joined native Lombards in resisting a Muslim attack on Salerno, and in 1017–18 Normans supported a Lombard rebellion against Byzantine rule in Apulia. The Normans excelled at fighting, and in the turbulent politics of southern Italy there was a demand for mercenaries. News of this filtered back to northern Europe, and more and more Normans came to the Mediterranean to seek their fortune and to fight Lombards, Greeks, or Muslims, according to the wishes and identity of their paymaster. Alongside the desire for financial rewards, however, the Normans also wanted land. The contemporary practice of land division in northern Europe dictated that, on a father's death, there was a good chance that his territory would be divided up between his sons, which meant those in large families were left with very little. Geoffrey Malaterra, a Norman-Sicilian monk writing around 1100, commented:

They [the Normans] saw that their own neighbourhood would not be big enough for them, and that when their patrimony was divided out, not only would their heirs argue amongst themselves about the division, but the individual shares would not be of sufficient size. So, in order to prevent the same thing happening in future . . . they decided that since the elders were, at that time, stronger than those younger, they should be the first to leave their homeland and to go to other places seeking their fortune through arms.[1]

---

[1] Geoffrey Malaterra, *De Rebus Gestis Rogerii Calabriae et Siciliae Comitis et Roberti Guiscardi Ducis Fratris Eius*, ed. E. Pontieri (Rerum Italicarum Scriptores 5:1; 2nd edn., Bologna, 1927–8), 9; trans. G. A. Loud, *The Age of Robert Guiscard: Southern Italy and the Norman Conquest* (Harlow, 2000), 2.

Southern Italy and Sicily were, in parts, extremely fertile and, through trade with Muslim North Africa, quite wealthy. The possibility, therefore, of gaining highly profitable lands appealed to those Normans with only limited prospects in northern Europe.

In conjunction with these practical reasons, which could, of course, apply to expansion elsewhere in the medieval West, the political circumstances in Normandy were a particular stimulus to emigration. In the course of the 1030s and 1040s the region was riven by bitter conflict as the young Duke William II fought to establish and retain his power. By the 1050s William had asserted himself and was beginning to exact retribution on his opponents and to consolidate his authority by force. In many cases his enemies were punished by exile or chose to flee with their families. Sicily offered the opportunity for a new start with the possibility of lands and power that could no longer be acquired at home. In about 1055, for example, William Warlenc, count of Mortain, was disinherited and fled to southern Italy, although he remained of sufficient standing for his daughter, Eremburge, to marry Count Roger I of Sicily. The new arrivals were generally termed 'Normans', but this blanket usage covers all of the northern European immigrants who were linked by language and culture. It is estimated that about 75 per cent of this group were from the duchy itself, with the majority of the remainder coming from neighbouring Brittany and Maine, probably from families with dynastic and political ties to Normandy. Because of the rather haphazard process of immigration, the Normans of southern Italy were, in political terms, a very disparate group. In contrast to the conquest of England, which involved Duke William controlling the entire process and dividing the country up according to his own wishes, the Normans in the south fought each other as well as the indigenous population as they tried to establish their own particular pre-eminence. It was not until 1130 that Roger II had the authority and the opportunity to pull together a sufficient number of lordships to become recognized as the first Norman king of Sicily and southern Italy.

The imposition of Norman rule involved a mixture of force, diplomacy, and assimilation. Their initial base was at Aversa, fifteen kilometres north of Naples, acquired in 1030 when the native Lombards granted the Norman warrior Rainulf a castle and the right to levy tribute from the inhabitants of the surrounding land. In 1038 he was invested with the title of count of Aversa, and the Normans began to figure more overtly in the political complexion of the region. During the 1040s the Normans and their Lombard employers wrested much of Apulia from the ruling Byzantines. The native population had become dissatisfied with Greek rule, and the invaders found it relatively easy to induce a change of allegiance. A key figure to emerge at this time was William of Hauteville, who had arrived from Normandy in the 1030s and whose extended kindred would come to dominate the region. He was an effective warrior (he became known as William 'Iron Arm') and his achievements were recognized by the local ruler, Prince Guimar of Salerno, who gave him a comital title and the hand in marriage of his niece Maria. In 1048 one of William's brothers, Robert, arrived in Italy. He soon established himself as the foremost warrior of the age (he was known as Robert Guiscard— 'Guiscard' meaning 'the cunning', a name of which he thoroughly approved) and became the leader of the Normans in Apulia. After he had repudiated his existing wife on the (probably sound) grounds of consanguinity, he married Guimar's daughter, Sichelgaita, thus giving himself close ties to the native population, a sense of legitimacy in the eyes of the Lombards, and the prospect that his heirs from the marriage would have a strong claim to the land. Through unions of this sort the process of assimilation into the upper echelons of the native population began. This policy of marriage to women of the indigenous ruling class proved an effective method of consolidating the newcomers' presence; significantly, we also find it practised later in England and the Christian-populated county of Edessa in the Levant.

An important aspect of the Normans' settlement of southern Italy and Sicily was a close and mutually beneficial relationship with the Church. At first, the arrival of a new power was perceived as a threat by the nascent reform papacy, but in 1059 a papal schism pushed the Normans and the papacy into an alliance. The pope recognized Robert Guiscard as duke of Apulia and Calabria (some of which was still under Greek rule), and Sicily (which was still in Muslim hands). Robert's pre-eminence amongst the Normans was thereby made clear—and the scale of his future plans also became evident. The duke swore homage to the pope, giving himself real legitimacy and a bulwark against other claimants, while the papacy gained a protector against rivals and, in future, attacks from the German emperor.

During the 1060s the Normans completed the conquest of

southern Apulia and in 1071 took the port of Bari, followed five years later by the capture of Salerno, which became Robert's capital. In the course of these conquests the Normans' military tactics and their treatment of the native population—the Greeks in Apulia and the Lombards in Campania—are highly revealing. In both areas they faced stiff resistance from the indigenous peoples, who resented the Normans' presence and abhorred their tactics of devastating the land, exacting tribute, and taking hostages. These were familiar practices in their homeland, but once victory was achieved the Normans in Italy chose not to exact punitive retribution on their opponents and quickly sought peace. They lacked the men to hold all of the fortified sites they had taken and, by extension, when they captured cities such as Bari and Salerno, they could not garrison them either. In order, therefore, to compensate for their lack of numbers and to try to ensure the loyalty of their new subjects, as well as preserving the prosperity of the cities, they kept much of the existing bureaucracy in place. Furthermore, while the rulers of these new lands were removed, other local families of standing were allowed to keep their property. In Salerno, the ecclesiastical establishment, coinage, and laws were left unchanged, and Robert astutely became the patron of the native princes' favoured abbey of the Holy Trinity at nearby Cava. Actions of this sort, in conjunction with his marriage to Sichelgaita, helped to ensure a relatively smooth transition to Norman rule in this area. In addition to demonstrating the Normans' political skills, these conquests revealed them to be a highly adaptable military force. The lengthy sieges of large fortified cities such as Bari (which resisted for two years and eight months) and the successful deployment of naval forces (again at Bari), together with their acknowledged effectiveness on the field of battle, demonstrated an all-round military skill that was unrivalled at that time.

The capture of Bari and Salerno formed the keystones of Norman power in southern Italy, but alongside this they had initiated another highly ambitious scheme—the conquest of Sicily. This would be of a different character from the campaigns on the mainland because two-thirds of Sicily was populated by Muslims. With the advent of the reform papacy—keen to extend papal authority—and given the Normans' developing ties with Rome, it was inevitable that there would be a religious dimension to the struggle not apparent in southern Italy. From 1059 onwards there were plans to recover the island 'from the hold of the unbelievers'.[2] In the course of the eleventh century Muslim rule in Sicily had disintegrated into a series of minor principalities, which meant the Normans faced a much weaker enemy than would have been the case in the past. (Interestingly, the armies of the First Crusade encountered a similar set of circumstances in northern Syria in 1097–8 and benefited even more from Muslim disunity.) In 1061 the Normans secured a vital foothold with the capture of Messina opposite the mainland, yet the final conquest of Sicily would take another thirty years. In part, distractions in southern Italy, such as attacks from the Byzantines, internal rivalries, and Lombardled revolts, often slowed down the process. On Sicily, fierce Muslim resistance, bolstered by occasional help from their co-religionists in north Africa, was also a barrier to progress. Most damagingly, however, the Normans were, once again, present in only limited numbers. Surprisingly, and contrary to the norm in the Middle Ages, this did not prevent them from pursuing a highly aggressive military strategy. During this period set piece battles were rare because, unless commanders enjoyed an overwhelming numerical advantage, they shied away from the inherent dangers of a decisive engagement (the effect of King Harold's death at Hastings in 1066 is an obvious example). Yet on several occasions in Sicily during the 1060s the Normans challenged and defeated much larger armies, probably on account of their confidence in their own highly trained and well-equipped forces.

At the siege of Palermo in 1072 they were boosted by Pope Alexander II's endorsement of the campaign through the gift of a papal banner, a blessing similar to the one that the Normans at Hastings had probably received six years earlier. This papal sanction of warfare was, as we shall see, one precursor to the First Crusade, but the crucial elements of a crusade—the taking of a vow, the penitential aspect of the exercise, and the offer of remission of all sins—were, as yet, missing. In the absence of the sharp edge of crusading ideology as it would subsequently emerge, and with the precedent of the Normans' pragmatic treatment of the conquered peoples in southern Italy, there was no large-scale massacre of defenders at Palermo. The Muslims were permitted to remain and to continue to worship according to their faith, although the central mosque became a Christian cathedral. Toleration of this sort helped to encourage other submissions

---

[2] Geoffrey Malaterra, *De Rebus Gestis Rogerii*, 29.

and greater acquiescence in future years. This was important because in the same way that many of the first crusaders returned to the West after completing their vows, so large numbers of the Norman army returned to mainland Italy, leaving another manpower problem. Sicily was ruled by Roger, Robert Guiscard's brother, and many of his relatives and supporters acquired territory on the island. Southern Italian Christians were offered land as freemen on good terms, but the native Greek and Muslim farmers were relegated to the status of villeins. Compared to the Holy Land, where a combination of the geographical proximity to Muslim-ruled areas and the religious significance of Jerusalem stimulated interactions based on threat and counter-threat, the fact that Sicily was an island, and the removal of the Muslim leadership that could have acted as a focus of resistance, meant that it would be extremely difficult for any invader to remove the Normans.

In order to administer to the spiritual needs of the newcomers, it was necessary to establish a new Catholic hierarchy, headed by an archbishopric (Palermo, founded in 1083) and suffragan bishops. Count Roger could, with pride, style himself 'the restorer of Christianity', and his patronage provided for a series of monasteries to be founded. Some followed the Catholic rite, but many were Greek Orthodox, which showed the Normans' willingness to cater for the needs of the native population in order to facilitate a smooth and efficient rule. Arab converts and Greeks tended to form the heart of Palermo's administrative class, and documents can be found in Latin, Arabic, and particularly Greek, which was the language of much of Calabria and southern Italy at this time. It is apparent, therefore, that changes outside the ruling classes of the island were of limited form in the early decades of settlement.

The Normans attempted to extend their authority across the Adriatic, invading the Byzantine mainland in 1081 and 1084–5, but distractions in Italy (papal-imperial conflicts and internal revolts) and disease caused them to withdraw. In 1085 Robert Guiscard died, ending the effort to defeat Alexius Comnenus. In southern Italy Robert's death was followed by a fragmentation of power. His successor, Roger Borsa, was a more peaceful man, but with figures such as Bohemond (Robert Guiscard's eldest son from his first, Norman, wife) looking for lands, and given the lack of centralized authority, there was little to prevent the slippage of power to the localities.

Private warfare became endemic in southern Italy, and there was a need to resort to measures such as the Peace of God to preserve ducal authority.

As the Norman occupation of southern Italy and Sicily moved into its second generation, it is possible to discern the emergence of a sense of identity amongst the settlers. Earlier ties with their homeland had in any case been fairly limited in nature, because the emigrants' lowly origins or the abrupt circumstances in which many had left northern Europe did little to foster sentimental ties or to encourage close cooperation in either direction. Orderic Vitalis, a monk writing in Normandy in the first half of the twelfth century, recorded links between religious institutions, but in general terms it would be wrong to imagine a particularly intense relationship between the Normans of northern and southern Europe. The events of the First Crusade also demonstrate this point because there was no attempt by the Anglo-Norman and Norman-Sicilian contingents to link up, nor did they cooperate in the establishment of the Christian settlements after the conquest. Furthermore, while the Sicilians preserved ties with Bohemond's conquest at Antioch down to about 1130, thereafter the Franks of the East chose to break these links and to act independently.

By the early decades of the twelfth century many of the Normans had married Lombards, and the ruling class was therefore of mixed stock. Graham Loud has shown how the words and names people used to signify their identity changed. Until the end of the eleventh century, men described themselves as 'sprung from the race of the Normans' or 'from the Norman race'. But from the early years of the twelfth century styles such as 'Adam, son of Gilbert the Norman', or 'Herbert, son of Herbert the Norman, called Ass's Head', or 'Castellana, the daughter of William the Norman' emerged. These people noted their origins, but were describing themselves as descendants of Normans, rather than Normans per se. Furthermore, within another generation mention of individuals as 'son of the Norman' disappeared, which indicates that the settlers now saw themselves as standing distinct from their Norman ancestry.

The processes of infiltration and assimilation that had been taking place produced a culture headed by Catholics, originally of northern French extraction, but with a substantial input from native Christians, particularly the Lombards, and with overt influences from Islam and Byzantium. Some of the most prominent features of the conquest of England, such as castle-building and the use of mounted knights, were also employed in the Mediterranean, but because of the complex history of the area and the slow rate of conquest, the standard institutions present in Norman England, such as the fief, homage, and vassalage, never became universal in the southern Mediterranean; knight-service arrangements were rare, and freeholds of land were much more common than fiefs. Only in the mid-twelfth century did Latin take over from Greek as the main language of record-keeping. Coinage was of Byzantine and Arab design with, once again, western images only emerging over time. Art is perhaps the most obvious area in which these cultures overlapped, as is evident from the Arab styling of the six royal palaces at Palermo. The design of these buildings copied forms found in Fatimid Egypt: the use of stalactite vaulting, fountains in courtyards, and decorations showing scenes from court life. In fact, between c.1123 and 1143 there was a close relationship between the Fatimid and Sicilian courts, encouraged by trade and diplomatic contact. Furthermore, Roger II (king 1130–54) adopted Arabic titular forms. Rather than simply being known as 'king', he opted for 'royal, sublime, Rogerian, supreme majesty, may God make his days eternal and give strength to his banners'. There was a Byzantine influence too: the splendour of the royal coronation robes, the mosaic decorations of the palaces, and the burial of leaders in ornate porphyry tombs all revealed the Sicilians' appreciation of their rivals' art, but also their need to be perceived as rulers of real substance—according, that is, to the cultural and political norms of the Mediterranean, rather than those of northern Europe. While Roger I (d. 1101) was Norman by birth and upbringing, Roger II did not venture north of the Alps because his horizons were firmly fixed in the central Mediterranean.

In 1127 Duke William of Apulia, who ruled mainland southern Italy, died without leaving a clear succession. Count Roger II of Sicily observed the disorder that followed William's death and anticipated an opportunity to impose his authority on the mainland. After a period of fighting and the careful exploitation of a papal schism, Roger was formally invested as king of Sicily and his claim over Calabria, Apulia, and Capua was acknowledged. The royal houses of Europe—a jealously guarded clique—had a new and significant player: by the latter half of the century the Sicilian realm emerged as a prominent power in the eastern Mediterranean, at times posing a serious threat to the Byzantine empire and, on occasion, attracting the enmity of the German emperors too. Under Roger and his successor, William I (1154–66), the strength and wealth of the Norman kings became fully consolidated, and by the 1170s the ruling house was of sufficient standing to attract marriages with the Angevin and Hohenstaufen dynasties. The Sicilians' expansionist aims can be seen in their attacks on the Byzantine empire (1148) and their short-lived control of parts of the north African coastline from Tripoli to Tunis, which lasted from 1148 to 1159/60. Ultimately, however, the end of the Hauteville family in the direct male line led to the heiress to the kingdom, Constance, marrying Henry VI of Germany. At that point, politically at least, the orientation of the Sicilian lands changed again to become, in the thirteenth century, closely associated with the western empire and its yet wider orbit.

In sum, the impact of the Norman conquest of southern Italy and Sicily was considerable. It created a rival for Byzantium, involved the displacement of the Muslims, and brought about the emergence of a new political and cultural force: a remarkable achievement for—in their origins at least—a disparate group of hired mercenaries and exiles.

The French in the Holy Land

On 27 November 1095 Pope Urban II addressed a church council at Clermont in central France. He outlined the distress of the Christians living in the eastern Mediterranean and called for a holy war to reclaim Christ's patrimony from the infidel. He offered participants a spiritual reward of unprecedented magnitude—the remission of all penance for their sins. The response to his appeal was remarkable, and over the next two years tens of thousands of people, from all over Europe and representing all levels of society, took the Cross and set out for the Levant. It was, however, French-speaking groups that formed the majority of these forces, with men (and women) from Boulogne, the Île-de-France, Flanders, Normandy, and Blois joining the southern French and the Normans from southern Italy and Sicily. After a three-year journey of approximately 4,000 kilometres, the armies of the First Crusade captured the holy city of Jerusalem in July

1099. The Franks, as the westerners became known collectively, had taken over an area with a bewilderingly complex ethnic and religious history. Prior to the crusade Sunni and Shi'i Muslims had ruled different parts of the region, but some lands had a substantial Greek Orthodox population; also present were other eastern Christian groupings such as Jacobites, Copts, Nestorians, and Maronites. There were also Jewish communities and a small number of Zoroastrians. Through the First Crusade the Franks imposed their political authority on the Holy Land and placed the Catholic faith and its people at the top of the ecclesiastical and secular hierarchies, replacing Islam and pushing the eastern Christians into a secondary position.

In the course of the conquest and over the early decades of the twelfth century, the settlers established four states, each of distinct character and with a different mix of native populations. The county of Edessa had a largely Armenian Christian population and came under the control of the northern French noble Count Baldwin of Boulogne in 1097–8. Bohemond of Taranto, a son from Robert Guiscard's first marriage (and thus excluded from the Sicilian succession), established the principality of Antioch in 1098 in an area of mainly Orthodox inhabitants. At Jerusalem, Godfrey of Bouillon (duke of Lower Lorraine) took the title 'Advocate of the Holy Sepulchre' in 1099. On his death in 1100, his brother, Baldwin of Boulogne, assumed a royal title, probably for reasons of religious and political prestige and in order to free himself from suggestions of papal dominance. Within two decades Godfrey and Baldwin's original supporters had largely died out, and there was an influx of nobles from the Île-de-France and Champagne, led by the Montlhéry family. This group had incurred the enmity of King Louis VI of France, whose military pressure forced the kindred to look overseas for opportunities and power—an interesting parallel to the circumstances of those Normans who settled in southern Italy after their exclusion from the duchy by William the Conqueror. The population of the kingdom of Jerusalem was very diverse, with some areas of Christian villages and others of Muslim settlements, as well as smaller groups of Bedouin and Jews. The fourth Frankish state was not established until 1109 when Bertrand of Toulouse took the coastal city of Tripoli as the capital of his new county, an area with a large eastern Christian population. Thus it was French nobles, or nobles of French descent, who established themselves as the rulers of the Latin East. But this did not mean that settlers from other areas of the West neglected to visit the Holy Land as pilgrims or to choose to live there. Furthermore, the origins of the first Frankish ruler in each area did not preclude westerners from other regions arriving to live in his lands or, given the high mortality rate among the ruling classes, to take control of them.

In common with the Normans of southern Italy and England, the Franks of the Levant were in a numerical minority and this dictated their approach to the process of settlement. Unlike the conditions obtaining after the conquest of England, or to some extent (given the emergence of Robert Guiscard as a leading figure) in Sicily, the Franks were a polyglot force that faced an enormously diverse native population. Furthermore, they never succeeded in quelling external opposition to their rule and faced a series of attacks from enemies such as the Fatimids (down to 1171) and then the Ayyubids of Egypt, the Zengids of Aleppo, and the Damascenes, as well as, at times, Christian polities such as Lesser Armenia and the Byzantine Empire. While it is true that England, for example, faced the military challenge of the Capetians, there was a further dimension to the threat to the settlers in the Levant because overarching the complexities of the political scene was the religious significance of Jerusalem. It must be remembered that, behind Mecca and Medina, Jerusalem is the third most important site in the Islamic faith as the place from where the Prophet ascended into heaven, and its recovery was accordingly a duty of the faithful.

With Jerusalem at the heart of the Christian faith, and at a time of intense religiosity in western Europe, the importance of defending Christ's patrimony loomed large in the settlers' minds and did much to dictate their relationship with their co-religionists in the West. How did the Franks adapt themselves to political and everyday life in the East and how did they engage with their homelands?

One perspective is provided by Fulcher of Chartres, the French-born chaplain to Count Baldwin of Boulogne who settled in Palestine and wrote a history, completed in various stages, of the First Crusade and the first decades (up to 1127) of the Frankish East. According to Fulcher in the earliest portion of his text, in October 1100, as Baldwin marched south to take the throne of Jerusalem, the Franks faced a difficult battle near Beirut: 'On all sides we were besieged by our enemies ... That day nothing went well ... Indeed I wished very much that I were in Chartres or Orléans and so did the others.'[3] Although these were men who had not returned home after the First Crusade, at this point they had not yet put down emotional or even practical roots to tie themselves to the Levant. Yet in the final part of his work, composed in the 1120s, Fulcher was able to write the famous lines:

We who were once Occidentals have now become Orientals. He who was a Roman or a Frank has, in this land, been made into a Galilean or a Palestinian. He who was of Reims or Chartres has now become a citizen of Tyre or Antioch. We have already forgotten the places of our birth; already these are unknown to many of us or not mentioned any more. Some already possess homes or households by inheritance. Some have taken wives not only of their own people, but Syrians, Armenians, or even Saracens who have achieved the grace of baptism. Words of different languages have become common property known to each nationality, and mutual faith unites those who are ignorant of their descent . . . He who was born a stranger is now as one born here; he who was born an alien has become a native. Our relatives and parents join us from time to time, sacrificing, even reluctantly, all that they formerly possessed. Those who were poor in the Occident, God makes wealthy in this land. Therefore why should one return to the Occident who has found the Orient like this? God does not wish those to suffer want who with their crosses dedicated themselves to follow Him, even to the end.[4]

While Fulcher may have been indulging in an element of recruitment (his text circulated in the West), he would have been unwise to have given an entirely false impression. He suggests, in fact, that the Franks viewed themselves as permanent settlers and that they had formed their own sense of identity born out of their common Christian stock and their achievements to date. Through Fulcher, we also glimpse the process of intermarriage with native women. For example, in the county of Edessa, as in southern Italy, marriage to women of the indigenous nobility was an important way for the newcomers to cement their rule over the local peoples, and the first three Frankish counts married Armenian wives.

The conquest of the Holy Land did, however, involve a significant difference from that of southern Italy. The religious fervour of the

---

[3] Fulcher of Chartres, *Historia Hierosolymitana*, ed. H. Hagenmeyer (Heidelberg, 1913), 360; trans. F. R. Ryan, *A History of the Expedition to Jerusalem 1099–1127*, ed. H. S. Fink (Knoxville, Tenn., 1969), 139.

[4] *Historia Hierosolymitana*, 748–9; trans. Ryan, *History*, 271–2.

crusade and the suffering of the Christian army marching to the East meant that, once towns and cities fell, massacres often took place. That at Jerusalem in July 1099 is the most infamous, but there were others, including Ma'arrat (1099) and Beirut (1110). The Christian population of Jerusalem had been driven out by the Egyptians in 1099, but soon after the crusaders captured the city, native Christians, especially Greek Orthodox, reappeared and began close cooperation with the newcomers. The principal shrine churches of the Holy Land were staffed by both Catholics and Orthodox, although throughout the Latin states it was the conquerors who held the ecclesiastical hierarchy in their grip. The basic practicalities of establishing the rule of a numerically inferior group of outsiders would, to the Norman Sicilians at least, have been quite familiar. The conquest of Sicily had been completed as recently as 1091, and Bohemond's takeover of Antioch began only seven year later. Notwithstanding the intensity of the Franks' crusading fervour, good relations with the native population—regardless of faith—were essential for the newcomers to survive and settle. There were not enough westerners to farm the land (or with the specialist knowledge of the agricultural or hydro-graphical techniques required in the East), and a sustained policy of massacres was simply not feasible. Bohemond's successor, Tancred, was sufficiently concerned that native labourers should remain on his lands that he arranged for their wives to return from Aleppo, where they had fled for safety. As in Sicily, the Muslim farmers were not usually mistreated, and, in fact, by 1184 the Muslim traveller Ibn Jubayr felt moved to complain of the farmers 'living comfortably with the Franks' and the fact that the hearts of his co-religionists had been seduced by easy living: 'God protect us from such temptation.'[5]

Because these new states were politically independent from western Europe, the key ties between the Levant and the West took two other forms: first, through shared faith, which obviously provided a link between all the settlers and Catholic Europe; second, a particular affinity with France. Because of French-speakers' domination of the First Crusade and the continued influx of settlers from the West, family ties between Franks in the East and their co-religionists in Europe began to form. As Louis VII of France considered his strategy on the Second Crusade, Prince Raymond of Antioch, a Poitevin by

[5] Ibn Jubayr, *The Travels*, trans. R. J. C. Broadhurst (London, 1952), 316.

birth and the uncle of Queen Eleanor of France, was said to hope that his ties with the queen would 'count greatly' in Louis's assessment.[6] Family links, as Fulcher of Chartres noted, could also lead to relatives coming to the East. The sister of King Fulk of Jerusalem, Ermengarde of Brittany, came out from the West in 1148 (aged eighty!) and became a member of the community at St Anne's church, Jerusalem, until her death in 1157. Traditions of crusading also emerged to further bond the two groups. For example, the family of the counts of Nevers could boast an uninterrupted run of crusading participation during the twelfth century, starting with William II's unsuccessful expedition of 1101. His sons William III and Rainald both took part in the Second Crusade; William IV died at Jerusalem in 1168, and his brother Rainald died at the siege of Acre on the Third Crusade in 1191. Affinities of this sort manifested themselves in many ways, but two of particular prominence were the settlers' requests for military assistance and the selection of husbands for eligible heiresses.

From the 1140s onwards, increasing Muslim pressure meant that the Franks' need for outside help grew, and so they turned to many of the leading figures of the West. In the 1160s, for example, King Henry II of England was the subject of an intense campaign to persuade him to take the Cross. Sicily, Pisa, Venice, the Spanish kingdoms, Germany, and the Byzantine empire were all approached at various times during the twelfth century, but France was always the favoured choice. Bohemond III of Antioch asked Louis VII for help in these emotive terms: 'Great sadness! How disgraceful it will be to all peoples and to you if this land, land in which your relatives spilt so much blood . . . may be violated by evil people.'[7] As king of France, a former crusader, and a man famed for his piety, Louis was regarded as the man who, of all rulers in the West, had the Holy Land in his heart. As the settlers' diplomacy grew increasingly sophisticated, they began to emphasize historical links between the Levant and their co-religionists in the West. In 1169 they sent an embassy to Louis offering him the keys to the walled city of Jerusalem. This was probably intended to remind the king that Charlemagne had received a similar offer in 800, and was asking Louis to accept—as Charlemagne did—a

---

[6] William of Tyre, *Chronicon*, ed. R. B. C. Huygens (Corpus Christianorum Continuatio Mediaeualis 63/63A; 2 vols., Turnhout, 1986), ii.754.

[7] Louis VII, 'Epistolae', *Recueil des historiens des Gaules et de la France*, ed. M. Bouquet, rev. L. Delisle (24 vols., Paris, 1840–1904), xvi.28.

formal role as the protector of the city and all the holy places within its walls. Louis and the Capetians were closely linked with the Carolingian tradition, and a window depicting Charlemagne's legendary pilgrimage to Jerusalem and the events of the First Crusade had been constructed at the royal abbey of Saint-Denis in 1147. In using Charlemagne's memory to try to secure Louis's support in 1169, the settlers had identified a figure of paramount importance to the Capetians' image and someone whose actions matched their own present needs. In the event, Louis declined the offer, wisely perhaps, feeling unwilling to assume the burden of defending Jerusalem at that time.

Ties between the Franks of the East and their ancestral homeland can be shown in the choice of potential spouses for eligible heiresses. While some intermarriage with local Christians took place, reasons of diplomacy and prestige also led the settlers to look abroad. On the six occasions that a husband was sought for a Levantine heiress up to 1187, five of the men selected were from France. Coupled with the choice of heiress was the need for military support. Crusades, by their very nature, were temporary affairs, and the settlers often needed short-term assistance for a specific goal such as the recapture of Edessa (1145–9) or the conquest of Egypt (1164–9), but when a request for a husband was dispatched, a different and, in many respects, more serious debate was opened. The husband would be expected to leave his own territory behind, to rule his new land, to father heirs, and to provide a fresh influx of military support. Alongside such positive developments, however, was the danger that the westerners might usurp the influence of the existing settlers. The establishment of this difficult balance caused many of the tensions between the settlers and the West, and problems in assimilating newcomers was a crucial weakness in the Frankish hold on the Holy Land.

One of the reasons for the bitter quarrels that so beset the kingdom of Jerusalem prior to the fall of the Holy City in 1187 was the hostility towards a newcomer, Guy of Lusignan, husband of Sibylla, the heiress to the throne. Guy was a Poitevin noble who married Sibylla in 1180 and six years later became king. Many factors contributed to Guy's unpopularity amongst a faction of the Jerusalemite nobility, but as a contemporary Frankish writer recorded, his obvious identification as an outsider was part of the difficulty. The *Chronicle of Ernoul* relates that when Guy became king, 'the Poitevins sang a song in Jerusalem which greatly incensed the men of the kingdom. The song went: "In

spite of the pulains, we shall have a Poitevin king". This hatred and
scorn gave rise to the loss of the kingdom of Jerusalem."[8] We can see
the tension between the arrival of westerners and the settlers' difficulty in accommodating them within the existing political frameworks. *Pulain* was a derogatory term used by the crusaders to
describe the Franks. Some in the West saw the settlers as 'soft' on
their Muslim neighbours and degenerate in their style of dress and
manners. In fact, political considerations probably lay at the root of
this antipathy: the superficialities of clothing would have been less of
an issue had the infidel been defeated. The disastrous failure of the
Second Crusade (1147–9) and the resultant accusations of Frankish
treachery did much to damage relations between the Franks and the
West for a time, and events such as this served to stimulate scrutiny of
the settlers and their alleged moral shortcomings. On the other hand,
although the case of Guy of Lusignan is often highlighted as an
example of such tension, in some cases outside candidates did come
to integrate smoothly. Raymond of Poitiers ruled Antioch highly
effectively between 1136 and 1149, and Henry of Champagne was a
popular choice as king of Jerusalem in 1192.

While the Franks conducted themselves as independent political
entities, their familial and religious ties to the West were deep. They
maintained contact with religious institutions in their homeland.
King Fulk of Jerusalem (1131–43) sent a piece of the True Cross back
to the church of Saint-Laud in Angers, thereby showing a continued
attachment to his native Anjou. The settlers also sought to sustain
spiritual ties with their place of origin. This can be demonstrated by
the foundation in Antioch of a church dedicated to Saint Hilary, an
early Gallo-Roman martyr and the patron saint of the city of Poitiers.
The church was erected by Prince Raymond, a Poitevin who had been
invited to the East to marry the heiress to the principality, Constance.
Raymond evidently felt a sufficient affinity to his 'home' saint that he
wanted to continue to venerate him in the East. Many members of the
religious hierarchy, certainly in the early decades of conquest, were
from France. They took with them their own liturgical traditions, and
we know that the liturgy of the canons of the Holy Sepulchre was

---

[8] *La continuation de Guillaume de Tyr (1184–1197)*, ed. M. R. Morgan (Documents
relatifs à l'histoire des croisades 14; Paris, 1982), 53; trans. P. W. Edbury, *The Conquest
of Jerusalem and the Third Crusade* (Aldershot, 1996), 46.

based upon northern French models brought over by the clergy in the contingents of the count of Boulogne.

The French monastic orders of Cluny and Cîteaux both founded houses in the Levant (in 1170 and 1157 respectively), but such was the strength of existing Christian life in the region and the dominance of the major secular institutions such as the Holy Sepulchre, that their presence remained at a relatively low level. The other important expression of religious life in the East was the Military Orders, and the French influence on their conception and growth was considerable. While the Hospital of St John had existed in Jerusalem under Italian control since the mid-eleventh century, after the Frankish conquest it was French personnel who took over and developed the Hospital into an international organization that specialized in the care of sick pilgrims and, by the 1140s, provided knights for the defence of the Holy Land. The Templars were founded in 1120 by a French settler, Hugh of Payns, in order to protect pilgrims travelling around the holy sites. Hugh soon turned to Bernard of Clairvaux to secure formal ecclesiastical approval and a written Rule for the order (1129). Once this was obtained, the Templars soon received many donations and volunteers. They established a presence in most countries of the West to become, along with the Hospitallers, a highly visible reminder of the struggle to retain Christ's patrimony.

Settlers from France were not merely members of the noble, knightly, or religious classes and their entourages or kindreds. Many thousands of westerners travelled east and remained in the Levant as farmers or traders, attracted by the offer of good terms of tenure, the possibility of social advancement, and the lure of living in the Holy Land itself. The work of Ronnie Ellenblum has shown that the old stereotype of the Christians living walled up in their cities, fearful of enemy attack and not farming the land, is, for parts of the kingdom of Jerusalem at least, demonstrably untrue. The Franks established themselves in rural areas, either in close proximity to existing eastern Christian settlements, or else in newly founded communities. Little evidence for this sort of settlement survives, but two documents containing lists of settlers are extant. It is possible to list 150 names of settlers at the village of Magna Mahomeria, dating from the 1150s and 1160s. Of those whose origins we can identify as European (rather than Levantine because there was internal migration too), 80 per cent were from France. The Île-de-France, Burgundy, Poitou, Berry, and the Auvergne supplied the farmers, although the lack of southern French representation is noticeable and perplexing. At the casal of Bethgibelin, the French accounted for 60 per cent of the westerners. The pattern that emerges is of an influx of new immigrants similar to what was happening in certain areas of Europe such as Sicily, the Languedoc, Catalonia, and Germany's eastern borders.

Alongside their presence as individuals and as the rulers of the land, the Franks also made an impact on the physical environment of the Levant. Again, the scale and form of this varied over time and space, but could encompass both ecclesiastical and secular architecture. In both these contexts the Franks might take over and adapt the buildings that they found. For example, sites such as the al-Aqsa mosque in Jerusalem were turned into churches. The castle of Saone in northern Syria, originally a Byzantine fortification, was massively developed by the crusaders. Some former Muslim villages were taken over, although in other instances the Franks created something new. Archaeological excavations at the village of Parva Mahomeria have revealed a planned village (*villeneuve*) with the majority of the buildings dating from the same construction period (probably *c.*1160). The village was organized along a central road with a fortified tower acting as a storehouse and place of refuge at the heart of the settlement. Many similar *villeneuves* were founded in southern France at this time. Western styles were also imported in the field of ecclesiastical architecture. The façade and western bays of the cathedral of Tortosa, for example, reflect the early Gothic architecture found in contemporary France and are of a form not previously seen in the Levant. Art could see an integration of styles. The Melisende Psalter (now in the British Museum) shows a range of influences. It was commissioned for Queen Melisende (1131–52), whose own ancestry was mixed through her northern French father and Armenian mother. The illuminations indicate a Byzantine provenance, but the text of the calendar and the psalter were probably northern French in origin, and the ivory covers and spine of the work were probably executed by Franks settled in the Levant.

The need for military help was the most prominent aspect of the settlers' political relationship with the West. Embassies throughout the 1170s and 1180s tried hard to convince those in Europe of the gravity of the situation in the Levant. Saladin had gathered the resources of Syria, Egypt, and northern Iraq and threatened to crush the Franks. This danger was compounded by the reign of the often incapacitated leper-king Baldwin IV (1174–85) and the bitter in-fighting this produced amongst the nobility. On 4 July 1187 Saladin defeated the Franks at the battle of Hattin, and soon afterwards he took Jerusalem and most of the Latin kingdom. News of this disaster prompted the Third Crusade, led by Emperor Frederick Barbarossa (who died *en route*), Philip Augustus of France, and Richard I of England (himself French by upbringing, of course). The expedition saw the capture of Cyprus and the establishment of the Poitevin Lusignan family as a successful and independent ruling house on the island. The government, ruling population, and the Church on Cyprus were transformed by the arrival of Frankish nobles and the Catholic ecclesiastical hierarchy. The Third Crusade also managed to re-establish a Frankish presence on the Palestine/Syrian littoral and resolved the disputed rule of Jerusalem with the choice of Henry of Champagne as king.

The Norman Conquest of England

The most obvious point of entry for the French into the history of Britain is the Norman Conquest of 1066. Unlike the invasions of Sicily and the Holy Land, where the French arrived *de novo*, for reasons of geographical proximity, if nothing else, there was already a long-standing French presence across the English Channel. In polit-ical terms the most significant departure date for this is 991, when Emma, sister of Duke Richard II of Normandy, married King Aethelred II of England. The extent of Norman influence in England expanded after 1013, when the arrival of Emma's second husband, Cnut, and the Danish invasion of that year forced her son Edward to flee to Normandy. When, in 1042, Edward took the throne of Eng-land, he was soon joined by his former hosts, and it was Normans and Bretons who helped to counter the power of the Godwin clan, the dominant force in English politics. Under King Edward, Robert, the former abbot of Jumièges, became bishop of London in 1046, and Ralph, Edward's nephew, became an earl in 1050. It should be noted, however, that Lotharingians and Danes had also arrived in England at this time, and there is no sense of the Normans forming an organized group working to prepare the way for a conquest.

The details of Duke William II of Normandy's claim to the English throne need little rehearsing here; suffice it to say that the Normans argued that King Edward had promised William the succession. On Edward's death in January 1066, however, Harold Godwinson seized the crown and refused to concede to William. The duke decided to invade and assembled a substantial coalition of Norman, northern French, Flemish, and Aquitanian troops, tied together by (in some cases) kinship and the desire for material rewards of land and/or money. His force numbered about 7,000, of which cavalry formed about one-third to one-quarter. At the battle of Hastings on 14 October 1066, after a brutal and closely fought struggle, King Harold was killed and the Normans triumphed.

William secured Winchester, Canterbury, and London—the key ceremonial, ecclesiastical, and commercial centres of England—and on 25 December 1066 he was crowned king at Westminster Abbey with the acknowledgement of the surviving Anglo-Saxon lords. It would take William at least a decade to subdue England beyond the dead king's familial heartlands in the south-east. Brian Golding has identified William's early policy as one of limited disruption and an attempt at continuity in order to facilitate and legitimize his succession. This practice bore some resemblance to the Normans' approach in Sicily. It also enabled the king to counter external threats to his rule from Scotland, Wales, and particularly Denmark. William's hopes were swiftly dashed, however, because he faced rebellions in the south-west in 1067–8 and, more seriously, in northern England in 1069–70. William's response, the 'harrying of the north', imposed his authority on the land in a brutal and savage fashion. Orderic Vitalis wrote:

He cut down many in his vengeance ... Nowhere else had William shown such cruelty . . . In his anger he commanded that all crops and herds, chattels and food should be brought together and burned to ashes. My narrative has frequently had occasion to praise William, but for this act which condemned innocent and guilty alike to die by slow starvation I cannot commend him.[9]

Lands were appropriated and redistributed to loyal supporters, and

---

[9] Orderic Vitalis, *The Ecclesiastical History*, ed. and trans. M. Chibnall (6 vols., Oxford, 1969–80), ii.230–3.

the castle, the symbol of Norman dominance, appeared in increasing numbers. Castles had scarcely been known in the English regions and their construction was an integral part of the Norman advance. They functioned as symbols of authority and centres of administration, and they acted as bases for expansion, settlement, and colonization. Many were found on frontiers, such as the Welsh marches, or in the north of England. The stone castles of Chepstow (c.1071), Richmond (c.1071), and Carlisle (1091) demonstrate this.

After the Conquest itself, and through the disinheritance and forfeitures that followed the rebellions, William was able to offer handsome rewards to those who had followed him. In fact, King William *needed* to reward those who had risked all in the Conquest to help take over and then to settle and hold England and its borders. Orderic Vitalis noted that William 'with so much fighting on his hands was most anxious to keep all his knights about him, and made a friendly offer of lands and revenues and great authority, promising them more when he had rid his lands of all his enemies'.[10] The crucial challenge for William was to persuade people to remain in a region that, unlike the gains in Sicily and the Holy Land, was close to their motherland. King Baldwin I of Jerusalem had warned his soldiers before the battle of Ramla in 1101: 'If you wish to flee, remember that France is a long way away.'[11] The impediment of distance did not exist in the case of England. Often it was younger sons who were willing to establish themselves and live in England, rather than more senior family figures who held the bulk of the patrimonial lands anyway. Once William had given lands to an individual noble, he in turn could enfeoff his own vassals too. Soldiers would acquire small estates in return for military duties, and nobles would also be accompanied by their household retainers who also needed to be provided for. Thus we can see a wide spectrum of Normans arriving in England.

In the early years in particular the English resented the greed of these newcomers, who, it seems, exerted an uncompromising and venal grip upon their subjects. This sort of behaviour caused rebellion, but William's men were determined to get their rewards, and the king desperately needed money to defend his land borders

[10] *Ecclesiastical History*, ii.220–1.
[11] Fulcher of Chartres, *Historia Hierosolymitana*, 412; trans. Ryan, *History*, 158.

and coastlines on both sides of the Channel. We saw above that similar accusations had been levelled against the Normans in southern Italy. In England, probably on account of the scale of their needs and their clear military superiority, the Normans imposed a particularly tight and prolonged pressure on the English. The conquerors' ability to tax and govern England was helped by the existing Anglo-Saxon structures. Unlike those in Sicily or the Levant, the new rulers of England were able to take over a sophisticated and well-established system of government. Wisely, the Normans left in place the administrative units of the shires and hundreds and their associated officials (the sheriff and the reeve) to facilitate tax collection and the delivery of justice. In this sphere of life, therefore, we can see considerable continuity of practice pre- and post-Conquest. Many English laws were left in place, although harsh measures to try to ensure the safety of the newcomers were put into effect and some legal practices were imported from Normandy, such as the introduction of trial by judicial combat in criminal cases, rather than the ordeal. The language of government also changed: royal writs, an Anglo-Saxon tool, were written in Latin rather than the vernacular after 1070. The issue of language was complicated, particularly in circumstances such as the legal process. At times we must envisage a situation whereby those presiding over the court spoke French, the legal process was in Latin, and the witnesses and jurors spoke English. We hear of tensions caused by language in other areas of life, for example in the Church, when a Norman abbot could not communicate with his English monks.

The English Church was profoundly affected by the Norman Conquest. In the Levant and Sicily, of course, there was no pre-existing Catholic hierarchy. In England, in terms of personnel, physical structures, liturgy, and spiritual direction, the Normans implemented sweeping changes. The influence of the reform papacy grew because, in the same way that it suited the invaders of Sicily to have papal endorsement for their campaign, the Normans secured the blessing of the curia in 1066. In return, the papacy would benefit from having a conduit to channel ecclesiastical reform into an area previously little touched by such ideas. The Normans themselves used the Church and its extensive lands as a source of finance for the expansion and defence of their dominions, and they employed bishops and abbots as prime instruments in the control of land and justice. After 1066, no

Englishman was appointed to high ecclesiastical office and representatives of the powerful Norman monasteries of Bec and Fécamp
began to fill the key positions in the hierarchy. The arrival of the
Normans also saw a considerable programme of church building and
development, most overtly demonstrated by the extensive use of the
Romanesque style. On occasion, however, this blended in with a
native influence, as the striking pillars of the nave of Durham
cathedral so vividly reveal.

Norman monasteries acquired significant landholdings in England
and again, over time, their personnel became established. Interestingly, however, the Normans, after some initial hostility and disregard
of native sensibilities, chose not to reject or degrade the existing
canon of English saints, but rather to take on their cause and to
support them. This was motivated by a mixture of piety and the
realization that protecting the prestige of a saint and his or her particular institution would also maintain that institution's wealth. The
Norman invasion also enabled the dominant monastic house on the
continent, Cluny, to enter England with the foundation of Lewes
priory in 1077.

The relationship between the Norman nobles and the Church provides one important indicator of the pace and extent of integration.
Within two generations, Norman magnates were choosing to be buried in the English monasteries that they patronized. Golding comments that this process 'argues for a growing cultural and spiritual
assimilation of the colonists [and] a statement of both continuity and
legitimacy'.[12] The level of assimilation varied from region to region,
with some districts subject to limited French influence and others,
especially urban areas, witnessing a far greater mix. Orderic Vitalis,
himself the son of a Norman clerk and an English mother, wrote of
'English and Normans living peacefully together in boroughs, towns
and cities, and intermarrying with each other'.[13] Orderic wrote these
words in the 1120s, probably reflecting the situation by that date;
certainly the picture he draws seems that of a settled and established
society, rather than one still feeling the after-effects of an invasion
and the forceful imposition of an external power. A major impetus to
this process of assimilation in England was the political situation. On

---

[12] B. Golding, *Conquest and Colonisation: The Normans in Britain, 1066–1100*, 2nd
edn. (London, 2001), 175.
[13] *Ecclesiastical History*, ii.256–7.

William the Conqueror's death, the division of his lands between England (ruled by William Rufus) and Normandy (ruled by Robert Curthose) pushed nobles into deciding where their priorities lay: few could balance cross-Channel holdings amidst the severe political tensions that emerged between the two brothers. Often, as in the case of William of Warenne, earl of Surrey, younger sons or brothers based themselves in England and, through marriage, land-holdings, and patronage of the Church, put down roots in their new land.

In 1106 King Henry I (1100–35) defeated Robert Curthose at the battle of Tinchebrai and established control over both England and Normandy. By the time of Henry's death the Normans were integrated within many aspects of life in England, yet changes in the ruling house over the remainder of the century saw the arrival of other French influences. In 1135 Stephen of Blois seized the throne from Henry's designated heiress, Mathilda. Stephen's hold on England and Normandy was never secure, and it is difficult to ascertain many enduring and specifically Blesevin influences resulting from the nineteen stormy years of his reign. His brother, Bishop Henry of Winchester, was a major artistic patron, but he encouraged the import of Sicilian and Byzantine-derived works, rather than anything overtly French. It is not until the period of stability provided by the Angevin Henry II (1154–89) that further continental influences become evident. Henry's father, Geoffrey, had taken Normandy from Stephen in 1141–4, and in 1152 Henry had married Eleanor, duchess of Aquitaine. When he became king of England in 1154, therefore, England was ruled by a man who had only one Norman grandparent. His lands were vast, and England became part of a continental empire with consequences for trade, administration, and politics. The reality of this situation brought the Angevin lands into a state of tension with France for decades to come. Given the French origins of Henry and his successor, Richard I, the cross-Channel influence on England was pervasive. Technically, the king of England was a vassal of the Capetians for his French lands. In reality, the Angevins held a far larger area of land than did the kings and had much greater wealth. But under Richard's successor, John (1199–1216), this would change, and in the early thirteenth century it was King Philip Augustus who began to gain the upper hand with the conquest of Normandy in 1204. The Angevin empire was crumbling and it fell back upon England as its core.

The French in Byzantium and Spain

At the same time as the arrival of Norman mercenaries in southern Italy during the 1030s and 1040s, there was also a demand for warriors in the Byzantine empire. The emperors of this huge and wealthy territory had many enemies, both inside and outside their lands. They used 'Frankish' mercenaries (mainly Normans, but also some Flemings and Germans) in their struggles and, as in southern Italy, the Normans were rewarded for their efforts with land. In some instances, however, especially in the case of Roussel of Bailleul in the 1070s, there was discontent. Roussel was given territory in Asia Minor, but he extended his brief beyond the protection of Byzantine possessions by trying to set up his own independent lordship. The rebellion failed and Roussel was brought to heel, although such was his military expertise that he was rehabilitated and deployed by Alexius I (1081–1118) against other enemies of the empire. The use of western mercenaries was a commonplace in Byzantium, and forms part of the background to the request by Alexius to Pope Urban II for French knights to come to fight the Turks in 1095. This, of course, was one of the triggers of the First Crusade, although the tensions created by that expedition between the Franks and the Greeks reduced the use of westerners in subsequent years.

While not technically involving movement 'overseas', one further aspect of the French abroad should be mentioned. In the course of the *reconquista* in northern Spain, significant numbers of French knights took part in the struggle, motivated by the prospect of plunder, land, and, from 1089, spiritual rewards of a limited remission of penance—rewards that had grown by the early twelfth century to resemble those associated with the crusade in the Holy Land. There was also a notable level of intermarriage between the southern French and northern Spanish nobility which further encouraged involvement in these military campaigns. Probably the most striking example of French—or, more specifically, Norman—activity in Spain took place in the mid-twelfth century. The counts of Barcelona had spent decades trying to capture and then consolidate their hold on the city of Tarragona in north-eastern Spain. Robert Burdet, from near Argentan in Normandy, was a warrior-adventurer who fought in the region. In 1129, in acknowledgement of his military prowess, he was enfeoffed with Tarragona by the local archbishop in order to defend the city from Muslim counterattacks. In time, Robert began to act independently, and he came into conflict with the archbishops and also the counts of Barcelona. He had, in effect, carved out an independent Norman principality in northern Spain. The ecclesiastical and secular hierarchies soon moved to end this situation, and the Normans were largely brought to heel by 1155, finally being expelled in 1177. Nonetheless, we can see the familiar themes of opportunity for land, military expertise, and a link with the Church apparent in this episode. The west coast of the peninsula was also subject to French interest, with raids by naval expeditions, sometimes by pirates, or on occasion, as in the conquest of Lisbon in 1147, as part of a crusade (in this instance the Second Crusade, when Anglo-Normans and Flemings formed the majority of the successful Christian army).

Conclusion

We have seen the considerable geographical range of French activity overseas during this period. A number of principal themes emerge from these episodes, although the intensity with which each featured varied according to time and space. First, all revealed a desire for land, particularly in the conquest of Sicily and the settlement of England and the Levant. Second, it is apparent that French, and especially Norman, military skill was highly valued in the eleventh and twelfth centuries. The importance of military prowess led to Norman involvement in Sicily, Spain, and Byzantium, while Norman and French fighting strength facilitated the conquests of England, Sicily and southern Italy, and the Holy Land. Third, French expansion involved only limited manpower. This dictated a cautious and practical approach to dealings with native peoples because (except in areas of the Levant) there was never a question of wholesale emigration to the new lands and the creation of areas populated exclusively by newcomers. Even in the Latin East many of the Frankish rural villages in the kingdom of Jerusalem were located adjacent to, or close by, Orthodox or other Christian settlements. The limited numbers also meant that after the armed struggle necessary to achieve victory, the settlers tried—with differing levels of success—to establish peaceful relations with the indigenous peoples. This would speed up the post-conquest process of consolidation, provide a workforce to produce crops, and, through the adoption of local government and administrative structures, enable the populace to be taxed in order to finance defence. A common feature of French settlement overseas was intermarriage with the local nobility, providing legitimization and stronger ties to the newly won land.

One of the most prominent aspects of the French overseas was a close relationship with the reform papacy. The Church was closely involved in all of the episodes that have been examined (except the rebellion of Roussel of Bailleul in Asia Minor) and endorsed such activities. Legitimization and spiritual rewards followed, and in return the authority of the papacy was extended considerably. Non-Catholic Christians in southern Italy and Sicily, the holy places of the East, the lands 'reconquered' in Spain, and the previously distant English Church were all brought back into the fold of St Peter. Except with respect to the crusade to the Holy Land, it would be wrong to overemphasize the importance of any special religious drive behind the actions of the French overseas. The conquests of England, southern Italy, and Sicily were primarily driven by secular motives. The partnerships with the Church were rooted in the conventional piety of the age, and the relationship was of mutual benefit to both parties. It was substantially through the institutions of the Church that the French exerted a profound impact in their new territories. In the case of England, this was in terms of personnel, liturgy, and patronage; in Sicily, Spain, and the Holy Land, it was even more deeply felt with the arrival of a new Catholic hierarchy. Interestingly, there was little conversion associated with the French expansion overseas. It is true that this was before the age of the mendicant friars, the medieval Church's main instrument of conversion, but Cistercian monks worked hard to convert pagans around the Baltic region in a way not found elsewhere. The key issue appears to have been one of acknowledgement of papal authority, and, through the French, this was established to great effect.

Within two generations of the conquests of England, Sicily, and the Levant, the settlers were establishing their own identities, based firmly on the character of their new territories and featuring aspects of the indigenous cultures that they had taken over. The relationship between the conquerors and their place of origin varied considerably. The circumstances of the Anglo-Norman realm dictated a limited separation from the homelands, but in Sicily there was relatively little contact with Normandy. The Holy Land, however, on account of its spiritual significance to all in Catholic Europe, was different, and strong ties of family and faith were formed between East and West. In sum, this was a period of extraordinary vitality, and through their energy, strength, and spirituality the French overseas extended their own horizons and those of the Latin West as a whole.

Conclusion

Marcus Bull

Aphorisms and pithy remarks often capture something of the time and place in which they are made. Modern-day historians regularly seize on them as neat encapsulations of what the people they are studying thought about their world. Our period was one in which relatively few people were in a position to record their utterances in writing or have them preserved by others, but some informative examples have survived. To 'hear' medieval voices corroborating, qualifying, or contradicting the ideas we develop from other sources is very engaging. More than this, medieval authors often chose to use direct speech to frame the sentiments of those they were describing and thereby to signpost what they themselves considered significant, which suggests that they were alive to the ability of the judicious or fateful utterance to compress a great deal of meaning within a few well-chosen words. The writers of letters aimed for similar effects. One example of the succinct but revealing remark is described in Geoffrey Koziol's chapter: in the exchange between Hugh Capet and Count Aldebert of La Marche, according to Adhemar of Chabannes, the basis of Hugh's royal status is attacked with the devastating line 'Who made you [Hugh and his son Robert] kings?'[1] Equally memorable as a put-down is Pope Gregory VII's outburst that the bishops of the French kingdom, in supporting their king, Philip I, were no better than 'dumb dogs who cannot bark'[2]—a poignant evocation of the problems that reformers always faced in effecting change on the ground, and a reminder for us of the usually close and mutually

[1] Adhemar of Chabannes, *Chronique*, ed. J. Chavanon (Collection de textes pour servir à l'étude et à l'enseignement de l'histoire, 20; Paris, 1897), 205.

[2] Gregory VII, *Das Register*, ed. E. Caspar, 2nd edn. (Berlin, 1955), ii.5. See also *The Correspondence of Pope Gregory VII*, trans. E. Emerton (New York, 1932), 39–42.

beneficial relationship that existed between the French kings and senior ecclesiastics in substantial parts of their realm. When Walter Map put into the mouth of Louis VII the famous comparison between the Capetian and Angevin styles of rulership—the one characterized by simplicity and moderation, the other by wealth, raw power, and vaunting ambition[3]—he was guilty of exaggerating the differences between the two dynasties' resources and political cultures. After all, Louis's son Philip was soon to mobilize 'warriors, horses, gold' against Henry II's sons, and to good effect. But it is the sort of impression that sticks. The same is true of Suger's statement that Philip I told Louis VI that the troublesome lords of just one castle, Montlhéry, had 'virtually made me old before my time'.[4] William the Conqueror's verdict on the Normans in the deathbed speech attributed to him by Orderic Vitalis has more bite than other contemporary descriptions of that people because it is presented as coming from the king's own lips. Orderic was not present when the Conqueror died, but he obviously believed that this was the sort of thing the king could, or should, have said: 'If the Normans are disciplined under a just and firm ruler [just like William, in other words] they are men of great valour . . . But without such rule they tear each other to pieces and destroy themselves.'[5]

Among the celebrated utterances of this period, one of the most famous is that attributed to Abbot Abbo of Fleury (988–1004) when he had made the long journey from his monastery in the Orléannais to Gascony in order to visit one of Fleury's priories, La Réole. According to Abbo's biographer, Aimo, the abbot was able to declare that within the priory walls, and by necessary implication in the surrounding area as a whole, 'I am more powerful than our lord the king of France'.[6] Perhaps Abbo should have been less sanguine about the remoteness of secular authority in that part of the world, for he ended up being killed when the resentments of the monks whom he

[3] Walter Map, *De Nugis Curialium*, ed. and trans. M. R. James, rev. C. N. L. Brooke and R. A. B. Mynors (Oxford, 1983), 450–1.

[4] Suger, *Vie de Louis VI le Gros*, ed. and trans. H. Waquet (Les classiques de l'histoire de France au moyen âge, 11; Paris, 1929), 38.

[5] Orderic Vitalis, *The Ecclesiastical History*, ed. and trans. M. Chibnall (6 vols., Oxford, 1969–80), iv.82–3.

[6] Aimo of Fleury, 'Vita S. Abbonis', *Patrologiae cursus completus series Latina*, ed. J.-P. Migne (221 vols., Paris, 1844–64), cxxxix.410.

was trying to reform spilled over into a riot. King Robert the Pious was not there to help him. More to the point, perhaps, neither of the princes who dominated the region, Duke William V of Aquitaine and Duke Bernard William of Gascony, was present and able to save the abbot. On one level, then, both Abbo's quip and the circumstances of his death attest to the difficulties that resulted when the power of those who claimed authority was largely a matter of personal prestige projected by means of itineration. Even relatively effective rulers, men such as Louis VI grinding away at the lords of Montlhéry and the other castellans of the royal principality, or Henry II relentlessly traversing his sprawling domains, were largely engaged in a sort of unremitting damage limitation exercise, in which they were reacting to events more than they were controlling their own destinies. But viewed from another perspective, Abbo's encounter with a distant region has other lessons. In the first place, he was himself the bearer of notions of authority as a high-profile representative of a fashionable and prestigious form of monasticism. Fleury had been deeply influenced by Cluny in the tenth century and shared many of its ideals. Abbo himself was a very prominent figure with wide contacts; he had, for example, liaised with William V of Aquitaine about monastic reform during his fateful journey southwards. The threads that connected people and places, in other words, did not only exist in the sphere of what we would call secular politics.

It is also noteworthy that Abbo, according to Aimo, chose to invoke the notion of royal power even as he was drawing attention to its limitations: La Réole was in the kingdom of the west Frankish king, after all, and he was 'our lord'. This seeming paradox of simultaneous absence and presence characterizes much of the history of France in our period. When historians differentiate between degrees of royal power by means of terms such as 'notional', 'nominal', 'potential', 'effective', and 'real', they do so because it makes a great deal of sense to place complex processes within linear patterns of change. But when tracking the nature and content of monarchical authority in this period, we should not anticipate a smooth and continuous transformation. More to the point, it is important to remember that we are not dealing with some constant quantum of power and authority that was somehow 'out there' ready to be fought over, the only issues to decide being how it was distributed between different parties at any given point, and the balance between 'potential' and 'real' forms of power within each manifestation of it. Over the course of these three centuries, France changed profoundly. It became more populous; its social structures became more diversified; and it became richer. There were important technological changes in military architecture and in agriculture. New attitudes towards money emerged in tandem with urban expansion and a growth in commercial activity. New values were attached to learning and the functions of literacy. What constituted power, therefore, and what made it possible changed as the social underpinnings changed.

Given the basic fact of change, however, it is also worth noting that France between c.900 and c.1200 experienced no abrupt, cataclysmic paradigm shifts of the sort that historians of later periods would label 'revolution'—even the much-debated 'transformation of the year 1000' and 'feudal revolution' were, if they in fact took place, quite drawn-out processes compared to the pace of change that has characterized the last two or three centuries. Change in medieval France, moreover, was inexorably bound up with forces for continuity which were, at the level of conscious expression, often articulated as a pronounced respect for tradition. The Cistercians encapsulate this tension perfectly: they were experimenting with new forms of monastic organization and embracing a new and fashionable spiritual vision even as they preached a strict return to the letter of the sixth-century Rule of Saint Benedict and, beyond that text, to the way of life believed to have been followed by the Apostles. As with the Cistercians, so with numerous facets of France's political, religious, cultural, and social experience: change and resistance to it sparked off each other.

If we focus on the numerous and constant interactions between old and new in central medieval France, and avoid over-reliance on value-laden terms for expressing the effects of change over time— words such as 'progress', 'development', even 'transformation'—then it becomes easier to counter the possible objection that France is an unsuitable circumscription in which to frame the events and processes of our period. True, a great deal of what was happening at this time fits within contexts that transcend the kingdom's borders: the various movements within the western Church as a whole are obvious illustrations. Equally, virtually all of the day-to-day lived experiences of the great majority of the population existed within physical and mental frameworks that accentuated the very localized, immediate, and visible. The (double-edged) attraction of pilgrimage as an encounter with the unfamiliar would have kicked in for most people only a few kilometres from their homes. So, the kingdom was just one way of perceiving space amongst many different frames of reference, and not one that actively engaged the imaginations of most people most of the time. But that does not mean that 'France' did not exist: the west Frankish kingdom of the early tenth century was a very different place from the France of the early thirteenth, but there is an unbroken thread that runs between the two. The word 'France' effectively boils down to scholarly code for a constantly shifting assemblage of group identities. The key point is that different kinds of group identity generally coexist unless, in exceptional circumstances, they become mutually exclusive and demand a conscious act of choice. Frenchness was a tonal, shape-shifting thing of impressions. This helped to give it a largely unproblematic quality, even for those who might have reservations about certain manifestations of it. For example, the Normans who followed their duke in seeing the Capetian kings and their 'French' followers as potential enemies were nonetheless happy to see themselves described as *Franci*, not *Normanni*, in the text that accompanies the images of triumph on the Bayeux Tapestry. Likewise, first crusaders from southern France were included within the generic description of 'Franks', with all its positive connotations, even as they simultaneously developed a more specific sense of regional identity around the word 'Provençals'.

If we look briefly ahead to the thirteenth century and beyond, we find the theme of change-within-tradition sustained. At the level of national consciousness, the Capetians consolidated their status to project themselves with increasing confidence as the radiating core of French identity. In contemporary England, national sentiments were substantially channelled into the notion of a 'community of the realm' which was separate from, and potentially in conflict with, royal authority. In France this binary pattern did not emerge with nearly as much clarity. The kings wrapped themselves in their own myth, and their subjects broadly fell in line. A good indication of this is the fact that crusading, directly or indirectly, saw off three kings in succession: Louis VIII died in 1226 on an expedition into the Midi to fill the power vacuum left by the Albigensian Crusade; Louis IX (St Louis) died in 1270 in Tunis on his second crusade (his first had occupied fully six years of his time); and Philip III died in 1285 returning from a campaign against Aragon which had the status of a crusade. The next king, Philip IV (1285–1314), never crusaded, but not for want of planning and dreaming. Philip IV perhaps represents the apotheosis of what the Capetians were able to achieve in their self-fashioning, in that he was as much the victim of the image as he was its legatee. The memory of St Louis, the unsurpassable model of all that was great in French kingship, obsessed his grandson, feeding his rather brooding religiosity and his pronounced fear of contamination—contamination by Jews, adulterous daughters-in-law, heretics, and the hapless Templars accused of trumped-up charges of idolatry. Within a generation of Philip's death, the cracks were showing. France became the scene for the series of conflicts which historians lump together as the 'Hundred Years War'. We tend to see this war as a national dispute between France and England, but it was much more an internal conflict about the political configuration of the French kingdom—the kingdom that had been forged back in the central Middle Ages. But that is a matter for the next volume in this series.

Further reading

General

There are a number of good introductions to the history of central medieval France which cumulatively cover our three centuries. For the earlier period, see R. McKitterick, *The Frankish Kingdoms under the Carolingians, 751–987* (London, 1983), which may be complemented by E. James, *The Origins of France: From Clovis to the Capetians, 500–1000* (London, 1982). For the later part of our period there are a number of valuable treatments: J. Dunbabin, *France in the Making, 843–1180*, 2nd edn. (Oxford, 2000) is an excellent synopsis and analysis of recent work, and is also particularly strong on aristocratic culture; E. M. Hallam and J. A. Everard, *Capetian France, 987–1328*, 2nd edn. (Harlow, 2001) is a clear introduction, particularly helpful on royal politics; and G. Duby, *France in the Middle Ages 987–1460*, trans. J. Vale (Oxford, 1991) is a patchy but stimulating overview by the foremost French medievalist of the final decades of the twentieth century. R. Fawtier, *The Capetian Kings of France: Monarchy and Nation 987–1328*, trans. L. Butler and R. J. Adam (London, 1960) is now showing its age but still repays close attention. Among individual kings, the best served in English is Philip Augustus: for a thought-provoking study of his reign, see J. W. Baldwin, *The Government of Philip Augustus: Foundations of French Royal Power in the Middle Ages* (Berkeley, Calif., 1986). J. Bradbury, *Philip Augustus, King of France 1180–1223* (London, 1998) is a more straightforward treatment, particularly useful on the king's military activities. For two studies of the relationship between the kings and the princes, see E. M. Hallam, 'The King and the Princes in Eleventh-Century France', *Bulletin of the Institute of Historical Research*, 53 (1980), 143–56, and K. F. Werner, 'Kingdom and Principality in Twelfth-Century France', in T. Reuter (ed. and trans.), *The Medieval Nobility: Studies on the Ruling Classes of France and Germany from the Sixth to the Twelfth Century* (Amsterdam, 1978), 243–90. T. N. Bisson, 'The Problem of Feudal Monarchy: Aragon, Catalonia and France', *Speculum*, 53 (1978), 460–78 is valuable for placing France in a broader context. A number of chapters in the *New Cambridge Medieval History*, vol. iii. *c.900–c.1024*, ed. T. Reuter (Cambridge, 1999) are directly relevant, especially those by C. B. Bouchard, J. Dunbabin, D. Bates, and M. Zimmermann. The forthcoming volume in the same series on the eleventh and twelfth centuries, edited by J. S C. Riley-Smith and D. Luscombe, will prove equally useful. A fairly clear synthesis of recent region-focused research is provided by J.-P. Poly and E. Bournazel, *The Feudal Transformation 900–1200*, trans. C. Higgitt (New York, 1991), though it should be noted that the book's central *mutationiste* thesis, expressed in its title, is the subject of vigorous debate. For a statement by the leading French opponent of the idea that there was a socio-economic and political 'mutation' around 1000, see D. Barthélemy, 'The Year 1000 without Abrupt or Radical Transformation', in L. K. Little and B. H. Rosenwein (eds.), *Debating the Middle Ages: Issues and Readings* (Oxford, 1998), 134–47. For further debate, see T. N. Bisson, 'The "Feudal Revolution"', *Past and Present*, 142 (1994), 6–42, with responses by D. Barthélemy, S. D. White, T. Reuter, C. Wickham, and Bisson again in vols. 152 (1996), 196–223, and 155 (1997), 177–225. Unsurprisingly, Normandy is the part of France best served by English-language studies. D. Bates, *Normandy before 1066* (London, 1982) is an excellent introduction. See also E. Searle, *Predatory Kinship and the Creation of Norman Power (840–1066)* (Berkeley, Calif., 1988); L. Shopkow, *History and Community: Norman Historical Writing in the Eleventh and Twelfth Centuries* (Washington, DC, 1997); and C. Potts, *Monastic Revival and Regional Identity in Early Normandy* (Woodbridge, 1997). For Brittany, see P. Galliou and M. Jones, *The Bretons* (Oxford, 1991), which may be complemented by two thoughtful monograph studies: J. M. H. Smith, *Province and Empire: Brittany and the Carolingians* (Cambridge, 1992); and J. A. Everard, *Brittany and the Angevins: Province and Empire 1158–1203* (Cambridge, 2000). The coverage in English of other areas is less extensive, but see D. Nicholas, *Medieval Flanders* (London, 1992); T. Evergates, *Feudal Society in the Bailliage of Troyes under the Counts of Champagne, 1152–1284* (Baltimore, 1975); and G. T. Beech, *A Rural Society in Medieval France: The Gâtine of Poitou in the Eleventh and Twelfth Centuries* (Baltimore, 1964). Among historical atlases, particular mention should be made of the informative *Atlas de la France de l'an mil*, ed. M. Parisse (Paris, 1994). There is much of interest in X. de Planhol, *An Historical Geography of France*, trans. J. Lloyd (Cambridge, 1994), although it contains errors of historical detail.

Constructing the medieval nation

Most of the scholarship on the emergence of France from its Frankish roots has been in German. The fundamental work is B. Schneidmüller, *Nomen Patriae: Die Entstehung Frankreichs in der politisch-geographischen Terminologie (10.–13. Jahrhundert)* (Sigmaringen, 1987). Another major study in German, C. Brühl's *Deutschland-Frankreich: Die Geburt zweier Völker* (Cologne, 1990), has appeared in a French abridgement as *Naissance des deux peuples: Français et allemands (IXe–XIe siècle)*, trans. G. Duchet-Suchaux (Paris, 1994). As its title suggests, the emphasis of C. Beaune, *The Birth of an Ideology: Myths and Symbols of Nation in Late-Medieval France*, trans. S. R. Huston, ed. F. L. Cheyette (Berkeley, Calif., 1991) is post-1200, but it contains some useful material on our period. The same applies to the classic E. H. Kantorowicz,

The King's Two Bodies: A Study in Medieval Political Theology (Princeton, NJ, 1957), as well as to J. R. Strayer, 'France, the Holy Land, the Chosen People, and the Most Christian King', in his *Medieval Statecraft and the Perspectives of History* (Princeton, NJ, 1971), 300–14, and C. T. Wood, '*Regnum Franciæ*: A Problem in Capetian Administrative Usage', *Traditio*, 23 (1967), 117–47. For Charles the Bald and the critical years of the mid to late ninth century, see the excellent study by J. L. Nelson, *Charles the Bald* (London, 1992). Many of the same author's important studies of Carolingian political thought, coronations, and ritual are collected in her *Politics and Ritual in Early Medieval Europe* (London, 1986). See also her 'Kingship and Empire', in J. H. Burns (ed.), *The Cambridge History of Medieval Thought c.350–c.1450* (Cambridge, 1988), 211–51. For ideas attaching to the royal dynasty, see the thoughtful study by A. W. Lewis, *Royal Succession in Capetian France: Studies on Familial Order and the State* (Cambridge, Mass., 1981). G. M. Spiegel has written a number of important studies of royal ideology, including 'The *Reditus Regni ad Stirpem Karoli Magni*: A New Look', *French Historical Studies*, 7 (1971), 145–74, and 'The Cult of Saint Denis and Capetian Kingship', *Journal of Medieval History*, 1 (1975), 43–69, both reprinted in her *The Past as Text: The Theory and Practice of Medieval Historiography* (Baltimore, 1999). See also her analysis of pro-Capetian historiography in *The Chronicle Tradition of Saint-Denis: A Survey* (Brookline, Mass., 1978). The classic study of the French kings' claims to possess healing powers is M. Bloch, *The Royal Touch: Sacred Monarchy and Scrofula in England and France*, trans. J. E. Anderson (London, 1973). Revisions to Bloch's position are found in F. Barlow, 'The King's Evil', *English Historical Review*, 95 (1980), 3–27, and P. Buc, 'David's Adultery with Bathsheba and the Healing Power of the Capetian Kings', *Viator*, 24 (1993), 101–20. For descent myths, see the stimulating study by S. Reynolds, 'Medieval *Origines Gentium* and the Community of the Realm', *History*, 68 (1993), 375–90, which may be consulted in conjunction with her important book *Kingdoms and Communities in Western Europe 900–1300*, 2nd edn. (Oxford, 1997). Aspects of the extension of Frankish ideology into crusade contexts are discussed in M. G. Bull, 'Overlapping and Competing Identities in the Frankish First Crusade', in *Le Concile de Clermont de 1095 et l'appel à la croisade: Actes du Colloque Universitaire International de Clermont-Ferrand (23–25 juin 1995)* (Rome, 1997), 195–211. For linguistic changes and boundaries, see P. Wolff, *Western Languages, AD 100–1500* (New York, 1971); P. Rickard, *A History of the French Language*, 2nd edn. (London, 1989).

Political culture

Many of the works listed in the previous section are also directly relevant to issues of political culture. The fundamental work on the subject is G. Koziol, *Begging Pardon and Favor: Ritual and Political Order in Early Medieval France*

(Ithaca, NY, 1992), which brings anthropological perspectives to bear on the conduct of royal and princely politics. See also the same author's 'England, France, and the Problem of Sacrality in Twelfth-Century Ritual', in T. N. Bisson (ed.), *Cultures of Power: Lordship, Status, and Process in Twelfth-Century Europe* (Philadelphia, 1995), 124–48. For anger as a political and social instrument, see B. H. Rosenwein (ed.), *Anger's Past: The Social Uses of an Emotion in the Middle Ages* (Ithaca, NY, 1998), especially the contributions by S. D. White and R. E. Barton. See also M. Bennett, 'Military Masculinity in England and Northern France c.1050–c.1225', in D. M. Hadley (ed.), *Masculinity in Medieval Europe* (London, 1999), 71–88. Two important articles by S. D. White apply insights afforded by legal anthropology to the issues of aristocratic culture and dispute settlement: '*Pactum Legem Vincit et Amor Judicium*: The Settlement of Disputes by Compromise in Eleventh-Century Western France', *American Journal of Legal History*, 22 (1978), 281–308; 'Feuding and Peace-Making in the Touraine around the Year 1100', *Traditio*, 42 (1986), 195–263. See also P. J. Geary, 'Living with Conflicts in Stateless France: The Typology of Conflict Management Mechanisms, 1050–1200', in his *Living with the Dead in the Middle Ages* (Ithaca, NY, 1994), 125–60. G. Duby, *The Three Orders: Feudal Society Imagined*, trans. A. Goldhammer (Chicago, 1978) is a classic treatment of representations of social ordering. For a detailed study of one long-lived and successful count, see B. S. Bachrach, *Fulk Nerra, the Neo-Roman Consul, 987–1040: A Political Biography of the Angevin Count* (Berkeley, Calif., 1993), which is particularly clear on the military dimensions of princely power. Recent views of the Peace of God are conveniently brought together in T. Head and R. Landes (eds.), *The Peace of God: Social Violence and Religious Response in France around the Year 1000* (Ithaca, NY, 1992). For warfare, the best overview is provided by P. Contamine, *War in the Middle Ages*, trans. M. Jones (Oxford, 1984). See also M. H. Keen (ed.), *Medieval Warfare: A History* (Oxford, 1999). There is much of interest in G. Duby, *The Legend of Bouvines: War, Religion and Culture in the Middle Ages*, trans. C. Tihanyi (Berkeley, Calif., 1990). For castles, see C. Coulson, 'The Sanctioning of Fortresses in France: "Feudal Anarchy" or "Seignorial Amity"?', *Nottingham Medieval Studies*, 42 (1998), 38–104. For Suger see P. L. Gerson (ed.), *Abbot Suger and Saint-Denis: A Symposium* (New York, 1986), and the stimulating study by L. M. Grant, *Abbot Suger of Saint-Denis: Church and State in Early Twelfth-Century France* (London, 1998). The roles played by women in political life are addressed in two useful collections of papers: A. J. Duggan (ed.), *Queens and Queenship in Medieval Europe* (Woodbridge, 1997); and T. Evergates (ed.), *Aristocratic Women in Medieval France* (Philadelphia, 1999). See also J. C. Parsons (ed.), *Medieval Queenship* (Stroud, 1994).

Rural economy and society

Two useful introductions to the rural economy by Georges Duby have been translated into English: *The Early Growth of the European Economy: Warriors and Peasants from the Seventh to the Twelfth Century*, trans. H. B. Clarke (Ithaca, NY, 1974), which emphasizes the roles of both lords and peasants in economic change; and *Rural Economy and Country Life in the Medieval West*, trans. C. Postan (Philadelphia, 1998). J. Gimpel, *The Medieval Machine: The Industrial Revolution of the Middle Ages*, 2nd edn. (Aldershot, 1988) includes a discussion of agricultural technology. P. Freedman, *The Origins of Peasant Servitude in Medieval Catalonia* (Cambridge, 1991) includes a good deal of information on the meaning of serfdom outside as well as within Catalonia. On the economic role played by the Cistercians, see C. B. Bouchard, *Holy Entrepreneurs: Cistercians, Knights, and Economic Exchange in Twelfth-Century Burgundy* (Ithaca, NY, 1991). G. Duby, *The Chivalrous Society*, trans. C. Postan (London, 1977) is a collection of many of this leading scholar's most influential articles, including those on noble family structure and the militarization of the nobility. For an overview of current scholarly approaches to knighthood and nobility, see C. B. Bouchard, *'Strong of Body, Brave and Noble': Chivalry and Society in Medieval France* (Ithaca, NY, 1998). Many of Bouchard's important articles on noble family structure have been collated and revised in her *'Those of My Blood': Constructing Noble Families in Medieval Francia* (Philadelphia, 2001). See also J. Dunbabin, 'Discovering a Past for the French Aristocracy', in P. Magdalino (ed.), *The Perception of the Past in Twelfth-Century Europe* (London, 1992), 1–14. The literature on feudalism is vast; the classic treatments are M. Bloch, *Feudal Society*, trans. L. A. Manyon, 2nd edn. (London, 1962) and F. L. Ganshof, *Feudalism*, trans. P. Grierson, 3rd edn. (London, 1964). A seminal article by E. A. R. Brown, 'The Tyranny of a Construct: Feudalism and Historians of Medieval Europe', *American Historical Review*, 79 (1974), 1063–88. was instrumental in putting an effective end to medievalists' indiscriminate use of the term 'feudalism'. S. Reynolds, *Fiefs and Vassals: The Medieval Evidence Reinterpreted* (Oxford, 1994) is a lively and controversial study. For chivalry, see M. H. Keen, *Chivalry* (New Haven, Conn., 1984) and R. W. Kaeuper, *Chivalry and Violence in Medieval Europe* (Oxford, 1999), in addition to the works of the leading French scholar on the subject, J. Flori. See especially his *L'essor de la chevalerie, XIe–XIIe siècles* (Geneva, 1986). See also C. S. Jaeger, *The Origins of Courtliness: Civilizing Trends and the Formation of Courtly Ideals, 939–1210* (Philadelphia, 1985), a thoughtful study that links aristocratic mores back to the values of antiquity.

The south

There is relatively little on the Midi in the earlier part of our period, so M. Zimmermann, 'Western Francia: The Southern Principalities', *New Cambridge Medieval History*, vol. iii: *c.900–c.1024*, 420–55 helps to fill an obvious gap. Though it is now rather old, there is still much of value in A. R. Lewis, *The Development of Southern French and Catalan Society, 718–1050* (Austin, Tex., 1965). J. H. Hill and L. L. Hill, *Raymond IV Count of Toulouse* (Syracuse, NY, 1962) is an interesting study of the foremost southern leader on the First Crusade. J. H. Mundy, *Liberty and Political Power in Toulouse, 1050–1230* (New York, 1954) was a groundbreaking work which still repays attention. For the later part of our period, the best treatment is L. M. Paterson's stimulating and evocative *The World of the Troubadours: Medieval Occitan Society, c.1100–c.1300* (Cambridge, 1993). A fine study of an important twelfth-century Occitan noblewoman also contains much of interest about the period and place more generally: F. L. Cheyette, *Ermengard of Narbonne and the World of the Troubadours* (Ithaca, NY, 2001). See also the same author's 'Women, Poets, and Politics in Occitania', in T. Evergates (ed.), *Aristocratic Women in Medieval France* (Philadelphia, 1999), 138–77. There are valuable collections of studies by three of the most eminent historians of the medieval south: P. Bonnassie, *From Slavery to Feudalism in South-Western Europe*, trans. J. Birrell (Cambridge, 1991); T. N. Bisson, *Medieval France and her Pyrenean Neighbours: Studies in Early Institutional History* (London, 1989); and J. Martindale, *Status, Authority and Regional Power: Aquitaine and France 9th–12th Centuries* (Aldershot, 1997). T. N. Bisson, 'Unheroed Pasts: History and Commemoration in South Frankland before the Albigensian Crusades', *Speculum*, 65 (1990), 281–308, is an impressive analysis of the sources for southern history. Twelfth-century Aquitaine is brilliantly evoked in J. Gillingham, *Richard the Lionheart*, 2nd edn. (London, 1989). See also the same author's *The Angevin Empire*, 2nd edn. (London, 2001). R. Benjamin, 'A Forty Years War: Toulouse and the Plantagenets, 1156–96', *Historical Research*, 61 (1988), 270–85, is full of interest. The Cathars are the subject of two excellent studies: M. Lambert, *The Cathars* (Oxford, 1998) and M. Barber, *The Cathars: Dualist Heretics in Languedoc in the High Middle Ages* (Harlow, 2000). The older treatment by W. L. Wakefield, *Heresy, Crusade and Inquisition in Southern France, 1100–1250* (London, 1974), is still of value. A. G. Remensnyder, *Remembering Kings Past: Monastic Foundation Legends in Medieval Southern France* (Ithaca, NY, 1995) is an important examination of how monasteries in the south retained ideas of belonging to a regnal community even when the actual power of the kings in the area was minimal. For the religious culture of the aristocracy of south-west France, see M. G. Bull, *Knightly Piety and the Lay Response to the First Crusade: The Limousin and Gascony c.970–c.1130* (Oxford, 1993). For the troubadours, see S. Gaunt and S. Kay (eds.), *The*

Troubadours: An Introduction (Cambridge, 1999), which includes essays on a wide range of topics. The classic discussion of the nature and significance of courtly love, now much revised, is C. S. Lewis, *The Allegory of Love* (London, 1936). Another influential treatment is A. J. Denomy, 'Courtly Love and Courtliness', *Speculum*, 28 (1953), 44–63. See also H. R. Bloch, *Medieval Misogyny and the Invention of Western Romantic Love* (Chicago, 1991); W. E. Burgwinkle, *Love for Sale: Materialist Readings of the Troubadour Razo Corpus* (New York, 1997). For a recent feminist assessment of the troubadour *canso*, see S. Gaunt, *Gender and Genre in Medieval French Literature* (Cambridge, 1995). The works of Marcabru have recently been edited in *Marcabru: A Critical Edition*, ed. S. Gaunt, R. Harvey, and L. M. Paterson with J. Marshall and M. Florence (Woodbridge, 2000).

The Church

There is no single-volume treatment in English of the French Church in our period. The best points of entry into the subject are therefore discussions of the western medieval Church in general. Two excellent introductions are B. Hamilton, *Religion in the Medieval West* (London, 1986), and J. H. Lynch, *The Medieval Church: A Brief History* (London, 1992). C. Morris, *The Papal Monarchy: The Western Church from 1050 to 1250* (Oxford, 1989) is a magisterial work that covers a wide range of topics. The best introduction to monasticism is C. H. Lawrence, *Medieval Monasticism*, 3rd edn. (London, 2000). There have been several important studies of French monasteries and their relations with the wider world: see P. D. Johnson, *Prayer, Patronage and Power: The Abbey of la Trinité, Vendôme, 1032–1187* (New York, 1981); C. B. Bouchard, *Sword, Miter, and Cloister: Nobility and the Church in Burgundy 980–1198* (Ithaca, NY, 1987); S. D. White, *Custom, Kinship and Gifts to Saints: The* Laudatio Parentum *in Western France 1050–1150* (Chapel Hill, NC, 1988); B. H. Rosenwein, *To Be the Neighbor of Saint Peter: The Social Meaning of Cluny's Property 909–1049* (Ithaca, NY, 1989); L. K. Little, *Benedictine Maledictions: Liturgical Cursing in Romanesque France* (Ithaca, NY, 1993); M. McLaughlin, *Consorting with Saints: Prayer for the Dead in Early Medieval France* (Ithaca, NY, 1994). See also S. Farmer, *Communities of Saint Martin: Legend and Ritual in Medieval Tours* (Ithaca, NY, 1991). For the Cistercians and the other new orders of the twelfth century, there is a useful survey in H. Leyser, *Hermits and the New Monasticism: A Study of Religious Communities in Western Europe 1000–1150* (London, 1984). M. G. Newman, *The Boundaries of Charity: Cistercian Culture and Ecclesiastical Reform, 1098–1180* (Stanford, Calif., 1996), is an important study of the connections between the order's internal workings and its social and political roles. G. Constable, *The Reformation of the Twelfth Century* (Cambridge, 1996) is very rewarding. For female religious, two valuable treatments that work from different but complementary perspectives are P. D. Johnson, *Equal in Monastic Profession: Religious Women in Medieval France* (Chicago, 1991) and B. L. Venarde, *Women's Monasticism and Medieval Society: Nunneries in France and England, 890–1215* (Ithaca, NY, 1997). See also P. S. Gold, *The Lady and the Virgin: Image, Attitude, and Experience in Twelfth-Century France* (Chicago, 1985). The literature on the growth of the schools, and the so-called 'Twelfth-Century Renaissance' in general, is vast. The classic treatment is C. H. Haskins, *The Renaissance of the Twelfth Century* (Cambridge, Mass., 1927). For an excellent up-to-date survey, see R. N. Swanson, *The Twelfth-Century Renaissance* (Manchester, 1999). See also D. Knowles, *The Evolution of Medieval Thought*, 2nd edn., ed. D. E. Luscombe and C. N. L. Brooke (London, 1988). For Peter Abelard, see the comprehensive and stimulating M. T. Clanchy, *Abelard: A Medieval Life* (Oxford, 1997).

The French overseas

For the Normans, M. Chibnall, *The Normans* (Oxford, 2000) is an excellent introduction. See also R. H. C. Davis, *The Normans and their Myth* (London, 1976). The literature on the Norman conquest of England and its aftermath is, of course, enormous: for useful introductions, see M. Chibnall, *Anglo-Norman England 1066–1166* (Oxford, 1986) and B. Golding, *Conquest and Colonisation: The Normans in Britain, 1066–1100*, 2nd edn. (London, 2001). Robert Bartlett, *England under the Norman and Angevin Kings, 1075–1225* (Oxford, 2000) is comprehensive and thought-provoking. M. Chibnall, *The Debate on the Norman Conquest* (Manchester, 1999) is an admirable historiographical survey. The Norman presence in Italy is discussed in D. Matthew, *The Norman Kingdom of Sicily* (Cambridge, 1992) and G. A. Loud, *The Age of Robert Guiscard: Southern Italy and the Norman Conquest* (Harlow, 2000). See also H. E. J. Cowdrey, *The Age of Abbot Desiderius: Montecassino, the Papacy, and the Normans in the Eleventh and Early Twelfth Centuries* (Oxford, 1983). There is much of interest in K. B. Wolf, *Making History: The Normans and their Historians in Eleventh-Century Italy* (Philadelphia, 1995). H. Takayama, *The Administration of the Norman Kingdom of Sicily* (Leiden, 1993) is dry but informative. For crusading, two general histories by leading experts are noteworthy: J. S. C. Riley-Smith, *The Crusades: A Short History* (London, 1987) and J. Richard, *The Crusades, c.1071–c.1291*, trans. J. Birrell (Cambridge, 1999). See also J. P. Phillips, *The Crusades, 1095–1197* (Harlow, 2002). For an in-depth study of those on the First Crusade, most of whom were French, see J. S. C. Riley-Smith, *The First Crusaders, 1095–1131* (Cambridge, 1997). The contacts between western Europe and the states created in the wake of the First Crusade are carefully examined in J. P. Phillips, *Defenders of the Holy Land: Relations between the Latin East and the West, 1119–1187* (Oxford, 1996). Our understanding of western migration to the Latin East has been transformed by R. Ellenblum, *Frankish Rural Settlement in the Latin Kingdom of Jerusalem* (Cambridge, 1998). P. W. Edbury and J. G. Rowe, *William of Tyre: Historian of the Latin East* (Cambridge, 1988) is a valuable study of an important author and his world. Aspects of the French presence in Spain are addressed in M. G. Bull, *Knightly Piety and the Lay Response to the First Crusade: The Limousin and Gascony c.930–c.1130* (Oxford, 1993). See also L. J. McCrank, 'Norman Crusaders in the Catalan Reconquest: Robert Burdet and the Principality of Tarragona, 1129–1155', *Journal of Medieval History*, 7 (1981), 67–82. J. Shepard, 'The Uses of the Franks in Eleventh-Century Byzantium', *Anglo-Norman Studies*, 15, ed. M. Chibnall (Woodbridge, 1993), 275–305, is an excellent study of an often neglected topic. See also E. M. C. van Houts, 'Normandy and Byzantium', *Byzantion*, 55 (1985), 544–59.

Primary sources in translation

Many valuable sources may now be consulted in accessible translations. The most important histories include Rodulfus [Ralph] Glaber, *Opera*, ed. and trans. J. France, N. Bulst, and P. Reynolds (Oxford, 1989); Suger, *The Deeds of Louis the Fat*, trans. R. C. Cusimano and J. Moorhead (Washington, DC, 1992). Guibert of Nogent's 'autobiography' may be consulted in *A Monk's Confession: The Memoirs of Guibert of Nogent*, trans. P. J. Archambault (University Park, Penn., 1996). *The Letters of Abelard and Heloise*, trans. B. Radice (Harmondsworth, 1974) includes Abelard's *Historia Calamitatum*, an important source for the history of the early twelfth-century schools. Galbert of Bruges, *The Murder of Charles the Good*, trans. J. B. Ross (New York, 1959; repr. Toronto, 1982) is a remarkably detailed account of the dramatic events in Flanders in 1127–8. Also of interest are Herman of Tournai, *The Restoration of the Monastery of Saint Martin of Tournai*, trans. L. H. Nelson (Washington, DC, 1996) and Hugh of Poitiers, *The Vézelay Chronicle*, trans. J. Scott and J. O. Ward (Binghamton, NY, 1992). Lambert of Ardres, *The History of the Counts of Guines and Lords of Ardres*, trans. L. Shopkow (Philadelphia, 2000) is an important example of aristocratic genealogical literature. The Normans feature in a string of important texts: Dudo of St Quentin, *History of the Normans*, trans. E. Christiansen (Woodbridge, 1998); William of Jumièges et al., *The Gesta Normannorum Ducum*, ed. and trans. E. M. C. van Houts (2 vols., Oxford, 1992–5); William of Poitiers, *The Gesta Guillelmi*, ed. and trans. R. H. C. Davis and M. Chibnall (Oxford, 1998); and Orderic Vitalis, *The Ecclesiastical History*, ed. and trans. M. Chibnall (6 vols., Oxford, 1969–80). *The Normans in Europe*, ed. and trans. E. M. C. van Houts (Manchester, 2000) is an excellent anthology of extracts from a wide range of sources. The crusades generated a good deal of written history: see *Gesta Francorum et aliorum Hierosolimitanorum*, ed. and trans. R. M. T. Hill (London, 1962); and Fulcher of Chartres, 'Chronicle', trans. E. Peters, *The First Crusade: The*

Chronicle of Fulcher of Chartres and Other Source Materials, 2nd edn. (Philadelphia, 1998), 47–101. Two accounts of the First Crusade by southern French eyewitnesses are noteworthy: Peter Tudebode, *Historia de Hierosolymitano Itinere*, trans. J. H. Hill and L. L. Hill (Philadelphia, 1974) and Raymond of Aguilers, *Historia Francorum qui ceperunt Iherusalem*, trans. J. H. Hill and L. L. Hill (Philadelphia, 1968). See also Guibert of Nogent, *The Deeds of God through the Franks*, trans. R. Levine (Woodbridge, 1997). For Louis VII on the Second Crusade the principal source is Odo of Deuil, *De profectione Ludovici VII in orientem*, ed. and trans. V. G. Berry (New York, 1948). Two important narratives of the Albigensian Crusade have recently appeared: *The Song of the Cathar Wars: A History of the Albigensian Crusade*, trans. J. Shirley (Aldershot, 1996); and Peter of les Vaux-de-Cernay, *The History of the Albigensian Crusade*, trans. W. A. Sibly and M. D. Sibly (Woodbridge, 1998). Translations of early and influential *chansons de geste* are *The Song of Roland*, trans. G. Burgess (Harmondsworth, 1990) and *Guillaume d'Orange: Four Twelfth-Century Epics*, trans. J. M. Ferrante (New York, 1974). For courtly love, the fundamental texts are Andreas Capellanus, *The Art of Courtly Love*, trans. J. J. Parry (New York, 1960), and Chrétien de Troyes, *Arthurian Romances*, trans. W. W. Kibler (Harmondsworth, 1991). See also Marie de France, *The Lais*, trans. G. Burgess and K. Busby (Harmondsworth, 1986). For the work of the troubadours, see *The Poems of the Troubadour Bertran de Born*, ed. and trans. W. D. Paden Jr., T. Sankovitch, and P. H. Stäblein (Berkeley, Calif., 1986). Most translations are of narrative histories or literary works, but other source types are available. One important genre is the letter collection, for which see Bernard of Clairvaux, *The Letters*, trans. B. Scott James (London, 1953; repr. Stroud, 1998) and Fulbert of Chartres, *The Letters and Poems*, ed. and trans. F. Behrends (Oxford, 1976). A much-debated saint's Life is Odo of Cluny, 'The Life of St Gerald of Aurillac', trans. G. Sitwell, *St Odo of Cluny* (London, 1958), 89–180. For miracle collections, see *The Book of Sainte Foy*, trans. P. Sheingorn (Philadelphia, 1995); *The Miracles of Our Lady of Rocamadour*, trans. M. G. Bull (Woodbridge, 1999). *Feudal Society in Medieval France: Documents from the County of Champagne*, ed. T. Evergates (Philadelphia, 1993) is mostly concerned with post-1200 material but contains some interesting documents from our period. The Mediterranean polities ruled by those of French ancestry are the subject of *The History of the Tyrants of Sicily by 'Hugo Falcandus' 1154–69*, trans. G. A. Loud and T. E. J. Wiedemann (Manchester, 1998); Walter the Chancellor, *The Antiochene Wars*, trans. T. S. Asbridge and S. B. Edgington (Aldershot, 1999); William of Tyre, *A History of Deeds Done Beyond the Sea*, trans. E. A. Babcock and A. C. Krey (2 vols., New York, 1943); and *The Conquest of Jerusalem and the Third Crusade: Sources in Translation*, trans. P. W. Edbury (Aldershot, 1996). There are numerous websites that contain translated source material. Considerable care needs to be exercised when exploring this resource: the status of many translations is not made clear, some are inaccurate, and some are old translations (and thus out of copyright) which have been superseded by more recent versions. For some useful points of entry into what is available see the Internet Medieval Sourcebook based at Fordham University: http://www.fordham.edu/halsall/sbook.html; The Labyrinth, based at Georgetown University: http://www.georgetown.edu/labyrinth; Netserf, http://www.netserf.org; and ORB: The Online Reference Book for Medieval Studies, http://orb.rhodes.edu.

Chronology

978	West Frankish army invades Lotharingia
980s	Castles and knights (*milites*) begin to appear regularly in the sources
980s–90s	Emergence of the Peace of God movement
986	Death of King Lothar; Louis V succeeds
987	Death of Louis V, the last Carolingian king of the western Frankish kingdom; Hugh Capet elected king
991	Emma of Normandy marries King Athelred of England
994	Fulk Nerra, count of Anjou, builds Langeais, the first recorded stone *donjon* in western Francia
996	Death of Hugh Capet and accession of Robert II ('the Pious')
999	Gerbert of Aurillac becomes pope as Silvester II
	First attested involvement of Normans in southern Italian affairs
*c.*1000	*Carruca* begins to be widely used
1008	The royal favourite Count Hugh of Beauvais murdered by Fulk Nerra of Anjou
1016	Fulk Nerra defeats Count Odo II of Blois at Pontlevoy
*c.*1020	Bishop Fulbert of Chartres describes the responsibilities of vassalage in a letter to William V of Aquitaine
1020s	Theory of the 'Three Orders' of society widely promulgated
1022	Outbreak of heresy at Orléans
1027	Council of Toulouges proclaims the first Truce of God
1030	Death of William V, duke of Aquitaine
1031	Death of King Robert I and accession of Henry I
1032	With the death of Raoul III, the kingdom of Burgundy is taken over by the German kings
	Henry I's brother Robert established as duke of Burgundy
1037	Death of Odo II of Blois
1038	Rainulf becomes count of Aversa, the first Norman to hold a title in southern Italy
1039	Establishment of the community of canons regular at Saint-Ruf, Avignon
1040	Death of Fulk Nerra
1044	Count Geoffrey Martel of Anjou defeats the count of Blois for control of the Vendômois and Touraine
1047	Duke William II of Normandy asserts his control by defeating rebels at Val-ès-Dunes
1049	Council of Reims
	Death of Odilo, abbot of Cluny since 994

1050s	Stonework begins routinely to replace wood in castle construction
	Practice of banal lordship becomes well established
1054	William II of Normandy decisively defeats royal and rebel Norman forces at Mortemer
	The Council of Narbonne condemns all shedding of Christian blood
1055	Foundation of the community of Cluniac nuns at Marcigny
1059	Robert Guiscard and Richard of Capua become papal vassals for their southern Italian lands
1060	Death of Henry I and accession of Philip I ('the Fat')
	Death of Geoffrey Martel, count of Anjou
1061	Normans begin the conquest of Sicily, completed in the 1090s
1063	Duke Guy Geoffrey (William VIII) of Aquitaine adds the duchy of Gascony to his domains
1064	French lords assist local Spanish forces in the capture of the Muslim city of Barbastro
1066	Norman conquest of England
1071	Normans capture Bari
1076	Foundation by Stephen of Muret of the community that subsequently relocates to Grandmont
	Normans capture Salerno
1079	Foundation by Gerard of Corbie of La Sauve-Majeure
1080	Archbishop Manasses of Reims deposed by papal legate
1084	Foundation by Bruno of Cologne of the hermitage that later becomes La Grande Chartreuse
1085	Death of Robert Guiscard
1086	Death of Guy Geoffrey (William VIII), duke of Aquitaine
1087	Death of William the Conqueror
1088	Odo of Châtillon becomes pope as Urban II
1095	Pope Urban II preaches the First Crusade at Clermont
1096	Attacks on Jewish communities in the wake of crusade preaching
1098	Foundation of Cîteaux
	Capture of Antioch by the First Crusade and foundation of the principality under Bohemond of Taranto
1099	Capture of Jerusalem by the army of the First Crusade
1100	Duke William IX of Aquitaine supports King Philip I against papal legates at the Council of Poitiers

	Count Baldwin of Boulogne assumes the title king of Jerusalem
*c.*1100	Beginnings of a period of rapid urban growth
1101	A second wave of crusaders, including the dukes of Aquitaine and Burgundy, leaves for the East
	Foundation of Fontevraud by Robert of Arbrissel
1106	King Henry I of England defeats his brother Robert at Tinchebrai to secure control of the duchy of Normandy
1107	Formal resolution at Troyes of the investiture conflict between the papacy and the French kings
1108	Death of Philip I and accession of Louis VI
1109	Death of Hugh, abbot of Cluny since 1049
1112	Murder of the bishop of Laon and uprising of the Laon commune
	Bernard of Fontaines (St Bernard of Clairvaux) joins Cîteaux
1113	Count Ramon Berenguer III of Barcelona marries Douce, the heiress to Provence, extending Catalan interest in the Midi
*c.*1113	Foundation of Saint-Victor, Paris
1116	Death of Robert of Arbrissel
1118	French lords participate in the crusade of King Alfonso I of Aragon-Navarre against Zaragoza
1119	Louis VI defeated by Henry I of England at Brémule
	Pope Calixtus II denounces heresy
1120s	Last regular appearance of servile status in documentary sources
1120	Formation of the Templars
1121	Foundation of Prémontré by Norbert of Xanten
1124	Louis VI and the abbey of Saint-Denis coordinate the French reaction to a threatened German invasion
1125	Hugh, count of Champagne, becomes the first high-profile recruit to the Templars
1126	Death of Duke Willliam IX of Aquitaine ('the Troubadour')
1127	Murder of Count Charles the Good of Flanders
1129	Establishment of first Occitan consulate, at Avignon
	Robert Burdet enfeoffed with the lordship of Tarragona
1130s	*Conversi* become an important part of Cistercian organization
1130	Recognition of Roger II as king of Sicily by Pope Anacletus II

1131	Count Fulk V of Anjou becomes king of Jerusalem
1130s–40s	Troubadour Marcabru active
1134	French lords among the Christian forces under Alfonso I of Aragon that are routed by the Almoravids at Fraga
1137	Death of Louis VI and accession of Louis VII
	Death of Duke William X of Aquitaine and the marriage of his heiress Eleanor to Louis VII
c.1140	Execution at Saint-Gilles of the heretic Peter of Bruis
1140s–70s	Troubadour Bertran de Ventadorn active
1143	First securely attested appearance of Catharism in western Europe, in Cologne
	The Templars become substantially committed to the Spanish *reconquista*
1144	First royal ordinance for the whole kingdom, concerning relapsed Jewish converts
1145	Mission of Bernard of Clairvaux to combat heresy in the south
1145–9	Second Crusade
1150s	It becomes common for peasants to buy their way out of labour dues
1151	Death of Suger of Saint-Denis
1152	Marriage of Eleanor of Aquitaine to the future Henry II of England
1153	Death of Bernard of Clairvaux
1155	Proclamation of a royal Peace of God
c.1155	Confirmation by Louis VII of the Customs of Lorris, the blueprint for the self-governance of rural communities
1159	Henry II's attack on Toulouse thwarted by the intervention of Louis VII
1160s	First concerted efforts to standardize practice within the Cistercian order
1163	First recorded accusation of ritual child murder by French Jews, at Pontoise
1165	Meeting of heretics and Occitan prelates at Lombers
	Canonization of Charlemagne by the antipope Paschal III at the behest of Emperor Frederick Barbarossa
1166	Alfonso II of Aragon, count of Barcelona, imposes his suzerainty in Provence
c.1167	Benjamin of Tudela observes a flourishing Jewish community in Occitania

1170	Murder of Thomas Becket
1170s–80s	Chrétien de Troyes active
1172	Feudal surveys in Normandy and Champagne
c.1173	Waldes, a Lyonnais merchant, begins preaching
1174	Court festival at Beaucaire
c.1177	Cathar assembly at Saint-Félix-de-Caraman
1179	Third Lateran Council enacts measures to combat heretics and mercenaries
1180	Death of Louis VII and accession of Philip II ('Augustus')
	William VIII, lord of Montpellier, licenses the teaching of medicine in the city
c.1181–95	Troubadour Bertran de Born active
1184	Waldensians condemned as heretics by Pope Lucius III
1187	Flemish *Grote Bref*, an account roll for the comital domain
	Jerusalem falls to Saladin's forces
1180s–90s	Philip Augustus encourages the growth of Les Halles as a market centre in Paris; Parisian streets are paved; the city wall is extended
1187–92	Third Crusade
1189	Death of Henry II of England
1190	Royal ordinance for the governance of the kingdom
1194	*Prisée des sergéants*, a survey of military service owed in the royal domain
	Death of Raymond V, count of Toulouse
1196	Death of Ermengard, viscountess of Narbonne
1199	Death of King Richard of England
1202	In the bull *Per venerabilem*, Pope Innocent III affirms that the kings of France have no temporal superior
1202–3	First surviving royal accounts
1202–4	Confiscation and substantial annexation by Philip Augustus of King John of England's French domains
1204	Count Baldwin IX of Flanders becomes emperor of Constantinople
	Death of Eleanor of Aquitaine
1208	Launching of the Albigensian Crusade
1213	Peter II of Aragon and Raymond VI of Toulouse defeated by the Albigensian crusaders at Muret
1214	Battle of Bouvines

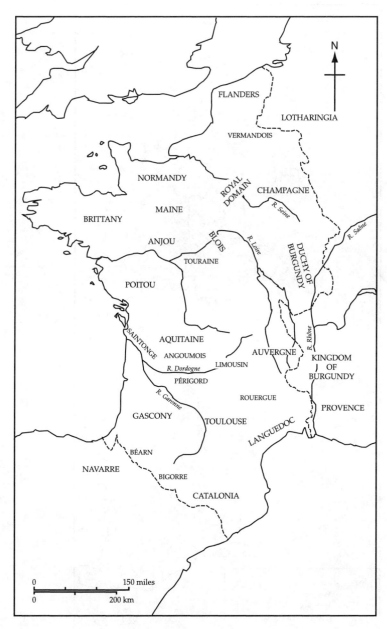

Map 1 The kingdom of France, c. 1000

Map 2 The church in the French kingdom and neighbouring territories

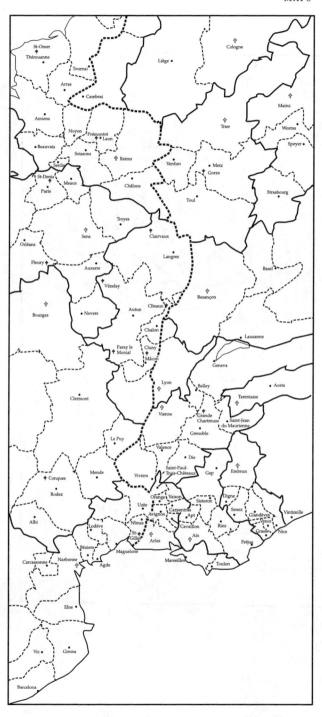

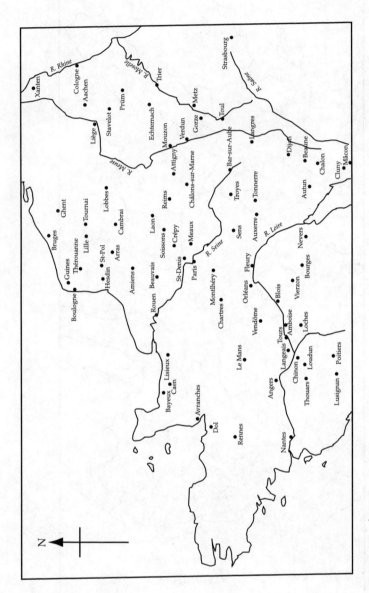

Map 3 Northern France

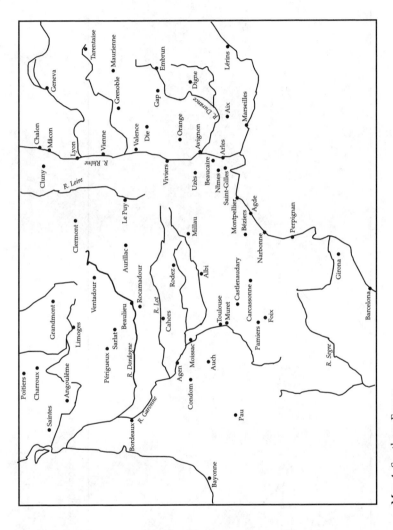

Map 4 Southern France

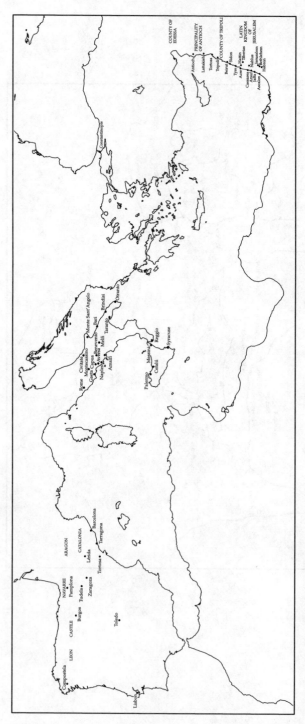

Map 5 The French in the Mediterranean, 1000–1200

Index